My Crazy Life Stories from A to Z

MARILYN LINKUL WINKA

Wasteland Press
Shelbyville, KY USA
www.wastelandpress.net

My Crazy Life Stories from A to Z
by Marilyn Linkul Winka

Copyright © 2017 Marilyn Linkul Winka
ALL RIGHTS RESERVED

First Printing – June 2017
ISBN: 978-1-68111-186-5

NO PART OF THIS BOOK MAY BE REPRODUCED IN
ANY FORM, BY PHOTOCOPYING OR BY ANY ELECTRONIC
OR MECHANICAL MEANS, INCLUDING INFORMATION
STORAGE OR RETRIEVAL SYSTEMS, WITHOUT PERMISSION
IN WRITING FROM THE COPYRIGHT OWNER/AUTHOR

Printed in the U.S.A.

0   1   2   3   4   5   6   7   8

"We do not stop playing because we are old; we grow old because we stop playing."

~Benjamin Franklin

MY CRAZY ACKNOWLEDGEMENTS AND DEDICATION

First I have to thank all of my family and friends for listening to my stories over the years, sometimes for the "umpteenth" time, and acting like they were funny and interesting each time!

Next, I have to thank all of the people (characters) in my stories for making my life interesting enough to write about. I hope that I did you justice when writing about you. Some of you may wonder why your name isn't in here or why it doesn't appear that often. It does not mean that you are any less important to me than those people whose names do appear a lot. It may simply mean you weren't involved in as many crazy parts of my life. And maybe you should be grateful for that.

I realize that my memory of events and relationships may be different than yours, but I can only write my truth. Everything that I wrote is according to my perception and from my memory. I did not invent, change, lie nor intentionally exaggerate or embellish anything. I hope that I haven't offended anyone by my portrayal of them or too greatly distorted experiences that we shared

Third, I thank my faithful Facebook followers for telling me that my posts are funny, often inspiring, and uplifting. If I can make people laugh and keep their spirits up then I think I have fulfilled my purpose in life. I am grateful that God sometimes uses me to inspire others or to lift their spirits a little.

I dedicate this book to all of the characters in my crazy life stories, especially my parents, Bill and Edith Linkul; my sisters Lois and Linda; my children Karen, Nancy and Amy; the men who have played the role of my husband: Terry, Steve and my dear sweet Jerry; my grandchildren Alexandria (Alex), Justin, Jake and Rachel; my sons-in-law Jim and Grant; my brothers-in-law Don and John; my Grandma Bertha; my dear step-mom Connie and my in-laws Al and Marge, who treated me like their own daughter; my dear aunts, uncles, cousins, niece and nephew; my BFF Barbara; my childhood friend Judy H.; my schoolmates; the many people I have worked with over the years; and all who have had to listen to my crazy stories "ad nauseam".

Oh, and a special thanks is owed to Wayne Sheridan, husband of my bank co-worker Vickie, for his awesome photography!

TABLE OF CONTENTS

My Crazy Foreword 1

My Crazy **A**nimal Stories 4

My Crazy **B**anking and Brokerage Stories 9

My Crazy **C**hildhood Stories 63

My Crazy **D**ating Stories 100

My Crazy **E**ating Stories 113

My Crazy **F**amous Stories 120

My Crazy **G**ermany Stories 130

My Crazy **H**oly Stories 142

My Crazy **I**nsane Stories 154

My Crazy **J**erry Stories 162

My Crazy **K**id Stories 177

My Crazy **L**inkul Stories 208

My Crazy **M**om Stories 226

My Crazy **N**aughty Stories 235

My Crazy **O**bnoxious Stories 242

My Crazy **P**erformance Stories 263

My Crazy **Q**ueen Stories 285

My Crazy **R**eptile Stories 289

My Crazy **S**chool Stories 293

My Crazy **T**ravel Stories 325

My Crazy **U**nderwear Stories 350

My Crazy **V**omit Stories 354

My Crazy **W**riting Stories 359

My Crazy **X**-rated Stories 361

My Crazy **Y**acht Stories 362

My Crazy **Z**oo Stories 375

My Crazy Epilogue 380

My Crazy Foreword

I have been told that I have a way with words. My favorite school subjects were always those that dealt with words: Reading, Spelling, Grammar, Composition, German, Latin, Spanish, and the various subjects I studied in college that led to my degree in Speech-Communication. Some of my teachers would say that "Talking 101" and "Talking Incessantly" were among my favorites, too.

My favorite games to play are word games. I have never liked games such as Monopoly, card games or any game that requires that I be good at strategizing. Instead, I love playing Scrabble, Words with Friends, Hang Man, Word Slinger and Puzzly Words.

My Mom was very good with words. She was an excellent speller and loved to play word games. To amuse herself she would often make lists of words that could be made from longer words. I can still picture her sitting in our kitchen on the metal stool next to the buffet and looking at our refrigerator and writing down words contained in the name Westinghouse. She played this game many times, always challenging herself to find at least one more word than she had been able to come up with the last time she played. I play this game sometimes myself, only with words other than Westinghouse.

I love to create stories. I think I get that from my Dad. When I was little, especially while we waited in the car for my mother to come out of her many doctor appointments, my Dad would tell my older sister Lois and me stories that he had made up when he was a boy. He told us that he had been hospitalized for osteomyelitis for almost a year when he was thirteen. He had very little to occupy his mind except to create stories. I remember the stories were about a boy and his adventures on a river, sort of Huck Finn style. I remember a hobo in one of his stories, and a bear in another. The boy in his stories always managed to prevail over any bad characters or physical challenges. The stories were really entertaining and inspired me to create stories of my own.

Anyone who has ever worked with me or who is my Facebook friend knows I love to tell stories about the crazy things I have done or experienced in my life. My life may be just as ordinary as anyone else's, but with me as the main character, it sometimes seems like material for a sit-com. My relatives, co-workers and friends have heard me tell my crazy stories over and over for years, and have often asked me to tell and re-tell them. My kids, my sister's kids and my grand-kids seem to especially like my "Famous" stories about all of the crazy things I did when I worked for Famous-Barr. I never tire of telling stories about "Famous", or the stunts I pulled at the other places I have worked.

I live alone now, except for my cat Edi, and I am retired, so I no longer have built-in audiences for when I feel like telling my stories, and I no longer have fodder for more work stories. I started posting funny stories on Facebook and have heard from many followers that I should write a book, so that is what I am doing.

It took me over a year to finish writing and editing. Because I am very verbose, I ended up with twice as much material as could fit in a normal size book. The stories that I had to pare down or eliminate altogether for publishing are printed out as a manuscript for anyone who wants to read more of my stories.

This book started out as a collection of stories about ordinary events in my life that turned out to be crazy stories, either because they really are crazy, or I am crazy for thinking anyone else thinks they are as funny as I do. As I put my crazy stories into writing - they had previously only been spoken - I decided to group them under letters of the alphabet according to their topics (sometimes stretching it a bit to make the stories fit under a certain letter, as you'll see). I stand by the fact that these stories are all true, or as close as they can be considering that some of them took place decades before I wrote them.

I hope you will not only enjoy my writing, but that you will be inspired to share your own stories, either in written form or just by telling them to someone you know will appreciate them. And most of all, I hope you learn this about me: that I may be all silly and crazy on the outside, but inside is a woman who may have taken too long to do it, but who realizes that God gave her a gift of being able to entertain and sometimes inspire others through my writing. I take my gift very seriously even though I have fun with it, too.

Thank you, Holy Spirit, for giving me a way with words, and may you inspire me to always use my gift to say what people need to hear.

My Crazy Animal Stories

Is Lassie My Guardian Angel?

From January 1952 until June 1953 my family lived in Overland, Missouri. My Mom didn't like living in the suburbs, since she didn't drive, and she was so far away from her family who lived in South St. Louis. My Mom was depressed during this time, so she took a nap every afternoon to get away from it all. If I didn't eventually settle down for a nap with her, she would let me go outside to play in the yard by myself. I was on my own a lot.

My older sister Lois, who was a second grader at All Soul's school, took a public transportation bus home every day. My Mom usually met the bus and took me along. One day she sent me to meet Lois by myself. As I waited for my sister's bus, I watched the many cars go by. One car pulled up right in front of me. As I recall, a man was driving, a woman was in the passenger seat, and a little boy was in the back seat. The little boy may or may not have been crying, but he was definitely licking an ice cream cone. It was vanilla, my favorite!

The woman rolled down her window and smiled at me. Then she said, "Little girl, would you like to go with us to get some ice cream?" My mother had warned me never to go with strangers, because they could be kidnappers. I looked at the little boy in the back seat and wondered if he had been kidnapped, lured by the same promise of ice cream. But then I looked back at the woman who was still smiling at me, and I thought of a delicious vanilla ice cream cone that could soon be mine. I was about to say "Yes!" when out of nowhere, a great big collie (who looked just like the famous television star Lassie), bounded up to me. I was afraid of dogs and this one seemed about to attack me!

I spun on my heels and ran as fast as I could towards home, screaming at the top of my lungs, with Lassie chasing me like I had done something to hurt Timmy or Grandpa! (If you didn't watch "The Adventures of Lassie" on television, you probably have no idea what I'm talking about.) Suffice it to say that this collie was hot on my heels as I ran to the safety of my Mom.

When I made it to my house, Lassie took off and I breathlessly told my Mom all about the collie, and how it had run me off from a chance to get a ride from these really nice people who were going to give me a free ice cream cone! I remember my Mom taking me into her arms and telling me that this dog was my guardian angel who had just saved me from being kidnapped! I think my Mom even cried as she explained that these "really nice" people had probably kidnapped the little boy that I had seen in the back seat, and that they were very likely trying to kidnap me too! She told me NEVER to go with strangers no matter how nice they seemed, and even if they offered ice cream. Then she explained how God sends our guardian angels to protect us from such harm, and how this time my guardian angel came in the form of a collie.

At the time this occurred my family didn't have a television and I had only watched television occasionally when I was at a relative's or a neighbor's house. After we moved back to South St. Louis and got our first television (when I was about six years old), I started watching "The Adventures of Lassie" on a regular basis. Whenever I saw that beautiful collie saving Timmy or Grandpa from danger, I thought of my guardian angel and how she had saved me from being kidnapped.

Final thoughts:

I wonder about the little boy who was in the back seat of that car. I hope he was not kidnapped; that he was just the kid in a really nice family who saw a little girl out by herself, and just wanted to make sure she got home safely.

Sir, Your Horse Is Dead!

I admit I really don't know that much about animals. And I admit that sometimes my thinking is really off-base. But this example of how clueless I can sometimes be is shocking even to me!

One Saturday I was driving home from having worked a half day at the bank. I was enjoying the drive home, since it was a beautiful, sunny spring day, the day before Easter. I was on the last stretch of road near my house. On my left there was a farm. I always enjoyed seeing their horses. Much to my horror, when I looked for the horses that day, I saw a dead one! The horse was just lying in the pasture. I surmised that it had just died and the farmer had not noticed it yet. I had lots to do at home to get ready for the next day, but I felt compelled to stop and tell the farmer that his horse was dead.

I drove up the gravel driveway to the farmhouse and was greeted by several dogs. I'm not a dog fan and am sometimes afraid of big dogs, especially in packs. I was afraid this day, because these dogs were all barking at me like I was trespassing or something. (I think there may have been a sign at the gate warning me that this was private property, but I was duty-bound to deliver the bad news to the farmer about his dead horse.) I slowly got out of my car, trying not to make eye contact with the pack of dogs. I nervously knocked on the farmhouse door. A tall, blonde Scandinavian-looking (and very handsome, I might add) man answered the door. Behind him there were several little blonde, blue-eyed children in "stair steps". I thought the children looked kind of scared. Right away I assessed the situation and determined this family had recently migrated here from Sweden or Norway, that the mother had perhaps died in childbirth (because otherwise she would have joined the family at the door) and that they seldom received visitors. In fact, I thought, they discouraged visitors; hence, the pack of watch dogs circling me. Young (and hot) "Farmer Swenson" (be sure to pronounce the "w" like a "v") looked at me inquiringly and said, "Yah?" He then said something to the dogs to quiet them, as I mustered up the courage to break the tragic news to him. "Sir, your horse is dead!"

"Farmer Swenson" looked out to the pasture as I pointed out the dead horse. I was babbling on. "I'm sorry to have to tell you this, but I just couldn't keep driving. I thought you should know your horse is dead." I looked at Farmer Swenson's face. He wore a big grin on it as he explained to me that the horse was just resting. "Oh my God", I thought. "The man is in denial." After all, the poor man had all those children to raise by himself. Who knows how recently he had been widowed. And now I had to further dampen his spirits with this tragic announcement.

I didn't know how to convince this poor man that his horse was indeed dead, and not just sleeping. Didn't he know that horses sleep standing up? Again, "Farmer Swenson" assured me the horse wasn't dead. He told me to honk my horn as I drove past the horse so I could see that the horse was not dead. Feeling that I had overstayed my dubious welcome, and afraid he might sic his watchdogs on me if I didn't skedaddle, I decided I had better leave. I got back into my car under the watchful eyes of "Farmer Swenson" and his brood of "Children of the Corn", and drove slowly down the gravel road. When I was parallel to the dead horse, I honked my horn as I had been instructed to do. To my surprise, the horse jumped up! It was a miracle! I wondered if the horse's name was Lazarus.

When I got home a few minutes later and told this amazing story to my family, they were incredulous that I didn't know that horses lay down to sleep sometimes.

My Crazy Banking and Brokerage Stories

I worked for the same bank under several different names. By that I mean that the bank had five different names due to name changes, mergers and takeovers and I had four different last names due to marriages, divorces and remarriages. I worked in the banking field for most of the years between 1967 and 1998 and then worked in the brokerage industry until 2012 when I retired. That's about forty years' worth of bank and brokerage firm stories. I am sure I could tell twice as many funny stories than are included in this book, but some stories are better left in the vault.

"Check" This Out—I'm in the Shriners' Parade!

Our bank processed checks for many smaller correspondent banks in the area. The Reconcilement Department's role was to reconcile the actual checks and deposit slips of these banks to printouts of the correspondent banks' debits and credits for the day. We called what we did "balancing" the banks. As part of this process we stacked batches of checks on a long counter. I don't remember why we did this.

On this particular night, I was assigned to reconcile Tower Grove Bank. (It was the biggest correspondent bank we handled). In other words, Tower Grove Bank had the largest number of checks, took the longest of any of the banks to reconcile and was our most important customer.

I was working at the end of the counter nearest to the windows that overlooked Sixth Street between Olive and Locust in downtown St. Louis. I had several rows of very tall batches of checks on the counter before me. While I was working, I heard the sound of drums coming from the street four stories below. I pulled the big window open, leaned out and took several stacks of checks with me. Checks flew out of the fourth floor window like confetti as I excitedly announced to my co-workers, "It's the Shriners' Parade!" I stood there for a few seconds, enjoying the parade, before I noticed that Tower Grove Bank's checks were all over the street, and that the Moolah Shriners were driving their little cars and running over them!

It was very important to send each and every customer check back to the bank along with our computer print-out. Once in a while our check-sorting machine "ate" a few checks, so the number of checks did not always reconcile to our report. I knew what had to be done that evening, because I did not want to fail, and not have Tower Grove Bank be "in balance". I hurriedly ran down four flights of steps, not wanting to waste any time waiting for the elevator. I ran out of a side door and onto 6th Street. I started weaving in and out of the line of little cars doing "figure eights" in the street, scooping up as many checks as I could. I looked up at the windows in my department on the fourth floor. Everyone was looking out at me. I waved and marched just like I belonged in the parade. I was actually enjoying myself. I have always loved marching in parades. (Once I even led an imaginary parade through the lobby of the bank, but that's another story).

I returned to my department and assured my supervisor that I thought I had retrieved all of the checks. I explained that some had tire marks on them, because they had been run over by the little cars, but they were all there, or so I thought. After tallying all of Tower Grove Bank's items and coming up short, I realized that I had not retrieved all of the checks. Some may have been stuck to the bottoms of those big clown shoes!

As I said earlier, when the items didn't balance with the report we sent to the bank, we said the bank was "out of balance". It was not a good thing to have the bank you were assigned to be "out of balance". It made our bank look bad to the small bank that was paying us to process their work. Just the evening before, my supervisor had admonished all of us to be more specific when reporting to a bank that they were out of balance. I felt bad that I had failed to balance Tower Grove Bank. The least I could do was be specific in my report. The reconcilement clerk had to write a brief explanation on the report and initial it, so that night I wrote on Tower Grove Bank's report:

Some checks missing. Fell out window into Shriners parade - couldn't get them all.
    Sorry, Mel.

(My initials were M.E.L. at the time, and I always signed my work as "Mel").

For years I have told this story to my family over and over again. When I tell it, I always act out the way I had marched in between the little cars, scooping up checks and waving just like I was an intended part of the parade. The story has been a family favorite and is always good for a laugh.

Flash forward about twenty-five years. I was working for another bank. I was no longer a clerk. In fact, I had worked my way up in the banking industry and was an Assistant Vice-President. (Eventually I was promoted to Vice-President). I was on the board of the American Institute of Banking (AIB), where I was also on the teaching staff. Not bad for the silly college girl who barely knew how to do her job, much less understand the seriousness of it.

The AIB board members consisted of bank executives from all over the Greater St. Louis area. We met in the swanky board room of a large downtown corporation. I took it very seriously and was so appreciative to be there in the company of mostly male bank executives. I had worked my way up from the ground level of banking and was still in awe of my unlikely current position, given my earlier history in the banking business.

We had finished with our serious bank business and were enjoying a few moments of socializing before heading back to our respective banks. All of the executives were talking about past experiences in their illustrious careers, and I wanted so much to be considered one of them, that when I heard that one of the men say he had been an executive from Tower Grove Bank, I blurted out my story. Everyone laughed. I ended with how I had written my stupid explanation of why the bank was "out of balance" on their report. The Tower Grove Bank executive said, "So you're Mel!" He went on to explain how he had told the story of "Mel" to other bankers many times, thinking "Mel" was a guy. I was floored to learn that I had been famous (or should I say "infamous") in the local banking industry for years and hadn't even known it.

An Elevator, a Mischievous College Girl and a Security Guard

When the elevator incident happened, I was still working in the Reconcilement Department. I worked from 4:00 PM until midnight and attended college full time during the day. Almost all of my co-workers were college kids. Working that job was like attending a college party every night without the liquor (except for the time I smuggled whiskey in, but that's another story). We got our work done, but there was a lot of down time while we waited for our work to arrive from the Federal Reserve Bank. We flirted harmlessly with one another, and there was a lot of double entendre talking and laughing while we worked.

We didn't really work that hard to deserve a break, but some of us took them anyway. The cafeteria was closed during the evening hours, but there were a few vending machines, plenty of empty tables and plenty of opportunities for me to be mischievous in the sparsely populated, darkened cafeteria.

On this particular evening I took my break with one of my supervisors. Tony was a young man attending St. Louis Parks College. He was friendly with the rest of us, as were all of the supervisors. I'm not sure he really had much authority over me. All I know is that as one of the supervisors he had to stay late to untangle the messes that I and my co-workers sometimes left for him.

Tony and I finished our break and were on the elevator when I got one of my crazy ideas. I asked Tony if he ever wondered what happened when you pulled the emergency handle on an elevator. Before Tony could even finish saying "Don't you dare!" I had pulled the handle. Much to my delight, the alarm went off. Much to my surprise, the elevator came to an abrupt stop about three feet above the floor, and didn't budge. Tony grabbed me and helped me jump down safely to the floor and led me back to our department. I remember he had such a serious look on his face. He told me to keep my mouth shut. Tony and I joined the others at the long counter where checks were being batched. Neither of us said a word when people started remarking about the alarm. Amid chatter about why the alarm was going off, and speculation that it sounded like the elevator had gotten stuck, Tony and I remained silent. I started getting scared. I was sure I had a guilty look on my face and that sooner or later the truth would come out that it was me who had caused the alarm to go off. Without saying anything to my co-workers I walked back to the elevator to see if I could somehow get the alarm to stop. When I got there, my favorite security guard, Ole George as I called him, was looking at the elevator with a puzzled look on his face.

Without having to think too hard about what I was going to say, in my most convincing "scared little girl" voice I said, "Oh, George, it was awful! I was on the elevator when all of a sudden it just stopped. I was so scared! I had to jump down to get off. Oh, George. It was awful!"

Ole George looked at me with such tenderness and concern that it should have broken my heart for lying to him. He asked if I was alright. I sniffled like I was crying a little and shakily told him that I thought I would be okay. I skipped off back to work without a care in the world while Ole George was left to figure out how to shut off the alarm. He eventually did I guess, or else he enlisted another guard for help, because soon all was quiet again.

For years afterwards, whenever I saw Ole George, he asked "How's my girl?" as though he thought I would still be traumatized by my scary elevator experience. I always played it up real good and told him that I was okay. I didn't have enough sense to feel guilty about fooling Ole George and maybe causing him some undue angst. I just knew it felt good to have Ole George looking out for me.

Drinking on the Job

As I said in my stories about marching in the Shriners' Parade and the elevator incident, my evening job at the big bank downtown when I was in college was more play than work. I worked with other college kids with little to no supervision. We had one "adult" supervisor, but she was having a fling with one of my co-workers, and the rest of us were between eighteen and twenty-one years old. You get the picture. It wasn't a traditional workplace.

Our shift was 4:00 PM until midnight and we often went out dancing and drinking afterwards. One of our favorite places to party after work was the "Red Onion", a night club in the Mansion House complex in downtown St. Louis. Most of us were under age, but we got in. Bars closed at 1:15 in those days, so we didn't have much time to party, having just gotten off of work at midnight, but it was a great way to end a night of fun with my co-workers. There were more guys than girls on the evening shift, so I and a girl named Kathy were pretty much the center of attention. Life was one big party as far as I was concerned. I skipped classes at UMSL by day so I could socialize and play cards. I worked with a bunch of fun college kids at night and partied during and sometimes after work. Ah, those were the days!

Our bank had a big employee picnic every June. All employees and their families were invited. It was a big deal. The bank reserved a whole park for the day and provided BBQ, ice cream, drinks, rides, booths, games with prizes--all the usual picnic stuff. It was an event not to be missed! The picnic was held on a Saturday. The Reconcilement Department worked every Saturday, and each of us was scheduled to work one Saturday a month. It just so happened that I was scheduled to work on picnic day in 1968. I was so upset. I had heard so much about the employee picnic, and now I couldn't go. I had a steady boyfriend (Terry), and we both loved to drink. We had been looking forward to the picnic and all of the free beer. I tried to get someone to switch Saturdays with me to no avail. There were several of us who had to work, and I assured them that I would see to it that we would have our own fun that day! On the day of the picnic I stole a bottle of whiskey from my Dad's liquor stash in the kitchen pantry. My Dad didn't drink whiskey or much of anything for that matter, but he kept a few bottles of liquor for company. I didn't think he'd miss it.

On Saturdays our work shift started at two o'clock in the afternoon and ended at 10:00 PM. Our "in house" picnic started as soon as we got there that day. We passed the bottle of whiskey around and then quickly stashed it in a drawer whenever it was time for a security guard to make his rounds through our department. I remember almost getting caught "red-handed". I saw the door to our department open and I shoved the bottle under my desk just as the guard stepped over the threshold. I must have had a goofy expression on my face as I greeted the guard and said something stupid like "Hi, how are you? We're all just fine. Yeah, we're all here just working away and not worrying about that silly old picnic we're missing".

I didn't realize at the time how lucky we were not to get caught. We could have all been fired. And I would have had a hard time explaining to my Dad that I got fired for drinking on the job, and with liquor stolen from him to boot!

It's all in the Wrist

I liked to show off back then. ("Thank God I have outgrown that", I just said facetiously). My co-worker and friend, Bill, used to take our breaks together. One night he showed me the ice cream freezer that held novelty ice cream treats. It was locked with a chain. He asked me if I could fit my wrist through the narrow opening and retrieve an ice cream treat for him. My wrists were very small and my arms skinny, so I did what he asked very easily. I handed him an ice cream and then took one for myself. It was fun to "outsmart" someone. That was my motive for stealing the ice cream more than wanting to eat it. Soon this became a habit. Bill and I would go to the cafeteria on break and eat our stolen ice cream. Word got around that there was a way to get free ice cream, and soon I was stealing ice cream for more people. After a while I tired of doing this, and besides, I did not want to get caught. The cafeteria manager may not miss one or two items, but would surely notice multiple items missing. So I stopped stealing ice cream and moved on to other pranks.

But before I go on, since I mentioned wrists, I must add another story about one of mine. Since the Reconcilement Department handled trays and trays of checks that could get your clothes dirty, sometimes the girls wore blue smocks over their clothes. I usually only wore a smock if I got too cold. We worked right outside of the computer room, which was kept as cold as a meat locker. One evening I was cold and I found the one remaining smock. I noticed it was missing a button from the cuff of the long-sleeved arm, but put it on anyway. Ever the show-off, I pointed out to someone that I could easily fix the missing button situation. I said, "Watch this!" as I used a heavy-duty stapler to close the open cuff. I hit that stapler hard for maximum effect. Only trouble was, not only did it not staple the two ends of the cuff together, it grabbed the thin skin of my wrist. Man, did that hurt! Someone suggested I go to the company nurse who was on duty in the evenings. So, I walked into her office. As always, she required that I sign in with my name, department and reason for my visit. Under "Reason for Visit", I wrote "Stapled wrist". She looked at my entry in her book, looked at my wrist and then at my face with her prim, no-nonsense look. I told her it had not been an accident. She kind of shook her head in disgust then removed the staple, cleaned the slight wound with alcohol and applied a bandage. She recommended that I get a tetanus shot. As I was leaving I saw her cross out what I had written in her book. She probably wrote in "mental issues".

Changing the Menu

One of my favorite cafeteria pranks was changing the menu. The cafeteria was dark during the evening hours and usually I and my companion Bill were the only ones in the place. Once in a while the janitors would be there cooking, but they looked the other way when I played with the menu, just as I looked the other way when they cooked.

I changed "loin of pork" to "groin of pork", meatballs to "chef's balls", and sometimes switched all the letters to read something entirely different, but always something either disgusting or nasty. "Sh*t on a Shingle" was one of my favorites, along with "Big Weiner on Bun". Some were even worse, but I'll leave it at that. Bill and I howled with laughter every time I changed the menu. We went back to our department bragging about my latest creation. Sometimes other employees would run up to the cafeteria just to see my handiwork. It was fun for me to imagine the day workers coming into the cafeteria the next morning to check out the daily fare. I loved shocking people and I loved making them laugh. I still do.

Sweetest Prank Ever!

My sugar dispenser prank should go down in history as best cafeteria prank ever!

One evening my friend Bill and I sat at a cafeteria table smoking, laughing and killing time. I had just finished a twin pack of cupcakes and was holding the cardboard piece from the package when I got an idea. "Watch this!" I said excitedly. I took off the cap to a sugar dispenser, put the cardboard piece in its stead, turned the dispenser over and set it down on the table. Then I carefully slid the cardboard piece out from under the upside-down dispenser and placed the top on what used to be the bottom of the dispenser. The next morning, some unsuspecting victim would grab the sugar dispenser, and all of the sugar would spill out from the bottom onto the table. It was genius!

Bill helped me rig up at least twenty other sugar dispensers in the same way. It would look like a Colorado ski resort in there the next day with tables and tables of mounds of snow-white sugar piled on them! The vision of what would happen the next day was enough reward for me. I still giggle when I picture someone picking up one of those sugar dispensers.

Second Time Around

I left the bank shortly after I got married in October 1969. When I went back to the bank in April 1973 to work full time, I had just turned twenty-five. I was getting a divorce. I had no money, no job, a newborn baby and a two-year-old. As you can imagine, I was very overwhelmed and scared. I didn't know where to go for a job. The bank where I had worked during college was the perfect place for me because it was familiar.

I cried all the way to work on my first day, but vowed that I could not cry at work. I told myself that as soon as the door closed behind me in the morning as I entered the bank, I had to forget about my kids and my circumstances. And only until the bank door hit me on the way out each evening, could I resume thinking about my kids. And I had to forget all about the bank by the time I was all the way out of the door. That's what got me through my first few months of being in the work force again.

I got a job in the Statements Department checking customer signatures while dropping the paid checks into the customer account files for later enclosure into their monthly statements. It was an easy job once you got the hang of quickly comparing the signature on a check to the one on the tab of that customer's file, as you quickly dropped the check into the file. But even an easy job was a lot for me to take on at the time, because I was so overwhelmed with just having to survive and raise two kids by myself. I remember going home after my first day on the job and sobbing into the telephone to my sister how I was never going to be able to file checks as fast as the other girls. My sister told me to practice, so I got a handful of cancelled checks from my own account statements and practiced looking at my signature on the bottom of the checks while dropping the checks quickly into the slots of my toaster!

As the months passed and I grew more confident and capable, my entry level job started to seem too easy for me. And I needed to make more money than I would ever be able to earn in the Statements Department. The job had served its purpose. It was time to move on. So I promoted myself. I secretly arranged for an interview for a job in the Central Securities Department and got the job. I was ready for a challenge and ready for more responsibility and money. Twelve months after coming back to the bank where I had worked during college, and gaining back the confidence that I had lost after being suddenly thrown into the role of single, working parent, I graduated to a new emotional level, too. My confidence and sense of fun were finally back! The year that I worked in the Central Securities Department was the year that I got my groove back.

One day shortly after I started my new job, my boss asked me if I liked my job. I answered "Yes, I do. Why do you ask?" He replied that he had seen the letters I had been sending out, and that they were being typed in all caps. I explained that it was easier for me to not have to hit the shift key when I typed the letters. He looked dumbfounded. He then reminded me that he had asked if I knew how to type during the job interview and that I had said "yes". (That's what I had said out loud, but in my head I had added "But not very well!"). Before he could say another word, I asked him, "Do I get the job done?" He answered, "Yes". So I replied, "Good, then we don't have a problem". With that, I went back to my work and he walked away, no doubt with a look of "What just happened here?" on his face. Most of the jobs I have had required typing skills. I never did learn to type well. I was still using the Hunt and Peck method and looking at the keys forty years later when I retired. Thank God I must have had enough "something else" going for me to be successful.

Customer!

The Central Securities Department was in an enclosed area of the main bank lobby. The area was called "The Cage". It was where the vault that was for the safekeeping of U. S. Treasury securities and municipal bonds was located. Part of my job in the Central Securities Department was to wait on retail investment customers and bank messengers who came to my window to take delivery of or drop off securities that completed transactions with our Bond Investment Department. Whenever a customer came to my window with an order to take delivery of securities, I would go to the gate of the vault in our secured area and yell out "Customer!" This indicated to the vault attendant that this was a priority. The vault attendant would then stop counting securities or whatever he or she was doing, (I once caught one of the vault attendants wiping a booger on one of the securities certificates) and come to the gate of the vault to fill my order.

One day I was really concentrating on my work at my desk (probably struggling to type a letter using the shift key) and I looked up to see an elderly gentleman at my window. I must have been really preoccupied with my work, because I got up, walked to the customer window and loudly yelled "Customer!" right in the elderly man's face! I had accidentally fast-forwarded to the part of the procedure where I was supposed to yell "Customer!" at the vault attendant. I didn't let my error rattle me, though. I just played it off like it was part it of my normal routine. The old gent never said a word about how I had greeted him, and neither did I. At least he fared better than the old man in the next story.

You Old Coot!

A different elderly man and I were at my window transacting business. When we were finished, he asked me where he might find some bond quote sheets. We kept a rack right outside of the cage to my left of the customer window. I could not see the rack from inside of the cage, but I knew where it always stood. I gestured toward my left of the window and told the old man that they were in the rack right over there. He looked in that direction and then back at me and asked "Where?" I was still standing at the window finishing up paperwork from our transaction and barely looked up as I gestured to my left again. He walked away as I resumed my attention to my work. Then I heard him ask "Where?" again! Exasperated, and without looking up from my work at all, I gruffly yelled "Right there!" I thought he was hard of hearing, and wouldn't hear when I added "You old coot!" I looked up and realized I had just yelled "You old coot!" right in his face! He had returned to the window! This time I really didn't know how to play off my blunder, so I just smiled, said "Have a nice day!", and went back to my desk. Later, when I walked outside of the cage to go to lunch, I noticed that the rack I had been referring to was no longer right by my window. Someone had relocated it. That poor "old coot" probably never did get his quote sheet, and I sure didn't score any points in customer service that day!

Fingering the Culprit!

One day, while still working in "The Cage", an officer who worked in the Bond Investment Department ticked me off. She had sent a memo to our boss claiming that our department had not handled something correctly, and our boss had bawled us out. I felt it was unjust and decided to let this officer know just how I felt about her scolding of our department. I went to the copy machine and took a copy of my hand with my middle finger extended. I placed the photo in an inter-office envelope and addressed it to her. (In hindsight, I realize that I probably didn't use a brand new interoffice envelope. I probably used an old one and just drew a line through our department name as the last recipient of the envelope. How stupid!) After this officer received the photo, she immediately called our boss, ranting and raving. She sent him the photo and he, in turn, asked our supervisor to find out who had sent it. I saw the supervisor coming around to talk to everyone, one by one. It looked like he was serious about something, and I got wind of the fact that he was trying to find out who the "middle finger" belonged to. It looked like the supervisor had a few people to talk to before he got around to me, so I rushed out of the department with a big work scissors hidden under my clothes. I ran to the ladies restroom and savagely hacked off all of my long fingernails. I also took off a ring that I often wore. I got back to my desk seconds before it was my turn to be interrogated.

My supervisor showed me the photo and asked if I had any idea who had sent the photo to the officer. The look on his face told me that he knew. I held up my hands and said, "Well, it obviously couldn't be me. My nails are much shorter than the ones in the picture, and I am not wearing a ring." He looked at me with a slight smile on his lips and agreed that it could not possibly be me. We both knew it had been me, but he was cool enough not to say otherwise. I never heard any more about the incident until many years later, after I had been gone from this bank for many years and come back to work with some of the same people, including my middle finger victim. I finally 'fessed up to some other people that it had been my finger in the photo. I heard they told her when she retired and that she said she had always suspected it had been me.

The Bomb Scare

Another foolish thing I did while working in the Central Securities Department involves my coming back late from lunch. I knew I was running late, but I really had to go to the restroom before coming back into "The Cage". So I reached into my window from the lobby, and set my purse and sweater down on the counter on the inside of the window. That way people would see my stuff, and assume I was back from lunch. I went to use the ladies room, entered my code into the keypad that secured the cage and walked to my desk in front of the window. My supervisor and two men from Security (the physical security department) were standing looking at my purse that I had covered with my sweater. I asked what was going on. One of the security guys told my supervisor and me to step back. He was poised to lift my sweater off of my purse when I said, "That's my purse. What's happening?" The security guys and my supervisor (the same one who had interrogated me about the middle finger photo) gave a sigh of relief as I explained that I had stashed my stuff there on my way to the restroom after getting back from lunch. They explained that there had been a bomb scare while I had been at lunch. The security guards had been going around looking for suspicious packages or objects. When they noticed the mysterious "lump" on the counter just inside of the security cage window, they thought it might be a bomb! They were relieved it wasn't a bomb, and I was relieved that in all the excitement, no one had noticed that I was late getting back from lunch!

After about twelve months in my position as Central Securities clerk, I got bored and promoted myself again; this time to the Personal Banking Department.

The Father of Rock 'n Roll

While I was working at the Information Desk in the Personal Banking Department, a slim, black man came to the desk and asked to see his Personal Banker. My job was to ask his name and the reason for wanting to see his Personal Banker, write this information on a piece of paper and then take the slip of paper to his Personal Banker. When the gentleman said his name was Charles Berry, it registered with me that he might be Chuck Berry, the Father of Rock 'n Roll! I knew Chuck Berry was one of our customers, because I had seen him in the bank before, but this time he looked sort of unkempt, so I wasn't sure it was THE Charles Berry. (Looking back, I realize that this may have been during his drug-taking days; hence, his bad appearance).

So, being as discreet as I could be, I quietly asked, "Are you who I THINK you are?" to which he replied "Well, who do you THINK I am?" I looked at the name I had written on the little piece of paper and looked at his face again, and shaking from excitement I said in a high-pitched squeal, "So you ARE who I think you are!" He just laughed, gave me that famous grin, and I knew for sure he was who I thought he was. I went to his Personal Banker's desk and said, "Sharon, you are not going to believe this, but Chuck Berry is here, and he wants to see YOU!" She looked up from her work, expressionless. I thought she might not know who he was, so I added "He's the Father of Rock and Roll!" She surprised me by calmly telling me to let Mr. Berry know that she would be a few minutes. I just stood there in awe and repeated that it was THE Chuck Berry who wanted to see her. She nonchalantly said, "Yeah, honey, I know. He comes here to see me all the time" and went back to whatever she was doing. While she was keeping the Father of Rock 'n Roll waiting, for goodness sake, I thought I would mitigate the shabby way his Personal Banker was treating him by asking for his autograph. I grabbed a pen and a blank, generic savings account withdrawal slip from the counter and handed it to Mr. Berry. He laughed and said he'd rather sign a deposit ticket, so I grabbed one of those. He signed it, and I brought it home to my two little girls. They were too young to know (or care) who Chuck Berry was, but I proudly taped his autograph to their bedroom door. I didn't take it down until we moved a few years later, but unfortunately, I didn't keep it.

Did You Get the Message, Ed?

One of the personal bankers, whom I'll call Ed, could be a little difficult to deal with at times. He always seemed to have a customer at his desk, so I had to take a lot of messages for him. One day I had taken a message for him from a customer who asked me to tell Ed to call him back ASAP! I wrote the man's name, phone number and message on one of those standard pink office telephone message forms and quietly laid it on Ed's desk. Ed's desk was a huge mess. It had disorderly piles of papers lying all over it. Later that day, Ed came up to me with a red face and angrily accused me of not giving him an important message. He had just been yelled at by the customer who had told me to have Ed call him ASAP, and was taking it out on me. I calmly told Ed that I had placed the message on the left side of his desk where I always placed his messages, within seconds of the customer's call. Ed went on and on, ranting and raving at me and told me that next time I had a message I should make sure I put it where he could see it! I told him that he should keep his desk neater so he could see his messages. He left my desk in a huff, and I went home in a huff that evening. Despite playing pranks on people, I took pride in my work, and didn't appreciate Ed's yelling at me. So I decided to get even with him. That evening I bought a large easel pad. I colored the background of one piece of paper pink and used a black marker to create a giant-sized telephone message slip. I rolled it up and brought it to work the next day. When I got the first message for Ed, I wrote it on the giant message slip. Ed was sitting alone at his desk. I took the huge piece of paper and violently pulled it down over his head, tearing it so that Ed was wearing it like a poncho. I asked, "Do you see THIS message, Ed?" and walked away. Ed was a little mad at me, but not for long. We really liked one another and he was actually a very good sport. We later had a good laugh about the giant message slip.

Ed was such a good sport that he practically begged to be pranked. One time I left a message for him to call a customer by the name of Jim Nasium and gave him the phone number of a local high school. When I handed him the message, he looked at the name and asked me who it was. I said. "Well, how should I know? Just call the number and ask if they have someone by that name." I went back to my desk and listened in as Ed made the call. He followed my instructions perfectly. When someone from the school answered, Ed asked "Do you have a Jim Nasium there?" and they said, "Why of course we do, sir. Why do you ask?" "Because I have a message to call him" was Ed's reply. The person asked "To call whom, sir?" In a gruff voice, Ed said "Jim Nasium. I'd like to talk to Jim Nasium!" "We have no one here by that name, sir". "But you just told me you did!" "Someone's playing a trick on you, sir!" Ed finally got it and hung up.

Another time I gave him the phone number of a massage parlor in a seedy neighborhood and asked him to call Ruby Rubbit. I listened in as he made the call. When the woman on the other end of the call started telling Ed how she would gladly give him a massage, Ed's face turned red. He also fell for the old classics to call Mr. Bear at the zoo's number and Rose Budd at a florist's number.

Stand Back, I Have Gas!

Another time I felt like pranking Ed for no good reason. He and I used to walk to the parking garage together after work. It was a block away. I had made a sign that said "Stand back, I have gas!" and managed to tape it to the back of Ed's coat without him noticing it. I helped Ed get his coat on that evening and he thanked me. As Ed and I walked and talked, I kept glancing at people behind us as they noticed the sign. It was hard for me to keep a straight face as I saw people pointing to him and laughing. I made sure Ed and I walked slowly so people would pass us up, ensuring that the maximum number of people would see the sign. Ed just kept talking, oblivious of the entertainment he was providing to the passersby. By the time we got to the garage, I couldn't keep it to myself any longer. I removed the sign from the back of his coat and showed it to Ed. I was laughing so hard, I could hardly see for the tears in my eyes. Then Ed started laughing. Soon we were both laughing uncontrollably. We laughed so long and hard and became so weak that we drug one another down to the floor of the garage. I think that was one of the hardiest laughs I have ever experienced. Yes, Ed was a very good sport.

Mrs. Sleeper

Never knowing when a co-worker would strike back at me with a prank because I played so many pranks on them, I was usually on high alert for this kind of thing. One day, I answered the phone and a woman said, "Hello, this is Mrs. Sleeper". Thinking this was a co-worker pranking me I said "So, Mrs. Sleeper, are you awake?" No response. So I laughed and said, "Wake up, Mrs. Sleeper! How can I help you?" The woman responded by asking if she still had a savings account with us. I asked for her first name and told her I would look it up. Sure enough, I found a savings account in her name. Still thinking I was being pranked and waiting for the woman to ask me something really stupid, I said "Yes, I see an account in your name. So what the hell do you want, Mrs. Sleeper?" She quietly told me that she had just wanted to know if she still had an account with us, and then she thanked me and hung up. I don't know if she was hard of hearing or if she had an unusually high tolerance for terrible customer service, but whenever I talked to her or saw her name after that day, I cringed with embarrassment and silently thanked Mrs. Sleeper for being too drowsy to bother to report me.

How Many Fo's Was That?

One time I had a black gentleman sitting at my desk opening a new account. When I asked for his address he said "Fo, fo, fo, fo Lee!" It took me a minute it to register that he was saying his address was 4444 Lee. Feeling playful, I asked "How many fo's was that?" to which he quickly replied "Fo". I then repeated "Fo?" and he replied "Fo". As I wrote his address on the form, I once again asked "Fo fo's?" He said "Fo" and we both had a good laugh!

Mr. Booger

As a Personal Banker I had many elderly customers who just liked to sit at my desk and visit with me. I truly enjoyed chatting with them. Maybe I put too much "personal" in the banking business, but I treated most of my customers like friends, even if they had very little money in the bank. I was particularly fond of an elderly gentleman who told me he had worked at the meat packing company where my Dad had worked. My Dad had worked as a bonus checker, figuring out how much of a bonus the meat packers had earned each week for exceeding the minimum production. He had to endure many arguments with the workers. My customer told me he remembered my Dad and had really liked him. He said my Dad was always fair. This created a bond between me and this man.

One day he came to visit me and I noticed that he didn't look like he was feeling very well. He told me he had a bad cold. I happened to look at the lapel of his coat while we were chatting and noticed a great big booger stuck there! Out of respect for this man, I tried to avert my eyes and just keep up with our conversation. But my eyes kept going back to the booger. It was like not wanting to see a bad car accident but not being able to look away. I felt myself starting to gag at one point and quickly excused myself. I went out of his line of sight and willed myself to stop gagging. When I thought I had it under control I went back to my desk to resume our conversation. I tried so hard to concentrate on what he was saying, but I could not. All I could think of is that big booger. I had to get up a few more times. He and his booger both stuck around way too long that day.

I wish I would have felt comfortable enough with this man to hand him a Kleenex and point out that he had a booger on his coat, so he could remove it. But I couldn't. Even as I write about that giant booger all these years later, I am gagging. That booger was at least four inches long. I can still picture it after forty years. I have told the story of that booger many times. I just can't get it out of my mind. It's sticking to my mind as much as it was sticking to his lapel. Why is it that I can't remember this man's name, but I can remember his damned booger?

Fire in the Hole!

While working in the Personal Banking Department, I was responsible for two fires. Or so I thought.

The first fire occurred at the Chain of Rocks Amusement Park just north of St. Louis. It was May of 1977. My daughter, Karen, was in first grade at St. Ambrose School on the Hill (the Italian neighborhood in St. Louis where we lived). Karen's school picnic was to be held at Chain of Rocks that year. It would be my first school picnic as a mother and I was really looking forward to going with Karen and her little sister, Nancy. A couple of my own school picnics had been held at Chain of Rocks and I loved that place!

As soon as I heard about the school picnic, I asked the Manager of Personal Banking if I could have the day off. She looked at the vacation schedule and saw that two Personal Bankers were already scheduled to be off on that day, so she told me that I could not take the day off. I acted like I had accepted my manager's decision, but secretly plotted to get around it somehow. There was no way I was going to miss my daughter's school picnic!

So, I planned to call in sick the day of the picnic. It would have been three or four weeks since I had asked for the day off, and I counted on my manager to have forgotten all about my request when it came time to call in sick. I don't like to lie, especially to a boss, so I had trouble sleeping the night before the picnic. I tossed and turned all night worrying that she would remember that I had previously asked for that day off to go to the school picnic, and that she would insist that I come into work that day. I hated being in this position! I prayed and prayed that God would somehow get me out of this dilemma. After a mostly sleepless night, my clock radio blared out to awaken me. The news was on. I awoke just in time to hear that the Chain of Rocks Amusement Park had burned down the night before!

Oh my! Did I do that? Did I have that much power? Was God punishing me for planning to tell a lie? Or did God answer my prayer like this to teach me a lesson to be careful what I prayed for? While I was heartbroken that the Chain of Rocks Amusement Park had burned down and that Karen's picnic was cancelled, I was very relieved not to have to tell the lie! I was actually glad to go to work that day.

The other fire, that I may or may not have caused, occurred about a year later. I told my co-workers that I was going to quit smoking. Even though most of them smoked, my co-workers were supportive of my decision to quit. It was very difficult to quit when so many of my co-workers were all around me, smoking. The toughest time that first day was before work when we all gathered around one of the Personal Banker's (Mary's) desk to have coffee, cigarettes and conversation to kick off the day. It was also very difficult at break time and after lunch not to light one up with the others.

I somehow made it through most of the day without succumbing, when all of a sudden I had an urge that just wouldn't go away. I didn't want to disappoint my co-workers or look weak in their eyes, so I snuck a cigarette out of my purse and went to a restroom on another floor to smoke it. It was a restroom that was hardly used, at least not by the ladies from my department, so I felt safe to sneak a smoke in there. I was standing in the restroom in front of the sink, smoking away, when I heard a voice outside of the restroom. It sounded like Yvonne, one of the Personal Bankers I worked with, coming towards the restroom. I quickly turned on the water, briefly passed the burning cigarette under the stream of water and threw it into the trashcan filled with used paper towels. It turned out that Yvonne did not come into the restroom. She and someone else were just passing by. But I took that as my cue to get out of there before anybody did come in and smell the smoke.

Soon it was time to leave work for the day. As far as my co-workers knew I had made it through my first day of not smoking just fine. That evening as I was getting ready for bed, I heard on the television in the next room that there had been a fire at the bank. Oh my God, I thought. I've done it again. God is punishing me again for being deceitful! I guessed that my cigarette had not gone out completely when I quickly ran it under the water, and now I had burned the bank down. Just like Chain of Rocks! I raced into the room to hear the rest of the story. The announcer was ending the story with saying that the fire had been put out quickly and that no real harm had been done. Still, I felt bad, and had another mostly sleepless night.

The next morning at work, while we were all sitting around Mary's desk talking before work, I discreetly asked if anyone else had heard about the fire. (I wasn't sure that I was going to disclose my part in it until I heard more details). Someone had heard the entire story and said that the fire had started in a computer room, a couple of floors up from where I had been smoking. I was so relieved that I blurted out the whole story of how I had been smoking in the second floor restroom, and that I had thought that I had started the fire. We all had a good laugh. Someone passed me a cigarette and held a lighter to it as I gratefully drew the smoke into my lungs and decided it was just too dangerous for me to try to stop smoking!

Unusual Bank Deposits

The old man who walked across the bank lobby shaking his trouser leg was perhaps our most disgusting customer. Every few steps he stopped and shook his trouser leg to let a few turds roll out, leaving a trail across the bank lobby. I didn't see this myself, but I have it from a really good source (Shirley). I say he takes the prize for most unusual bank deposit!

Then there's the guy who was so drunk that he peed into the ATM. This I saw for myself. ATM's were new and my bank was demonstrating ours during the annual Downtown St. Louis block party held every August. I had signed up to demonstrate our ATM's from 9:00-10:00 pm. By the time I came on duty some of the people that came into the bank for an ATM demo were three sheets to the wind. I heard one guy call out to his inebriated friend, "Watch this!" as he proceeded to take a leak right on the machine. I said, "Sir, that is NOT what we mean when we say you can make a deposit in an ATM!" Maybe he had heard the banking term "liquid assets"? Or maybe a downtown party event where there is a lot of alcohol being served is not the time or place to demonstrate banking procedures.

The Crotch Money Incident

When I was working in the Central Securities cage as a securities teller, part of my duties was to receive payment in exchange for securities that had been purchased through our Bond Investment Department. Securities transactions were at least $5,000 to $10,000, so mostly customers had the amount due for their purchases directly charged against their checking or savings accounts. Occasionally they paid at my window, by check. The one and only time I was paid in cash I was caught off guard.

That day a beautiful young lady was at my window saying she needed to pay $10,000 for a Treasury bill she had purchased. I noticed she had a large dog with her. This was highly unusual. She must have convinced a guard to allow her to bring the dog in. I was too naïve to guess why she had the dog with her. She looked around nervously and proceeded to reach into her pants to pull out one hundred one-hundred-dollar bills. I was horrified and embarrassed, but I took the bills from her. I cringed as I wrote out a temporary receipt and told her that I would take the bills to a teller for a credit advice payable to the Bond Department. I told her that when I returned with a copy of the credit advice I would hand over her Treasury Bill.

I walked out of the cage area and across the lobby towards the teller line. I was very nervous. I had never held that much cash in my hands. As I neared the area near where the lady and her dog were standing (outside of my window), the dog broke loose, came bounding up to me and started sniffing me. I guess he could tell that I now had the money that still smelled of his owner. Yuck! I must have looked terrified (because I am afraid of big dogs and didn't want to call attention to the fact that I had so much cash in my hands). Just then, Lee the Security Guard came to my rescue. He motioned for the lady to take control of her dog and then escorted me to the teller line. He gently told me that I should have asked for a guard to escort me to the teller line, and I explained that no one had ever told me what to do if I received cash.

Sometimes you have to go through something distasteful to learn a valuable lesson. Handling "crotch money" was my distasteful but learnable moment in banking.

Skirting the Issue

I was walking from the parking garage to the bank building. I was about twenty-five years old when this happened. I still remember the outfit I had on that day. It was a cream and burgundy print short-sleeved top and matching flouncy short skirt. While I walked out of the garage and merged onto the sidewalk with the other pedestrians, an older gentleman tapped me on the shoulder, saying "Excuse me young lady. I'm sorry to have to tell you this, but your skirt is all caught up in the back, and your underwear is showing!" I thought he was some kind of a pervert and was just saying this to talk about underwear. I reached around to the back of my skirt, and much to my horror, I felt the back of my skirt tucked into the waist! He was right. My underwear was showing! I quickly "untucked" my skirt and thanked the man for telling me.

I continued on my walk, walking as fast as I could. I wanted to get away from this man and all of the people walking behind me as soon as possible. I sensed that the old man was walking really close, right behind me and to my left, in my "blind spot" if he and I had been cars on a highway. I kept walking faster and faster, but the old man hung in there. I couldn't shake him loose. It was the longest block in the world. I wondered why this old man didn't give me a little space. It just made the whole experience so much worse to have him walking with me.

Finally I made it to the doorway of the bank. I was so relieved that I would now be free of this man and the whole mortifying experience. But no such luck. The old man followed me into the building! Now I was a little scared. Was he stalking me because he had seen my underwear and liked what he saw? But when we reached the bank lobby he walked towards the left to the attached building with a coffee shop and an elevator leading to some legal and accounting firm offices, so I figured he worked for one of them. Or maybe he was one of their clients. I hoped I would never see him again.

Later that morning, I was in the cafeteria with a bunch of my co-workers. I started telling them my story, when all of a sudden the old man walked in. I couldn't believe my eyes. I whispered in horror to my companions, "Don't look now, but the old man I am talking about just walked in!" Someone glanced at him and told me he thought the old man worked at the trust company. The trust company shared the bank cafeteria. I had never seen him before and never wanted to see him again knowing he had seen my underwear!

Well, I didn't see him again. That is, until about seventeen years later. By this time I worked for a different bank and I was walking with other employees in a charity walk through Clayton. I had just had a minor surgical procedure the day before, so I could not walk very fast. I had started out walking with some co-workers, but had soon fallen behind. I found myself walking with an older gentleman and we struck up a conversation. He told me he had just retired from a downtown trust company and was now working part time in the trust department of the bank where I worked. As we walked and talked we discovered that we had both worked for the same company years ago; I for the bank, and he for the trust company. All of a sudden it hit me. It was him—the old man who had seen my underwear seventeen years ago! Of course I didn't say a thing about the "underwear" incident, but I was afraid that if I continued to walk and talk with him, he might suddenly put two and two together and remember me and my underwear. And I know you won't believe this, but he was walking at my left and slightly behind me. Had he recognized me and was he hoping to get another glimpse of my underwear? The adrenaline of my embarrassment helped me step up my pace. Seventeen years had apparently slowed him down a little. This time he couldn't keep up with me. I quickly got so far ahead that he could no longer see me, much less my underwear!

My Googly Eyes

Another time I somehow got hold of a pair of googly eyed glasses. I had them hidden by my side as I walked through the bank lobby. As soon as I passed the Customer Service Department where some friends of mine worked, I put on the glasses. My friend Becky happened to be looking toward the open door way as I walked by. I yelled to her, "Look, Becky, I have googly eyes!" Usually Becky would have laughed, but this time she just stayed poker-faced. "What is wrong with her today?" I wondered to myself. I decided to walk past her office again, from the other direction, and try again to get a rise out of her or anybody else in the department. From this direction I could see several other employees, and noticed that they were all facing the corner of the department right next to the open doorway. None of them laughed or even changed the expressions on their faces as I screamed "googly eyes, googly eyes!" Then to my horror I followed their stoic gazes to a woman who was standing at the front of the department. I didn't recognize her. I didn't fully comprehend what was going on, but had enough sense to get out of there. I removed the glasses and ran back to my desk. I called my friend Becky and left her a message to call me ASAP! A few minutes later Becky called. She asked "What in the hell were you doing?" Then she explained that the lady was from the Social Security Administration and had been brought in to educate the Customer Service Department on how to handle direct deposit. That explained why not one employee had moved a muscle in their faces, broken their gazes or even slightly smiled when I yelled "googly eyes, googly eyes" over and over like an idiot. Becky told me that the woman from Social Security had not reacted whatsoever to my googly-eyed appearance, and had continued to speak, as the embarrassed employees tried to keep a straight face.

As I write this story, I have laughed so hard that I almost gave myself an asthma attack. Maybe you had to be there to fully appreciate the lunacy of this episode, but I count this as one of the craziest things I have ever done.

Surprise!

Soon after getting my Officer title, I was promoted to the Executive Financial Center to serve our wealthier customers. Working in the Executive Financial Center wasn't as much fun as working in the Personal Banking Department. I did manage to do a few crazy things while I worked there, though. I once led an imaginary parade through the bank lobby. There was some marching music playing on the lobby sound system and I just instinctively started marching. Then when I saw that people were watching, I hammed it up. I led the marching band with my imaginary baton, twirled it around and even threw it up in the air, catching it expertly. I missed the fun days in Personal Banking and just wanted to get away from the stuffiness of the Executive Financial Center for a bit.

The Officer who sat next to me in the Executive Financial Center was named Dennis, who could be pretty uptight sometimes, but he also liked to have fun. One day we had a meeting and Dennis told me to go ahead without him, as he had something he just had to get done before he left. The Executive Financial Center was on the other side of the door that led to the Commercial Lending area. The Commercial Lending Department was temporarily empty at the time due to it being remodeled. We could cut through there to get to our meeting.

The others in my department were already in the meeting place. As I entered the area alone, I got a brilliant idea. I would hide in an empty closet and pop out as soon as I heard Dennis come through the door. He could be kind of high strung at times and it would be fun to scare the wits out of him. I was in the closet giggling to myself in anticipation as I waited for my quarry. I heard the door open and I sprang into action. I jumped out yelling "Surprise!", but it wasn't Dennis. It was a Senior Vice-President and a commercial loan customer checking on the progress of the renovations. I was the one who was surprised that day!

My Comedy-in-Banking Career Continues at Cash Bank

I quit banking in January 1987 to return to college, finish my work towards a degree and pursue a career in radio broadcasting. At least that was the plan. My dream was to host a local radio show, "Mad Marilyn at Midnight". Unfortunately, when I graduated in

January 1988, I had no real connections and very little experience in the radio industry, so I ended up giving up my dream of being a radio personality. I decided that I should stay in the banking industry, but try to find a position that would be challenging and not only use my banking experience, but more importantly, use my creativity and leadership skills.

I could have gone back to my old bank and taken a position as a Personal Banker again, but pride and a desire to do something different led me to send my resume to other banks in the area. I wanted a fresh start at a bank that wouldn't automatically peg me as a Personal Banker. After a few interviews for positions that didn't really fit the bill, I answered a newspaper ad for a position with a bank in Clayton, MO. I'll call it Cash Bank. They were starting a brand new department called Telephone Banking and were looking for a Sales Manager. They were looking for someone with a strong banking and sales background, and for someone who could be creative. That was a good description of me, so I sold them on me and got the position. Mostly I did a good job for the five and-a-half years that I managed the Telephone Banking Sales staff. I specialized in sales training and my department soon became a training ground for the branch staff. I used creativity to motivate the sales people and we broke many records. But there were a few incidents that made me seem more crazy than creative. Some stories are in other sections, but here are a few.

That's No Dog, That's Our Boss!

The Telephone Banking Department had Saturday hours from 9:00 AM until Noon. The two managers (me and Debbie, the Customer Service Manager) and several supervisors rotated supervising so that I only had to work one Saturday out of every six or so. It wasn't so bad working on Saturdays because there was no one in the bank except for our small Saturday crew. We dressed casually, in jeans and sneakers, which really affected our behavior; at least mine.

One particular Saturday, it was my turn to supervise. I remember I had a cold that day and didn't feel well at all. I was complaining about my head feeling stuffed up when one of the employees offered me some over-the-counter cold tablets. I took two tablets, forgetting that some medicine acts the exact opposite in my system. (See my New Year's Eve story under Kid Stories for more details). These cold tablets came with a warning that they could cause drowsiness. Instead of making me drowsy, they made me crazy. All of a sudden the craziness kicked in and I went over to the employee's cubicle to show him how crazy his cold tablets had made me. He was on a call. I got down on the floor and started barking like a dog and pretending to "nip" at his heels. Somehow he managed to keep his composure. I kept barking and laughing like a lunatic and he kept holding it together. Soon other employees were laughing too. The employee told me later that the customer had asked if there was a party going on, to which he had replied "No, that's just my manager. She's down on the ground barking and trying to bite me!" The employee kept a straight voice, if that's such a thing, and continued the call without once losing his composure. Luckily the customer didn't say much more about the party going on in the background or the whacky manager, and apparently never reported the incident, because I never heard any more of it.

Day Tripping

Another time, one of my employees left a large empty box behind his desk, blocking part of the pathway I took to walk around the department. He had just unpacked some supplies and hadn't had time to properly discard the box, but I decided to teach him a lesson about never blocking the aisles for fire safety reasons. So I decided to fake-trip over the box. I stuck my foot in the box and began the fake trip when my other heel somehow got caught in the hem of my skirt. The foot in the box slid forward and with the other foot caught up in the hem of my skirt, I tipped over and landed face down on the floor. Everyone around me gasped out loud. Some kept right on talking to their customers, with horrified looks on their faces, while others asked me if I was alright or what had happened. I got up right away, unharmed, and explained that I was okay and that I had just been trying to teach the employee a lesson. I think the only lesson anyone learned that day was to never try to fake trip when you are a klutz and wearing very high heels and a longish skirt.

I always had fun when I worked in Telephone Banking. We were always having contests to motivate the staff to take more calls and make more sales. Mostly I behaved myself, and didn't do anything too inappropriate, except for the two incidents I just described. But there is one more story I'd like to include in "My Comedy-in-Banking Career Continues at Cash Bank".

Abe Lincoln Once Owned this Piece

Probably around the third or fourth year of my almost six year career with Cash Bank, we hosted a barbeque for a newly-acquired bank from Peoria, Illinois. The executives from our new Peoria bank locations were bussed to St. Louis for some meetings and a catered barbeque dinner to introduce them to the St. Louis management team. As a manager, I was invited and encouraged to make these people feel welcome; a part of the Cash Bank family. After the dinner, our CEO asked me if I would be interested in leading a little tour of the second floor (executive floor) of the bank. I said yes, although I did tell him that I really didn't know too much of the bank's history. He laughed and told me to just wing it. So that's what I did. I could have just led the visitors around and blandly pointed out who sat where, but that was not creative enough for me. I wanted to lead a tour they would not forget.

The second floor of the bank was gorgeous and displayed many beautiful pieces, some of which were obviously antiques. One of the visitors remarked on a beautiful piece of furniture, and without really thinking, I blurted out that I thought the piece of furniture had once belonged to their state's favorite son, Mr. Abraham Lincoln. Now, please keep in mind that I did not exactly tell a lie. I said that I "thought" it had belonged to Abe Lincoln. I saw our CEO after the tour and he asked me how it had gone. Again, without thinking, I just blurted out that I had "winged it" just as he had suggested I do. Then I added that I may or may not have been a little misleading about where some of the beautiful furniture and décor may have come from. He just grinned. I think he had a great sense of humor, just not as zany as mine.

The Brokerage Biz Can Be Fun, Too!

As I got older and maybe somewhat more mature, my on-the-job high-jinx lessened. When I made the transition from banking to the brokerage industry, I had lots of serious studying to do, which left little time for my usual silliness-on-the-job. But once I got my securities licenses out of the way, I was back in the tomfoolery business.

The High Chair!

At the bank brokerage company where I started an investment call center, I managed a staff of four young brokers – young enough to be my children, but I don't know if I can say that I was the most mature of the bunch. One of my employees, S., was fun to pick on. S. fell for practically everything and took it good-naturedly. One day, when the department was still brand new and we were just getting to know one another, I decided to play a trick on S. By design, S. came in to work a little later than the rest of us did, so he missed an early morning presentation on how to use the new chairs that had just arrived. He offered to come in early that day for the meeting, but I assured him that I would pass along any tips that the manufacturer's rep might give us on how to get the most out of our new ergonomic chairs.

I let the others in on my plan to mess with S. When he came in that day I told him that the chairs had a special feature to help manage employees' time away from their workstations. I explained that after an employee had been out of his chair for five minutes, the seat would automatically adjust upward, and would have to be manually lowered back into position before the employee could sit again. This feature was supposed to alert management if an employee was abusing time away from his desk, and to help the employee manage his own time. I went on to explain that the chair levels were somehow recorded and reported to upper management every time they were adjusted back to the proper level. I agreed that it was a weird concept, but that upper management really wanted to reduce the time that employees were away from their workstations.

I then proceeded to send S. away from his desk to run numerous little errands for me. He was always so eager to impress me that he liked when I chose him to do things for me, such as making copies, dropping off something at another office, getting supplies, etc. He would do anything to gain brownie points. Each time he left his chair, one of us would adjust the seat to be really high. S. raced back from every errand, because I had urged him to try not to let the seat go up. No matter how fast S. was, he always returned to a high seat. He adjusted it each time, and almost as soon as he sat down, I had another errand for him. He seemed oblivious to our snickers as I sent him on one errand after another. Each time he got back too late. At one point I heard him mutter "This is so stupid" as he adjusted his seat one more time. I could see he was getting frustrated. The three others and I kept making comments to further rattle him, such as "You're going to have to be faster, S. You're making our department look bad." Finally he had had enough. He came back from an errand only to find a raised seat once again, but this time he just climbed up and sat in it without adjusting it to the proper height. S. was short in stature so he had a hard time reaching the high seat. As high as his seat was, he almost fell out of it when he stooped down to answer a phone call. Finally we could not stand it any longer. We all started laughing until we had tears running down our faces. It took S. a minute to realize why we were laughing. He was a good sport when we explained it, though. After that, every once in a while one of us would adjust his seat up when he left it, as a reminder of that day.

The Mucophagist Among Us

Several months later, one of the female employees complained to me that S. was picking his nose on the job. I decided to teach him a lesson. I wrote a long email supposedly from Human Resources about a widespread employee hygiene problem that had come to their attention. I forwarded a copy to my employees. The email addressed the fact that there were too many employees getting sick, which was costing the company money, and demanded that managers enforce a strict hygiene policy which included no booger picking at work! It even went so far as to say that there would be MA meetings available for those employees who had obsessions with picking their noses. The "M" stood for mucophagy, the medical name for booger-picking. The other employees did not take it seriously, but I think S. did. After a minute or so, I sent an email to S. only, and informed him that I had signed him up for the Mucophagy Anonymous meetings, because an informant had given me a heads up about his nasty habit. In the email I explained that he should not take this as my "picking" on him, pardon the pun, but that I was just concerned about his obsession. I also stated that he was not to tell anyone that he was going to the meetings, since it was an anonymous thing. I walked out by the employees just in time to hear S. ask if anyone else had gotten a follow-up email from me. I quickly pulled him aside and told him this whole nose-picking business was serious and that he was not to discuss it further with the other employees. One by one, in private, the other employees told me that they thought my email had been funny and that S. seemed to be taking it seriously. He had made several comments that indicated that he thought that HR was really going overboard about the nose-picking. They also observed that he had not picked his nose, at least not publicly, since the email.

The next day I sent S. another fake email from HR giving the time and location of the first MA meeting. It said that each participant was being asked to bring a box of Kleenex to the meeting as there was going to be a guest speaker who would teach the attendees the proper way to remove "natural material" from one's nose. A short time later S. came into my cubicle, which was away from the rest of the department, and told me he had something to discuss with me. He looked really concerned and embarrassed. He asked if he really had to go to the MA meeting if he promised never to pick another booger at work again. He begged me to get him out of attending. I told him I would try. I got back with S. a short time later and informed him that HR had denied his request to be made exempt from the meetings. I warned him that if he didn't attend the meetings that HR would probably put him under some sort of surveillance, and that I hoped my asking if he could be exempt didn't already put him on some sort of list. When I saw how seriously S. was taking me, and realized that I had perhaps gone too far, I started laughing. Again, S. proved he was a good sport. I could have gotten into big trouble if S. had called HR himself, but he didn't (call) and I didn't (get into trouble).

Peeing on Demand

One of S.'s successors was a young man named E. E. was bright and could sometimes be a little arrogant. I liked E., but because of his arrogance, he fell right into my hands as a perfect person to prank. I sent him a fake email from Human Resources. This email said that he had been chosen for a random drug test and that he should drop off a container of his pee at the non-existent "nurse's office". I described the location for the "nurse's office" as the empty space that was being set up for a department. The department had not moved in yet and there would probably not be anybody there when E. dropped off his container. The email went on to say that E. should use a clean "to go" cup (pardon the pun) that he could obtain from the bank cafeteria. He was to label the cup "(His full name)'s Pee" and just leave it on the counter in the "nurse's office". He was further instructed to try to fill the cup half-way with his first pee of the day at work (not the day's first pee as one is normally asked to collect). It said that he would receive results in a day or two, and that he was to keep the entire matter private. I could just picture E. walking around the bank with a cup of pee and hoping no one would notice. And the fact that the cup would be marked "(His full name)'s Pee" made me laugh out loud just thinking about it!

But this is one prank that did not go off exactly as planned. I had foolishly provided a phone number that E. could call if he had any questions. In hindsight, I should have referred him to his manager (me) if he had any questions. The extension was made up. I didn't know that any internal call to the fake extension would be forwarded to a working number. E. came to see me and told me he knew it was me behind the prank. I laughed and asked how he had figured that out. He told me he had called the "nurse's office" at the extension provided in the email, and figured out he was being pranked as soon as his call was answered by someone who worked with computers. They told him that he had not reached the nurse's office; that there was no such thing. He told me that he had planned to tell me that he had called HR, and that they were investigating who was behind the prank, but that he could not go through with that plan. Phew! I dodged a big bullet that time! Even though my prank didn't work, I still got a big kick out of picturing how it could have worked.

I'm sure there were other pranks that I pulled, or incidents that might be considered to be "crazy" enough to include here, but these are the stories that stand out in my memory from when I worked for that bank broker-dealer. Luckily I never got caught. In fact, I was promoted to Vice-President, emphasis on "vice".

Stock Broker Shenanigans

Another entity took over (in fact two different bank holding companies took over within one year) and the investment center that I was managing was disbanded. I was hired on the bank side of the company as a Private Banking trainer. After about eleven months of mostly misery in this position, I left the bank for the last time to start my own business as a training and development consultant. My business never really got off the ground. I was without a job for over a year when I started working for a discount brokerage firm in November 2000 as a call center broker. I went from being a Vice-President at the largest bank in America to being a call center representative at a then little company I'll call "The Firm". I never regretted my decision to come to The Firm though. In fact, I managed to have lots of fun while I worked there. After all, as owner, founder and CEO, Robert as I will call him for the sake of his privacy, always told us, "If you aren't having fun, it's time to leave".

Every year Robert called the branch managers from all around the country into St. Louis for the annual branch managers meeting weekend. There was always a very nice awards banquet on the Saturday evening. The St. Louis (HQ) employees were invited to attend the banquet so they could chat with the people that they normally only dealt with by telephone, and to cheer for their accomplishments. These events were always fun to attend, especially if you got to be part of the entertainment like I did a few times.

Good-bye, You Are the Weakest Link!

I have always taken every opportunity I could get to perform or somehow entertain my fellow employees no matter where I worked. I appeared in a video that was shown at the first branch manager awards banquet that I attended, so when they needed someone for the next year, guess who was recruited to star in a video called "Who Wants to Be a Millionaire?"

The hostess of the popular "Who Wants to Be a Millionaire?" was a lady named Ann Richards. She was a middle-aged, tall, slender blonde with a very short haircut and the mannerisms of a strict school teacher. Of course, she had a British accent, because she was from Great Britain where the television show had originated. You may recall that her signature phrase in a clipped British accent was "You are the weakest link. Good-bye!"

I did not look like Ann Richards, but my husband Jerry had superimposed my head on her body on the computer and printed the image. I had taken the picture to work and had it posted on my cubicle. I don't exactly remember whose idea it was to have me play Ann Richards in the video to be shown at the big meeting (maybe it was mine), but I was very excited to do it. The video would consist of a few scenes depicting how it was at the other brokerage firms and how they did not compare to the quality of service that The Firm offered. If you wanted to be a millionaire, in other words, you should use our brokerage services (implied but not guaranteed of course). At the end of each scene, Ann would say to the other brokerage firms, "You are the weakest link. Good-bye!" Ironically, one of the firms that we made fun of in this video has just purchased *The Firm.*

Robert had just been featured on the cover of a business magazine. In the picture he was standing on the roof of the two-story building that served as The Firm's headquarters at the time. He was casually leaning against a brick structure on the roof with his arms folded. For the first scene, the guys who were shooting the video wanted a shot of Ann Richards up on the roof mimicking Robert's cover shot. After work on the day of the video shoot, I combed my new short hairdo, applied stage makeup, slithered into a sophisticated black dress a la Ann Richards and donned heels. I looked a lot like Ann if you squinted and pretended that I was about thirty pounds lighter. The video guys asked me if I was game to climb up to the roof. The only way to get up there was up a rickety set of open metal steps. The first step was very high from the floor. Keep in mind that I was in my fifties, had a short skirt and high heels on and wasn't in the best physical shape. The first video guy went up and reached down for my hand. The second guy walked close behind me, ready to give me a boost or catch my fall. It took a little coaxing and a lot of effort on my part, but I made it up to the roof. I was huffing and puffing and sweating. But like the professional that I was (or at least the one I was acting like I was) I endured the scorching sun for numerous takes. The shot turned out really good. I hoped Robert wouldn't mind that I had copied his stance and facial expression exactly. The next part of the video was to take place in Robert's office. We didn't count on him still being there, since it was early evening. We asked permission to use his office for the next scene and he readily agreed. Robert always expressed his concern about taking comedy too far when making these videos, but he watched as I did my presentation. Using my best imitation of Ann Richards I ended the scene with "Goodbye, you are the weakest link". Robert told me I looked and sounded just like Ann.

There were hundreds of employees at the meeting where the video was shown, and rather than being nervous, I was excited to be in the spotlight that day. I was dressed as Ann Richards for the meeting and introduced the video. The video got a great response. After the video presentation, I was standing in line in the ladies' restroom when a young employee asked me if I was the real Ann Richards who had just appeared in the video. That was the highest compliment I could have gotten for my performance! About a year later, the "Who Wants to Be a Millionaire?" television show was looking for Ann Richards look-alikes to be contestants on the show. I inquired at work if I could get a copy of the video we had made to send in as my audition tape. I got a phone call from Robert himself and he said that rather than using The Firm's videotape, he would have the company video guys shoot an audition tape for me. He said he thought I had a good chance of being selected and wished me luck. Unfortunately, I was not selected for the show. When I watched the show, I was very disappointed, because the contestants they chose did not look any more like Ann than I did. Oh well, I'm glad Robert liked me as Ann Richards!

The Horn, the Horn, Awakes Me at Morn!

When I worked in the call center I worked the 6:00 AM – 2:00 PM shift. I didn't like getting up at 4:15, but I did like getting home from work by 3:00 in the afternoon and not having to deal with much traffic. I am generally a morning person. As soon as my clock radio comes on, I hit the ground singing. So by the time I walked into the call center I was geared up and ready for the day. I was buoyed up from the loud music I played and sang along to on the ride to work. The "kids" that I worked with stayed up late partying or watching television, and did not seem at all like morning people. It was usually dark in the department when I walked in, because the "kids" couldn't stand to have the bright lights on that early in the morning. I came in with my chipper "Good Mornings", singing or humming the last song I had heard on the radio and flipped on the overhead lights to grumbled protests. I explained that I needed the lights on in order to properly see my computer screen, which was true.

One morning I was unusually wound up by the time I got to work. I flipped on the lights, said my "Good Mornings" and even did a little tap dance on the floor mat in front of my desk just to let everyone know I was there and ready to brighten their day! Everyone seemed especially sullen and I heard barely a mumble that morning. We had celebrated several birthdays the day before, and I spied some leftover party hats and noisemakers (that I had brought in). I picked up one of the noisemakers - a horn - and loudly blew it to get a rise out of someone, anyone. Boy did it work! I heard my manager's voice gruffly and loudly yell out, "Who blew the F'n horn?" He didn't abbreviate the "F" word like I just did. He fully pronounced it, which was very unusual for him. I had never heard him yell, much less curse. I must have really caught him in a bad mood. My favorite co-worker Ryan looked at me and later told me that I had looked like a deer in the headlights as I held up the offensive horn and slowly dropped it into the trash. I then turned around towards my desk, quietly put on my headset and logged into my computer and phone. The department was dead silent, except for some very quiet answers to customer phone calls. After a few minutes went by, we heard our manager apologize to all of us. I felt so bad for apparently making him so angry that he went out of character and cursed in front of the entire call center. I quietly went over to his cubicle and told him that I was the horn-blowing culprit and that I was very sorry. He told me that he thought it had been Ryan. I laughed and said "You didn't suspect the nice old lady, did you?" He just looked down and went back to his work. I could tell he was embarrassed and didn't want to talk about it. Ryan and I had a good laugh knowing that our manager had thought it was him, and that if I had kept my mouth shut he would have never known it was me. I thought the incident was hilarious. I managed to rile everyone up that morning and wasn't even a suspect until I opened my big mouth!

This is Country Bumpkin Marilyn. How Can I Help You?

We had pretty "high tech" phones in the call center. Our phones had a feature that allowed a call center rep. to record and store up to ten greetings, and select one to answer calls instead of having to verbally greet each caller. I didn't like this feature, and since it was not mandatory for us to use it, I didn't. But one day during downtime, I decided to have a little fun. I recorded several different greetings. I recorded greetings featuring Sister Mary Marilyn answering the phone with "Blessings to you, dear child", to Doofus Marilyn answering the phone with "Uh, how do you work this thing? Uh. Hello? Hello?"

My intention was to have Ryan listen to them and make him think that I was really going to use them, and to then delete all of them. Ryan listened to and laughed at all of them. Then, knowing how technically challenged I was (and still am) he admonished me to make sure I had deleted all of them. I was in the middle of assuring him that I had deleted all of them when a customer call came in. Apparently I had not yet switched my phone back to the mode where I had to physically answer it so the call went straight to the pre-recorded greetings, which I thought were non-existent. As I heard this happening I thought that the worst that could happen is that the customer would hear no greeting at all until I "flipped the switch" back and spoke my greeting. Much to my horror I heard my pre-recorded voice greeting the customer in the most hideous backwoods country accent. Apparently I had not deleted that one. So I decided to continue with the accent so the customer wouldn't suspect that I had been goofing around. Ryan and others who sat near me could hear me giving stock quotes and other information in my country bumpkin accent and probably wondering what was the crazy new old lady doing now?

Water on the Head!

Another partner in crime at the firm was a young woman named Julie. We were always playing pranks on one another, trying to make each other laugh, and in general were usually up to no good when we were together. One day Julie walked behind my chair on her way out of the department. She tugged at my hair as she walked by to try to make me laugh while I was on a call. I ended my call and decided to follow her into the restroom so I could play some kind of a prank on her. I entered the restroom and saw that only one stall was occupied. Perfect, I thought. I wouldn't have to squat down to look for Julie's shoes. I knew exactly where my victim was! I ran the water in the sink and got both hands full of water. I quickly ran over to the empty stall, reached my hands over towards Julie's head as she sat in the other stall and shook all the water on her. Then I made a beeline out of the restroom. I was surprised that I hadn't heard her squeal, laugh or make any noise, because Julie is definitely not the silent type. I hid myself behind a sign in the hallway right in front of the restroom and waited for a dripping wet Julie to come out. It was hard not to laugh out loud as I stood in wait. Finally, the restroom door opened and I popped out from behind the sign, ready to laugh in Julie's face. But instead of Julie, it was a lady whom I'll call Cindy, who was a respected manager and longtime employee, whom I did not know very well. I saw that there were beads of water on her eyeglasses and her hair was a little wet, but I couldn't laugh out loud. In fact, I just kind of stood there, paralyzed. Cindy didn't act like she even saw me. I ran back to my department and found Julie. "Where were you?" I demanded, and then proceeded to tell my story. Julie and I laughed so hard we almost wet ourselves!

A few years later, when I worked in the Compliance Department, employees were asked to contribute stories about Cindy to be read at her retirement party. I decided to share my story about making it rain on Cindy's head. I didn't attend the retirement party, but afterwards I talked to some of the people who had attended, and they told me that someone had read my story that night and that Cindy had laughed. I was relieved that she had found it funny. I didn't think I'd ever see Cindy again, but still, I was glad that she hadn't gotten mad or anything. A short time after she retired, Cindy came back to the firm to help out with a project. She and I talked one day, and I asked her if my story had offended her in any way and I apologized for getting her wet. She laughed and assured me that she thought it had been funny. What a good sport!

The Scarf Dance

The worst thing that I ever did at the firm was the scarf dance. My friend Julie was now working in the Training Department and I was working in the Compliance Department. I was leaving for the day and Julie still had another hour to work. Her desk was behind a glass wall and I routinely stopped by on my way to the elevator and waved to her at the end of the day. This particular day Julie was on the phone, looking down at her desk. I wanted to get her attention, so I whipped off the long scarf I was wearing and proceeded to do a racy dance with it, waving it around then sliding it between my legs and doing other crazy moves. It was pretty bad. Julie's head was still bent down as she concentrated on talking on the phone. Suddenly I saw someone coming down the hall. I abruptly pulled the scarf out from between my legs, but it was too late. The employee had seen me. I assured myself that I had seen a small smile on her face as she left the hallway. Julie looked up, and I made a beeline to the elevator and got out of there. As if leaving could erase what I had just done.

The next morning I described the whole incident to Julie. We had a good laugh as I recreated my racy scarf dance. Later that morning I received an email from the head of security. It stated that he had reviewed the camera by the elevator as he routinely did and had come across what he called my lewd dancing. He said the company had no tolerance for that type of behavior and explained that he had no choice but to report me to the Ethics Committee. He went on to instruct me to appear before the committee at a specific time that morning, and he provided a phone number to call to confirm that I would be there.

I was mortified and scared out of my mind. I pictured what I would say in front of the Ethics Committee. I would start out by apologizing profusely and promising never to do anything like that again. I was prepared to humbly offer my resignation if need be. As I dialed the number provided in the email I wondered when the Ethics Committee had been formed. I had not heard of it, but I was not surprised that there was one. Monitoring workplace behavior had become more stringent than ever in the past few years. Maybe there was no longer a place in the workforce for someone as irreverent as I was. Maybe my scarf dance was my last workplace prank. By the time I dialed the last digit of the four-digit extension for the "Ethics Committee", I realized that the phone number looked familiar. Just then I heard Julie's voice answer the phone! After talking and laughing with Julie, I called the head of security and we had a good laugh, too. Julie got me and she got me good! I deserved to be scared out of my wits for not only dancing lewdly in public, but in reparation for all of the inappropriate behavior I had exhibited ever since I joined the workforce many years before! Kudos, Julie. I couldn't have done it better!

My Crazy Childhood Stories

The Lady Next Door

I loved the lady who lived next door to the house where I lived from the day my parents brought me home from the hospital until I was nearly four years old. Mrs. K. was a widow. I'm not sure how old she was when I knew her; maybe in her sixties? All I know is that I loved her and that she was like a grandma to me.

Apparently I visited Mrs. K. on daily basis, and more than once a day. My Dad even installed a gate in between our houses so I could go back and forth easier. Mrs. K. used to give me cookies. I was quite a talker, and according to what my parents later told me, I told a lot of tall tales to Mrs. K.

Adults really liked me because I told lots of tall tales. But one day I wasn't likeable at all. I remember that day, and I really don't think it is a contrived memory based on what my parents told me about it. I can actually picture Mrs. K. mopping and waxing her kitchen floor that day. The chairs were moved out of the kitchen and I sat on one in the next room while she slowly cleaned her way towards me. I asked her for a drink of water and she told me "No!" because the floors were not dry. Apparently I didn't like her answer so I spit at her! She sent me home. Later when she and my Mom were sitting in their own backyards and talking as they did every evening in nice weather, Mrs. K. snitched on me. She told my Mom that I should be spanked for spitting at her! I remember getting scolded and being forced to apologize to her, but I was not spanked.

    One night when I was three I had to spend the night with Mrs. K. I wish I knew why, but there's no one to ask. I think my Mom had to go to the hospital for some reason. It was my first night away from my home or family. I slept in Mrs. K.'s bed with her. In the middle of the night I awoke to the overhead light suddenly being switched on and Mrs. K. yelling at me. I had had an accident in her bed! Mrs. K. grabbed me by the back of my neck and pushed my face down to within a few inches of the "accident". She yelled with frustration, "I ought to make you eat it!"

    I was so scared and very ashamed. I don't think I'll ever forget that scene. Mrs. K. certainly lost her cool that night. Maybe she wasn't the grandmotherly type after all. Maybe she barely tolerated me when I came to visit her every day. I'm just glad she didn't make me eat "it" that night. And I'll bet she was glad that her house was permeated with many years' worth of the smell of her son's cherry-vanilla pipe tobacco.

    (I learned in Psych 101 that according to Freud, if you were traumatized during your toilet training years that you might forever be stuck in that level of mental maturity. Maybe this story explains a lot about me).

Star Struck at Age Three?

There was another neighbor on Juniata Street that I loved visiting. She was the movie star Betty Grable's aunt. I don't know the woman's name, so I'll just refer to her as Betty Grable's aunt. My older sister Lois often played with a Kindergarten classmate, a girl named Gloria, who lived next door to Betty Grable's aunt. Lois used to let me tag along sometimes and Gloria and she took me to Betty Grable's aunt's place at least once, so I knew where she lived. One day I just decided to go see her all by myself. I was only three years old at the time. I just passed by that block the other day and marveled at how far away our house was from Betty Grable's aunt's place. It was quite a long walk for a three year old.

Betty Grable's aunt lived in a two-story flat on the second floor. I only remember the kitchen, possibly because that was the only room I ever saw. It had a beauty shop shampoo sink next the kitchen sink. Perhaps she had once owned a beauty shop and saved this one sink for occasional customers who came to her home. I remember getting my hair shampooed there once, but I am not sure if I was with Gloria and Lois at the time or if it was the day I went there alone.

I have a clear memory of sitting at her kitchen table in a chair and eating candy while I sat there talking this lady's arm off. I wonder what I talked about. I probably told some real whoppers! I must have been a good story teller, because old ladies used to ply me with cookies and candy and let me talk for hours. In this case I told stories for at least two hours. I didn't realize how long I had been there until my sister came to the door and told me to get home. My Mom had been looking for me for a long while and was ready to call the police when someone thought to check Betty Grable's aunt's apartment. I got a big lecture about always telling my Mom where I was going. I don't remember, but I was probably also told to never go into someone's home again without my Mom's permission, because I don't recall ever going back to Betty Grable's aunt's apartment again.

Pulling the Dentist's Leg

Our family dentist, Dr. O'Brien, also used to enjoy my stories. One time when I was probably about three years old, my Mom waited in the waiting room while he checked my teeth. I'm surprised I kept my mouth still long enough for him to even get a good look at my teeth. He told my Mom that I had told him some very interesting things. Apparently I had told him that my Mom fed me garbage and that she kept me under the kitchen table because I was a horse! I don't know why I would have said those things. Maybe he asked what foods I liked. At the time, I didn't really like much food. I loved Oreos and saltine crackers, often eating them one after another for a sweet and salty snack. (And you thought "sweet 'n salty" was a recent culinary phenomenon!). I also liked bologna sandwiches with mustard, devil's food cake, soft-boiled eggs with lots of salt, Campbell's chicken noodle soup and my Mom's home-made potato salad. I hated vegetables except for corn. With my vivid imagination, I may have thought my Mom was serving me garbage when she served anything except the few things I liked. And I do remember playing under the kitchen table while my Mom did the weekly ironing. She probably told me to play there so she could keep an eye on me. It did sort of feel like I was being corralled. Maybe I wasn't telling tall tales to pull the dentist's leg. Maybe I was telling the truth, or at least the way I saw it when I was three years old.

My Own Personal Witch

One of my truths when I was three years old was that a witch actually appeared in our kitchen. To this day, I swear, I saw her. She came right out of one of my sister's Golden books and stood in our kitchen, behind everyone else so they couldn't see her. Only I saw her, and no one believed that I had.

It was the only time she appeared to me, but she haunted me for many years. She lived under my bed and came out only when everyone in the house had fallen asleep. I slept on my stomach. She often reached out and touched my upper back, always on the right side, or the back of my neck, just to let me know she was there. I was so afraid of her. Until I was about twelve years old, I had to sleep with a cover on my upper back, even if it was a hot summer's night, and it had to be pulled up high enough to cover my neck. Otherwise, I felt too vulnerable to the witch's touch.

I made the mistake of letting my sister Lois know that I was afraid of the witch. Sometimes we'd be in the kitchen when it was dark outside. If my back was to the window, she would suddenly point to the window behind me and loudly exclaim, "Look! It's the witch!" I would scream bloody murder and she would laugh until one of my parents scolded her for making me scream.

That witch lived with us on Juniata Street and then again on Wyoming Street, but not on Bryant Avenue. I guess she didn't want to live outside of the city limits any more than my Mom did, because

I don't remember her being with us when we lived out in the suburbs.

Leader of the Brat Pack

We lived in Overland, MO, a suburb of St. Louis, from when I was almost four years old until I was a little over five. Our house was midway down Bryant Avenue from Lackland Avenue, which was a very busy street. There was a grocery store (Di Carlo's?) on the corner of Lackland and Bryant, across Lackland Avenue. I am pretty sure that I was told to never cross Lackland Avenue by myself.

But one day, while my Mom napped and I had nothing to do I snuck out of the house and had an idea to walk to the grocery store to get a free candy bar. My Mom, sister and I had been there recently while there was a man from a candy company stocking a rack. Lois and I had struck up a conversation with him and he gave us each a free candy bar. (All these years, until today, I thought maybe he gave us the free candy bars as a marketing ploy, but now I wonder if the darned things weren't stale or something and he was just getting rid of them to get rid of us!) Anyway, I loved the idea of getting a free candy bar again. So I rounded up Bobby and Boo (real name, Linda), my next door neighbors, who were five and three years old at the time and my neighbor on the other side of my house whose name was Dennis, I think, and who was four years old like me. And there was one other kid, who I remember nothing about except that he was a neighbor, he was a boy and he would do anything I said he should do.

I told the kids that I would lead them to the grocery store and we would each get a free candy bar. I remember the kids walking behind me in single file. When we got to the busy street, I told them to all hold hands and wait until I said it was clear to run across the street as fast as they could. Somehow we made it across the street. I really don't know how. The next scene I remember is standing at the check-out counter and telling the lady that we were there for our free candy bars. Not only did she tell us that we were not getting free candy bars, but she scolded us for coming to the store without our mothers. She recognized Bobby and Boo, and said she was going to call their mother. She made us wait in the store until Bobby and Boo's Mom (Mrs. P.) came to escort us safely home. As she walked us home, Mrs. P. stopped at each house and explained to each mom what we had done. Each mom grabbed her kid and told the rest of us that the kid was grounded for the rest of the day. I was the last kid to be turned in.

I don't know how long my Mom made me stay in the house, but it wasn't long. Knowing me, I whined and badgered her to let me go outside to the point where she just let me out of the house for the sake of peace and quiet. I decided to spring the rest of the kids out of prison since I had gotten out early for bad behavior. Bobby and Boo were first. I remember they were standing behind their screen door looking all sad because they couldn't come out to play. I proceeded to whimper and scratch the screen like a puppy until I drove Mrs. P. crazy, and she let her kids out. Two down and two to go! Off we went to Dennis' house. We sprung him in no time flat. Then I and my little band of followers went to Little-What's-His-Name's house and got him out too.

I was pretty proud of myself for outsmarting the grown-ups that day. I was a whiz at wearing parents down when I really wanted something, but not so good at wearing the lady at the grocery store down. If only I had had one minute alone with her to convince her that giving us free candy would be good for business. But when she recognized Bobby and Boo, I didn't get that time. And now I have a sudden craving for a Zero Bar!

The Mysterious Mouse Bite!

I was four or five years old when a mouse bit me. We were living in the house on Bryant Avenue in Overland. My Mom had me in the kitchen with her while she ironed. The phone rang, and before answering it, my Mom told me not to touch the hot iron. I really don't remember where the phone was in that house, but I feel like it was in another room, because my Mom did not see me when I touched the hot iron. Yikes! It was very hot, and a blister formed on my pointer finger right away. I didn't want to get in trouble for disobeying my Mom, so I had to think quickly how to explain the blister before my Mom came back.

I had also been told never to stick anything in the electrical socket or else I could get really hurt. Maybe sticking your finger into a socket gave you a big, red, hurtful blister like the one I just got. I wasn't sure. I was going to go with that story until I realized that my finger was too big to fit inside of the tiny holes of the socket. Besides, I would have gotten into trouble for sticking my finger in the socket.

I had seen in numerous story books that mice lived inside walls, so maybe I could say that a mouse had bitten me, but I didn't see any mouse holes in our kitchen walls. My Mom was ending her phone conversation, so I had to quickly settle on a plausible story.

I looked at the open kitchen door. It had sort of a hole in the bracket where the little "thing-a-ma-jig" fit when you turned the knob. That would have to serve as the mouse hole. Just as my Mom came in I put my finger in the "mouse hole" and recreated my original little gasp of pain that she had just missed.

I held up my throbbing, reddened finger to her and cried a little. I told her that a mouse had bitten it. Then I pointed to the mouse hole and explained that I thought I had heard a mouse in there, so I had stuck my finger in. (I had never been told not to stick my finger in that place, so I probably wasn't going to get in trouble for disobeying). My Mom ran my finger under the cold water and didn't say much more about the mysterious mouse that apparently lived inside our kitchen door. When my Dad came home from work that afternoon, my Mom told him all about the mouse and how it had bitten me. My Dad inspected the "bite". I remember my Dad saying "A mouse bit you, huh?" and he had a twinkle in his eyes. Then he went over to the door, looked into the "mouse hole" and said, "Yep. There's a mouse in there all right!"

I was only four or five, but I knew what was going on. I could tell by the amused looks on both my Mom's and Dad's faces that they didn't really believe there was a mouse that had bitten me, and that they knew I was telling another one of my wild stories. I think they let it go because they knew I had learned my lesson to never touch a hot iron again.

I Eat Telephone Poles!

If you haven't noticed yet, I'll tell you that I am an attention-seeker and have a need for everybody to like me. I've always been like that. On the way to school when I was in Kindergarten, I found myself walking with a little girl named Mary Beth, who was in my class. I liked her very much, because she was also an attention-seeker and I thought she was funny. In order to gain her admiration I told her that I ate telephone poles. Naturally, she didn't believe me. So I decided to prove it. I was sure it would impress her if I took a big bite out of the wooden pole that we were about to pass. I sunk my front teeth into the pole. I can still remember how the wood splintered between my two front teeth and cut my gums a little. It tasted horrible—dirty wood shreds mixed with a little blood. I proudly displayed the wooden bits in my mouth before spitting as much of it out as I could. Mary Beth didn't look impressed. In fact, she said something to the effect that I was stupid. We were friends after that, though. Maybe she respected me a little for biting wood to impress her.

I invited her to my sixth birthday party. After the presents were opened, the cake and ice cream eaten, and all of the planned games played, the kids got a little restless. My Mom left the living room for a minute and Mary Beth decided to entertain us all by jumping on our brand new faux leather arm chair. The chair was chartreuse and my Mom was very proud to have a nice new piece of furniture that had been delivered just the day before, in time for my party. I knew that Mary Beth shouldn't be jumping on our furniture, but I didn't want to jeopardize my hard-earned friendship with her by telling her to stop. My Mom returned to the living room and was horrified to see Mary Beth jumping on our new chair. She told Mary Beth to stop. Mary Beth didn't look too happy. Neither did my Mom.

After all of the parents came to pick up their little angels, my Mom ranted and raved about how "nervy" Mary Beth was, and how I was not allowed to invite her over ever again. Mary Beth and I were in different classes from first grade on, so our Kindergarten friendship didn't blossom into anything further. It had nothing to do with her jumping on the chair. We always remained fond of one another, even years later when she became a part of a clique and I didn't. Every once in awhile on the playground, or if we passed one another on the street, she would wink at me and ask me if I still ate telephone poles. And I asked her if she still jumped on furniture.

The Great Bank Robbery

My friend Judy H. and I were best friends for about four years until she moved away from our neighborhood. We took dance lessons at an in-home studio three houses away from where I lived and across the alley from where Judy lived. That's how we met.

We did lots of crazy things together, which I will talk about in separate stories. I had actually forgotten the story of the Great Bank Robbery until I sat next to Judy H. at my forty-fifth high school reunion. (Judy and I ended up going to the same high school after being separated for about four years. She was in the class behind me, but her class and my class always hold our reunions together). It's funny how things work out. This crazy little blonde girl, who was my childhood friend and then moved away, ended up sitting next to me at a high school reunion many years later!

Judy asked me if I remembered the bank robbery incident. In her mind, it was the Great Bank Robbery that was the title of a movie about the robbery of Southwest Bank in St. Louis in the 1950's. She remembered that it was winter when the incident occurred and that we were both wearing our matching vinyl mittens that we had just bought at the corner grocery store where we often hung out. When she mentioned the mittens, I suddenly remembered them and the robbery. The mittens were white with thin blue plaid lines on them. They were cheaply made, very stiff and probably cost one dollar or less. I'm not sure how we talked our parents into letting us buy them, but I remember that these mittens were our pride and joy.

On the day of the robbery, Judy and I were walking around the neighborhood looking for some trouble to get into, and we found it. The way I remember it, a speeding car nearly hit us as it pulled up to the curb a few yards in front of us. The men in the car got out and started running. As they did so, they dropped some of their loot. I don't remember paper money, but I do remember coins-- lots of them. Judy and I saw the money and started scooping the coins up with our mittens. Our hands were not very nimble because of the mittens, so it was very difficult to get many coins. But neither of us had "enough sense to come in out of the rain" as they say, so neither of us had enough sense to take off the damned vinyl mittens. Just then a speeding cop car arrived. They caught the men and put them in handcuffs.

Meanwhile Judy and I kept trying to scoop up coins and get them into our pockets. The cops yelled at us to stop and get out of their way. Judy and I just kept scooping until one of the cops yelled at us again. He explained that the thugs in the police car had just robbed Southwest Bank.

Years later, in Judy's mind, the robbery incident was the one that was portrayed in the movie with Steve McQueen. I told her that "our" robbery had taken place in a different year. That's too bad. If we had indeed been involved with the Great Bank Robbery incident, maybe they would have let Judy and I appear in the movie.

Our brush with real live cops and robbers ended without us getting to keep any of the coins. We got yelled at by our parents for interfering with an arrest and there was not even a mention of a movie!

Collecting Money for Mr. Diamond's Funeral

During that same time, Judy and I used to spend time hanging around a local dry goods store. It was called Diamond's and was located on the southwest corner of Morganford Road and Connecticut Street. Mr. and Mrs. Diamond ran the store themselves. During slow times, Mrs. Diamond would take a smoke break at the counter and talk to Judy and me. Between Judy and me, I was usually the instigator, but Judy was the talker. She talked on and on, while Mrs. Diamond mostly listened and I watched Mrs. Diamond suck the smoke in and blow it out. Sometimes Mr. Diamond would get a little impatient with our hanging around and would gently suggest that we "go out and play".

One day we came into the store and saw a sad-looking Mrs. Diamond in the store all by herself. She explained that Mr. Diamond had passed away. Because we loved the Diamonds, especially Mrs., we wanted to help her. Judy and I went door-to-door in the forty-three-hundred block of Connecticut, where Judy lived, to take up a funeral collection. Those who bravely answered their doors when they saw the two neighborhood pests expressed their sadness upon hearing of Mr. Diamond's death, but politely declined our request for money. By the time we got towards the end of the block, we were feeling pretty defeated. Not one penny had been collected, but I think Judy enjoyed being able to tell the news of Mr. Diamond's demise.

There was a man named Mr. T. who lived a few doors away from where Judy lived, which was across the alley from where I lived. My introduction to Mr. T. when my family moved into the neighborhood had not been a good one. My older sister, Lois, had told me to stick my tongue out at him because she thought he looked mean. It turns out she was right about him. He was as mean as he could be. Mr. T. scolded me big time, calling me a brat. I avoided him ever since that incident. Four years later I was standing on his front porch with Judy, about to be scolded again. Judy did the talking while I kind of hung back. I was really intimidated by this man. When Judy explained why we were collecting money, Mr. T. exploded in a tirade about how he wasn't going to give a penny to us. He accused us of collecting money so we could buy snow cones, which was funny, because I never bought snow cones. My family couldn't afford it. In those days a snow cone truck came to our neighborhood every evening in the summer. It seemed like every kid in the neighborhood got to buy snow cones except for my sisters and me. So I took it as a double insult when Mr. T. accused us of collecting money for snow cones. He slammed the door in our broken-hearted faces. After that I really, really disliked Mr. T. Whenever he saw me or Judy after that day, he would mutter just loud enough for us to hear, "Damn snow cone kids!" After being insulted at his house, we quit "Operation Diamond" and scraped together a small amount of change from our own piggy banks. We gave Mrs. Diamond something like seventeen cents and told her we hoped it would help pay for Mr. Diamond's funeral. Shortly after that, the store closed. Judy and I had failed Mrs. Diamond, but I'll bet she loved us for trying.

Mr. T., when I get to Purgatory (I'm sure you'll still be there when I arrive) I'm going to hold up the biggest snow cone I can find, but not give you any, stick my tongue out at you again and call you a damn snow cone kid!"

Call the Police!

Judy H. and I both had vivid imaginations. We were also pretty good about having "crushes" on older men. In another story I talk about our obsession with a teenaged boy named Freddy, whom we nicknamed Freddy Freckleson. Freddy worked at Cook's Market. And we both had a huge crush on Sergeant O., a policeman who lived at the other end of my block. He was extremely handsome, and because he was a cop, we really adored him.

One day Judy and I were walking around the neighborhood looking for some trouble to get into, and as we did on the day of the Great Bank Robbery, we found it. I can still remember which alley we were walking in. I looked into a basement window, because I did and still do like looking in people's windows. Not in a creepy, "Peeping Tom" way, but just to see how other people live. That day when I looked into the basement window I saw a white sheet, covering a dead body! I told Judy what I saw and she looked in the window and verified that what I had seen indeed was a dead body, all covered up with a white sheet just like what we had seen in movies and television shows!

There was only one thing to do - report this crime to our superhero, Sergeant O. We ran to his house and rang the doorbell. In seconds our handsome hero appeared at the door. I was probably talking a mile a minute and Judy, who had asthma, was probably doing the same in between wheezes. Sergeant O. told us to calm down and tell him exactly what we had seen. I explained that I had glanced into a basement window and had seen a white sheet covering a dead body. Sergeant O. asked us to lead him to the crime scene. He didn't bring along any yellow crime scene tape, which was kind of a disappointment, and he didn't call for back-up, which may have been a clue as to how seriously he took us. When we arrived at the scene, Sergeant O. squatted down, looked into the window, straightened back up and announced that what he saw was a work bench that had been covered with a white sheet. I don't remember if he talked to anyone in the household or if he even took a second look. All I remember is that he told us that we shouldn't jump to conclusions and that it definitely was not a dead body. I was a little disappointed. If we had discovered a dead body, Judy and I would have been all over the headlines. TWO SOUTHSIDE GIRLS DISCOVER MURDER VICTIM! Or maybe, "LINKUL GIRL BREAKS BIG MURDER CASE!" After all, I was the one who originally discovered the body, and I was the one who suggested we enlist Sergeant O's help. Oh, well, I would just have to find another way to save the world and to impress Sergeant O. at the same time. My day came soon after.

There was an old woman who lived above Cook's Market on the corner of Morganford and Wyoming, a block from my house. I passed by that intersection every day on my way to school in the morning and again on my way back to school after lunch. I waved to her every day and thought about her a lot. I really felt sorry for her because I imagined that she had nothing better to do than sit in the window, watching people walk by. (In those days there were a lot of people walking around).

Because I have always had a vivid imagination and have always been empathetic (some people would say just "pathetic"). I often thought of scenarios where I would go visit with the lonely old woman. I just knew that my daily waves made her day. It even crossed my mind that maybe she was being held captive in that tower. The least I could do is wave to her to help get her mind off of her captivity!

One Saturday Judy and I were walking around the neighborhood looking for trouble, and again, we found it. I looked up at the window in the tower as was my habit, and saw the woman sitting there as usual. Only this time there was a big, bad man standing behind her, trying to choke her! I thought, "Oh my God! Maybe he is the one who is holding her captive, and he is going to kill her because he thinks she's trying to wave for help!" I grabbed Judy by the hand and raced a few houses away to Sergeant O's.

If memory serves me correctly, it was Mrs. O. who answered the door this time. We breathlessly explained that there was a murder in progress and we needed Sergeant O's help immediately! She probably rolled her eyes and called out something like "The dumb kids from down the street are here again. This time, they think somebody's getting murdered right now!" Sergeant O. was packing heat this time. As we started walking to the active crime scene we excitedly told him what we had seen. By the time we got to the scene, no one appeared in the window. Fearing the worst, my heart raced and tears formed in my eyes as Sergeant O. commanded

Judy and me to wait in front of the building as he knocked on the door leading to the old woman's tower apartment. It seemed like a lifetime while we waited for Sergeant O. to return. All sorts of things ran through our minds and out of our mouths. I can almost hear Judy now telling passersby to clear the area; that there was a crime in progress. I probably silently prayed the rosary for Sergeant O., thinking that there might be a gun battle. Finally, Sergeant O. emerged from the building with that slight smile that he always had for Judy and me in these circumstances. That smile was probably one of slight amusement mixed with a little aggravation.

Sergeant O. explained that the old lady was fine. The "big bad man" had turned out to be the old woman's son. He was there for a visit. Instead of trying to choke her from behind, he had merely been hugging his mother. Again, Sergeant O. reminded Judy and me to not jump to conclusions, but allowed that if we ever needed his help, he was there for us.

God bless, Sergeant O. We interrupted his time off and led him on wild goose chases, but he still smiled at us, and never called us the "Snow Cone Kids". (See my story called "Collecting Money for Mr. Diamond's Funeral!" for an explanation.)

Freddy Freckleson, the Ketchup Bottle Pyramid and the Shopping Game!

Cook's Market was located at Morganford and Wyoming, about a block from my house. In the summer after fifth grade, my BFF Judy H. and I started hanging out at Cook's Market on a daily basis. I think the major attraction, besides our love of food, was a teenaged boy named Freddy who worked there. Freddy wore glasses, had red hair which he wore in a buzz cut and had freckles all over his face and arms. For some reason we thought he was cute. We nicknamed him Freddy Freckleson. Freddy was a stock boy. Judy and I used to oversee him stocking the shelves and talked his arm off. Judy was even more of a talker than I was (am). I'm pretty sure poor Freddy tired of us, but he never told us to go take a hike. Well, maybe he did a few times, but we kept coming back. We were persistent like that, and couldn't imagine anyone not wanting our company.

One day Freddy had been charged with building a pyramid of ketchup bottles. It was fascinating for us to watch our beloved Freddy Freckleson carefully balancing layer upon layer of glass bottles on pieces of cardboard. He told us we were making him nervous. Did that deter us? No. After all, we couldn't imagine anyone not wanting our company.

I don't know what actually happened, but all of a sudden there was a loud crash, shards of glass and red sauce flying all over the place! Had Judy or I bumped into Freddy or the pyramid, or did Freddy Freckleson finally freak from foolish friendly fraternizing? I'll never know now, because I don't know how to get in touch with Freddy Freckleson. All I know is that Freddy Freckleson freaked, and Judy and I fled. He probably said a different "F" word, if not out loud then in his cute little freckled head. That was the end of our flirtation with Freddy.

But it wasn't the end of Judy's and my love affair with Cooks Market. As I said earlier, the summer after fifth grade (the end of fourth grade for Judy) we found ourselves with nothing to do. So, because we had the most vivid of imaginations and were definitely social beings, we invented a game that fulfilled our need for something fun to do every day. And it took place in Cooks Market!

There used to be a daytime television game show that involved shopping carts. I don't remember the name of the show or even the premise of the game. All I know is that it inspired our game, "Shopping for Mom". The premise of our game was to get a shopping cart, hold a list (fake) and pretend to be shopping for "Mom". One of us would read aloud an item from the list while the other would retrieve the item from the shelf and toss it into the basket. Just to make sure that the store workers and general population of grocery shoppers thought we were legitimately grocery shopping, we would say things like "Yeah, Mom told us to get Folgers coffee" or "Yeah, that's what Mom said to get". We would fill the basket to the brim, admire our bountiful basket and then put everything back on the shelves. The entire process took about an hour. We did this every day for several weeks. Why no one from the store said anything to us, I'll never know.

Then the terrible news came that my dearest friend Judy was moving to another neighborhood! I was devastated. Judy was my whole life, at least from 9:00 AM until 9:00 PM during the summer (minus lunch and dinner times). What would I do without her? Well, I would carry on without her; that's what I'd do. I bravely took my grocery list to Cooks Market every morning and put the items in the basket myself. I no longer called out the items or said "Mom said we should get…", but I added a twist to the game. I started "buying" things that my own Mom would never buy, like Brach's Bridge Mix or huge bags of cheese curls just to make the exercise more pleasurable. I was soon up to two or three baskets a day. I was addicted. But what else was an eleven year-old, brokenhearted girl to do with her summer days? After my daily fake shopping trips I spent the rest of the days and evenings riding my bike through the neighborhood streets and missing Judy H.

After several of these shopping trips without Judy, the game began to lose some of its appeal, especially the part where I had to return all of the items to their shelves. I got lazy and stopped returning the items to the shelves. It was just too much work. I didn't stop to think that somebody from the store had to put all of those items back on the shelf if I didn't. Maybe poor old Freddy Freckleson had that privilege if he was still working there.

One evening while I was legitimately shopping at Cooks for my Mom, probably picking up a half-gallon of milk or a loaf of bread, I was walking towards the door to exit the store when I heard a loud commanding voice. "Little girl in the white shorts, stop where you are. We know what you've been doing!" My whole life flashed before me. All I could see is an image of me being led away in hand-cuffs, and all I could hear were the sounds of sirens as I slowly made my walk of shame back to the checkout counter. The store manager was standing there. I asked him what I had done and he explained, in front of several interested bystanders, that they had been watching me for a while and they knew that I had been leaving full grocery carts in the store. The manager went on to say that he was going to call my parents. He asked for my telephone number. I begged him not to call my parents. I told him I would rather have him call the police than call my parents. (I know. That doesn't make sense, because the police would talk to my parents, but remember that I was eleven years old and very scared of disappointing my parents).

I promised to never come back to the store if he would just not call my parents, and he agreed. Just as I clearly remember that I was wearing white shorts that evening, I remember that it was a Thursday evening. When the manager dismissed me, I ran home just in time to watch the weekly episode of "Leave It to Beaver". My family watched television as a family every evening from 7:00 until 10:00. My viewing spot was on the floor, a few feet away from the television. My Mom and older sister sat on the sofa. My Dad sat in the only arm chair. Sometimes my baby sister sat in her little chair or on one of my parent's lap. So I was right out in front of the entire family, which I normally liked because I love to be in the spotlight, but not that evening. I felt like they could see right through the back of my head and see the shame that I had brought down on my family. I couldn't really concentrate on "The Beaver". I forced out a few half-hearted chuckles and excused myself. I spent a lot of time in the bathroom that evening, sweating bullets and trying to calm my racing heart down a notch. I did keep my promise for over two years not to ever darken the threshold of Cooks Market again. That was no easy task considering it was my job to make the quick "in between" grocery trips at least once a week, usually for a loaf of bread.

I certainly couldn't go to Cooks, so I would alternate between two stores that were about four blocks away in different directions. I remember running to the stores so I would get back home within the same amount of time that it would have taken me to go to Cooks and back, so my Mom would think I went to Cooks. Other times I admitted going to one of the stores further away, explaining that I just wanted a change of scenery. Sometimes my Mom would specify that she wanted me to go to Cooks for a particular item because of the cost. So, since I was required to bring home the change and the receipt for every purchase, in that case I would have to make up a story for why I didn't have a receipt. I remember telling my Mom one time that the wind had blown the receipt out of my hand, along with some of the change. On a few other occasions I said that the cash register had been broken so there was no receipt to be had. For the most part, my Mom let me go where I wanted to pick up an item or two as long as I brought home the change.

One day, at the beginning of the school year when I was in eighth grade, my Mom asked me to go to Cooks for something. I remember exactly where I was (sitting on the edge of my bed, planning how I would fake going to Cooks) when my Mom asked me the big question: "Marilyn, why don't you go to Cooks anymore?" I was almost as scared as I had been when I had been caught at Cooks two years before. I started crying and told my Mom the whole sordid story. My Mom was such a kind and loving woman that she sat down next to me, put her arm around me and told me she was glad I had finally told her. Then we stood up, she took my face in her hands and told me that I was going to Cooks that very day. I told her I couldn't, and she told me that I must. I told her I needed a minute. She left the room and I got out a large head scarf and a pair of sunglasses and looked at myself in the mirror. I thought I was pretty unrecognizable.

I fancied myself a spy as I stealthily entered the store. I made a beeline for a tall set of shelves and partially hid while I scouted out the territory. The manager was nowhere in sight. I ran from hiding place to hiding place, keeping a sharp eye out for the manager, until I reached the bread aisle. I snatched up a loaf and ran to the checkout counter. I had to wait in line, which seemed to take an eternity. I looked around nervously until it was my turn. I kept my head down as I handed over the money and collected the change and the receipt. I had sweat beads all across my forehead and upper lip. I must have looked like such a fool. It was the first week of September and probably a pretty hot day. Here I was wearing a huge headscarf! I ran across the exit threshold halfway expecting to hear "Little girl in the stupid headscarf and sunglasses, stop where you are. We know what you've been doing. Don't think we have forgotten just because it's two years later!"

I'm glad my Mom made me admit the truth and face my fears. She was an excellent Mom and knew what was best for her foolish little girl. I wish she was here right now so I could thank her for the way she handled the problem, and so we could share a few laughs over how silly I was.

Two Cowboys and the January Thaw

If anybody thinks I'm not quite right in the head after reading some of my crazy stories, please consider that I may or may not have been adversely affected by playing in raw sewage for three days when I was ten or eleven years old.

It was January 1958 or 1959 when a sewer pipe in my neighborhood burst. We were experiencing a "January Thaw", which we seem to experience every year in St. Louis. The "January Thaw" usually takes place after a really cold spell, sometimes with snow, when the temperatures suddenly mimic spring. The sun comes out in full force and everything kind of thaws out for a few days. The burst pipe created a stream of water at the other end of the block. The water from the burst sewer pipe was augmented by melting snow. I can still remember the sound of the rushing water. To me, the stream of water looked and sounded like a roaring river somewhere out West. I always liked pretending to be a cowboy, so this roaring river seemed like the perfect place to pretend that I was camping out and maybe even panning for gold. I had my trusty bike, which could substitute for my horse named Rusty. I went home to pick up a few "play" dishes that my sister and I used when we played house and an old foil pie tin (from a frozen pie) and rode off to pick up my sidekick, Judy H. I told Judy all about the roaring river and my idea to camp out like cowboys for the day. She was in. She saddled up her bike-horse and followed me.

There was an outdoor space behind a rotting wooden fence in the yard behind a used car dealer lot where we kids used to hang out with Mr. Pickle, the oft-inebriated owner. This space, which sometimes served as our summer clubhouse, would serve as our cowboy camp. We were not allowed to visit Mr. Pickle in his office anymore, after my sister and I had seen him quickly hide a bottle of booze in his top drawer one day when we came to visit. But this little outdoor space by the fence was probably okay. Our cowboy camp was just a few feet from the roaring river. We could tie up the horses and have a little privacy, since the partial fence kind of shielded us from passersby. We could easily get to the river for water for our horses, our coffee and vittles and for panning for gold. It was perfect!

Judy and I had just bought matching vinyl mittens that would serve us very well, since we were going to be playing in the water, because it was icy cold in spite of the sun. We both had our red rubber boots on, along with our "car" coats (what they used to call short winter coats in the 1950's).

We played "cowboys" all day, going to our respective homes only for a quick lunch. We spent most of the time playing in the water. We filled the play dishes and pie tin with water and dirt for our campfire meals. We used the river to wash our dishes and then to pan for gold, using the same foil pie tin from which we had "eaten" our cowboy stew and beans.

We had so much fun that first day that we agreed to resume our game of cowboys the next day, which was a Sunday. After Sunday Mass we came back to our camp to feed the horses, feed ourselves and pan for more gold. We went home for supper on the second day just as tired and happy as we had the first day.

We had a day off from school the next day. I'm not sure why. It was 1958 or 1959, too early to have been celebrating MLK Day. Whatever the reason, I was so happy to have a third day to play in the roaring river of the Old West. As I recall, the third day was a lot warmer than the first and second days had been. We took off our "car" coats and mittens and rode our horses around the neighborhood, returning to camp to eat vittles, wash the dishes and pan for gold in the roaring river.

It wasn't until supper time on the third day that I described to my family how Judy and I had made camp with our horses and panned for gold in a roaring river for the past three days. When I mentioned the roaring river, one of my parents asked about the water I was referring to. When I told them about the burst pipes and the stream it had created they had a fit. "Do you mean you were actually touching the sewer water?" asked my Dad. "You didn't drink any of it, did you?" my Mom asked in horror. "Boy, you and Judy are sure stupid", was something my older sister might have said. I assured the family that I hadn't really drunk the water. I had put the play dishes that had been in the tainted water to my lips, but not really drunk the water.

My Mom called Judy's Mom to see what she knew about our hazardous playtime. Each of them had thought that we were just riding our bikes around the neighborhood all day and maybe hanging out at the other one's yard to play when we weren't riding. We had been in range of our mothers' calls (yells, not phone calls) to lunch and supper, so that had not been a tip-off that we were not playing in each other's yard. They had noticed that our vinyl mittens were kind of muddy and that our red rubber boots had gotten wet, but that was nothing to set off any alarms either. There had been some snow on the ground that was melting in the "January Thaw". In other words, they had no idea that we had been living in a cowboy camp on Mr. Pickle's lot or that we had been playing in sewer water all weekend.

Our Moms may have over-reacted, but they made us throw out the tainted vinyl mittens. My Dad turned on the outside faucet and washed my red rubber boots really good. My Mom washed my "car" coat and the rest of my play clothes. I remember having to take a hot bath and being told to scrub myself really good to get rid of the contamination. My Mom took my temperature and made me take some Castor Oil for good measure. She watched me for several days to make sure I wasn't coming down with hepatitis or anything. Nothing bad ever happened as a result of my playing in sewer water, except for one thing. My prized vinyl mittens had been thrown out!

So, mothers, tell your children not to be cowboys, especially if they are going to be panning for gold in sewer water!

Skating in the Basement, Hopping on Trains and Dancing on Vaults

My older sister Lois and I got along very well most of the time. She was three and a half years older (four grades ahead of me in school) so I had to defer to her a lot. She was very creative; always making up games for the two of us to play. Some of her games included "Queen and Beggar" where she sat on a throne and granted favors to her subjects (me) and I knelt in front of her and begged; "Mass", where she was the priest and I was the communicant; "Newspaper", where she was the Editor, Star Reporter, Advertising and Business Manager, and I was the delivery boy; "Skating Star", where she skated and I clapped; and "Dancing Star" with the same assigned roles as "Skating Star".

Once we had been playing "Skating Star" in our basement for so long, Lois' legs and my hands were tired. I asked Lois if I could please have a turn being the skating star. She reluctantly granted my wish. I was so happy to finally get to be the star in one of our games. I got my metal roller skates out and clamped them onto my shoes. Then I inserted the metal key to tighten the clamps just so. Finally I fastened the strap around my ankles, not too tight, but tight enough to support my ankles. Sometimes if you didn't have the clamps on just right, your shoe would slip out and all that kept your skate on was the leather strap around your ankle. This was kind of dangerous, since you were still rolling on the other skate, while dragging the loosened skate around by the ankle strap. Finally I was all set to skate as the star. I started humming my first routine song and making the first long stride with my right foot when I noticed Lois standing up and starting to walk out on my performance, saying, "I quit!" She explained that she was tired of playing "Skating Star". All that could be heard from the basement after that was "Mo-o-m! Lois is quitting just when it's my turn to skate!" No music, no sound of metal skates on concrete, no thunderous applause or acclaims of my greatness; just me whining about the unfairness of the situation and my Mom telling Lois that she wasn't being very nice. I think that was the last time we played "Skating Star".

Lois and I loved hearing our tap shoes go clickety-click, clickety-clack in time to the music, which was only our humming. One day we put on our tap shoes and carefully walked about a block away on Alfred Street to the Wilbur Vault Company. It was in site of our house, so we had to be careful so our Mom wouldn't see what we were about to do. There were many sets of two vaults stacked on top of another. We climbed up onto the top vault and started humming and tap dancing. The sound of our tap shoes on the vaults was music to our ears. Our tapping echoed loudly with every time step and "step-ball-change"! Actually it was so loud our Mom heard it, saw what we were doing and called us home! We were scolded for wearing our taps on rough pavement, for trespassing and for doing something so dangerous!

One summer after our vault dancing adventure, probably during the summer when I was eleven years old and without my partner-in-crime, Judy H., I got the idea to climb to the very top of four (not just two) vaults stacked on top of one another. Lois would never have the guts to do what I was about to undertake. I would be the star of my own game, "Mountain Climber"!

It was evening time. I probably knew that my Dad would be reading the newspaper after dinner and too focused on that to look out the front window to see me climbing on the vaults. I don't remember, but I must have also known that my Mom, Lois and little sister Linda would also not see me, because Wilbur Vault Company had been declared "off limits" after Lois and I did our famous vault dance a couple of years before then.

I somehow made it to the top of the mountain and looked out over my kingdom. Yes, I was on top of the world in all my glory, and no one, not even Lois, could topple me. I glanced over at my house. No one was out front. I felt so free and alive, but also a little guilty. I knew I wasn't supposed to be there, and I knew it was a sin to disobey my parents. Still, as sinning always does, it felt so good!

All of a sudden the sky darkened and there was the loudest clap of thunder I had ever heard. I noticed that the wind had also kicked up. I screamed and scrambled down as fast as I could. Frankly I don't know how I got down from the high mountain of vaults without hurting myself. All I do remember is screaming at the top of my lungs, "I'm sorry!" over and over again as I ran to the safety of my home. I don't know if I was saying "I'm sorry" to God or to my Mom. All I know is that my Mom was at the front door asking me what was wrong as I quickly came inside through the front door. I screamed a warning to my family, "There's a tornado coming. Get downstairs now! Please, get your rosaries and get downstairs!" My family heeded my warning, and we all went to the basement. I was crying as we started to pray the rosary. Was I crying because I had disobeyed God and my Mom, or because I was so relieved that I was home, safe, and with my family? (I would say, probably a little of each). That was my last climb to the top of Wilbur Mountain.

I was a lot younger when I started hopping trains. Judy H. was still around. Just beyond Wilbur Vault Company, there were railroad tracks. A few times, with some of the older neighborhood kids, Lois and I ventured down by the tracks to see if we could find "Snowball", a local hobo who was rumored to live there. We never saw "Snowball", but in my mind I know exactly what he looked like. He was a black man, as legend had it, which unfortunately was rare to see in South St. Louis in the 1950's. He wore shabby clothes and carried a tied up bandana on the end of a broken-off tree branch. It was rumored that "Snowball" liked his privacy and would run you off if you were a kid roaming around the railroad tracks. I always wondered why his name was "Snowball". Maybe his hair was snow white? I don't know. All I know is that we had a snowball's chance in hell of ever finding him.

One of the first times I went to the tracks with the other kids to see if we could spot "Snowball", a man who in my mind was dressed like an engineer, saw us and yelled at us to get out of the area. The man scared me off alright! I did not like getting yelled at, and I knew my parents would not approve of me playing in such a secluded and dangerous place. I didn't go back for a while.

Sometimes I used to play with a girl named Carol who lived right next to the train tracks. They were practically in her backyard. Once I was standing in her kitchen when a train went by and all of the dishes in their cabinet rattled and clinked. One day I was playing with Carol at her house and we decided to go to the tracks to try to find the elusive "Snowball". Again, a man dressed like an engineer saw us and yelled at us to get out. He said we were trespassing. I was really scared this time, because I didn't want to go to jail. So I lied. I told him that we were looking for our paper dolls that had blown off Carol's front porch. I figured this was a legitimate excuse for trespassing: to retrieve one's property. After all, paper dolls were expensive at twenty five cents a set at the dime store. I bent over like I was desperately searching for something, but as good as an actress that I thought I was, he wasn't buying it. He started to run after us. Carol and I high-tailed it back to her house and I didn't go back to the tracks for a few years.

When I was in eighth grade, my BFF Barbara and I returned to the rails. She was going to run away from home. Suitcase in hand, she had come to my house to see if she could stay with us, but my Mom told her no and advised her to go back home. I knew she couldn't do that. When you leave a note saying you are running away from home, you can't just go back. You have to wait at least a half hour! (Unless it's supper time and you're really hungry). Anyway, I understood Barbara's plight and offered to take her to the railroad tracks and hop a train with her. I don't think my intention was to stay on the train once it started rolling, because it was near my family's supper time, but I would be there to send her off. I felt there was no going back for Barbara. She had pulled the trigger and it was too late to get the bullet back!

The train was at a standstill when we got to the tracks. Ironically, according to the lettering on the outside of the cars, it was headed towards Texas, where Barbara moved many years later! We looked around, and seeing no one, we got up into an open car and waited. All of a sudden we felt a lurch and the train started moving ever so slowly. I looked at Barbara, and this normally dark-complexioned girl's face was white as a sheet. Truthfully I was scared, too, but kept a brave face on. I was the mastermind of this plan after all! I took a second to assess the situation. I was on my way to Texas and didn't even have a toothbrush. And more importantly, I hadn't said goodbye to my Mom. I wondered if I should jump off the train before it got up too much speed. Apparently Barbara was thinking the same thing. A split second later we both jumped down from the car. I asked if Barbara was going home, because I was done with this adventure. It was suppertime and I was hungry, and I'm sure Barbara was, too. It was time for Barbara to undo her running away from home.

The Coat Check Caper

My BFF Barbara and I volunteered to work the coat check station at the parish center for the New Year's Eve dance. We were only fourteen years old, and it seemed like a fun thing to do on New Year's Eve. We'd get to listen to music and enjoy refreshments and best of all, we'd earn tips! The parish center was brand new and this was the first big dance to be held there, so things maybe weren't as organized as they should have been. We were stationed in a small room with an open window facing the dance floor, where they had a big coat rack with a shelf on top to hold the men's hats. Barbara and I hung the coats and set the hats on the shelf. I don't remember there being any claim checks. The room was small and the coat rack was in full view, so maybe people were supposed to be able to identify their coats and hats from the window. It was all going pretty smoothly until we realized that there were no more hangers and no more room on the coat rack. A big surge of people came in so we started double-hanging the coats.

The dance got underway and all Barbara and I had to do was stay in the room to watch the coats and hats. We could look out the window to watch the adults dance and we could hear the music, but it wasn't really our kind of music. Somebody provided us with sodas and pretzels. We spent the evening talking and maybe even making fun of the way the adults danced, and thinking how we'd spend all of the tip money we'd be getting.

All of a sudden the heavily-laden coat rack gave way! Most of the coats and hats tumbled down, landing in a heap under the rack. The dance was almost over. Soon people would be coming to claim their coats and hats. Barbara and I frantically picked up the coats from the floor and tried to rehang them as quickly as we could. We were in the midst of trying to rehang the coats and reshape the hats when people started lining up outside the room to claim their stuff. It was impossible for anyone to see where their coats and hats were. Shuffling through the coats made some of them fall again. Soon the floor was covered with fallen coats and crumpled hats. It was bedlam! And there was a horde of people waiting, many of them kind of impatient.

Finally we announced that people should just come in and find their own coats. People were throwing coats around and even stepping on them. Barbara and I were doing our best to re-shape the crumpled hats, holding them up in the air and asking who they belonged to. We kept apologizing and said we were doing our best to get the coats and hats to their rightful owners, but the tip box was nearly empty. Finally, one of the men who was known to "tip the bottle" on occasion (like every weekend) saw that the tip box was nearly empty. He thanked Barbara and me for our good service and gave each of us a twenty-dollar bill as a tip! That was a lot of money back in the early sixties; even a lot today to give as a tip for having his coat stepped on!

When I told my parents all about the fiasco and how Mr. N. had given Barbara and me twenty dollars each, my parents told me we had to return the money. They knew that Mr. N. had a hard time supporting his family because of his drinking, and they said that Mrs. N. probably didn't know he had been so generous to us. So Barbara and I went to Mr. N's house on New Year's Day to return the money. Mrs. N. answered the door. She was so grateful that we returned the money. By the look on her face, I think Mr. N. probably got an earful when he got up from his hangover that day!

Not Invited to the Wedding (but we did get to see your gifts)

My BFF Barbara and I did some pretty crazy stuff together, especially as teenagers. We spent hours every summer evening and on weekends, no matter what the weather was like, roaming the streets of our neighborhood, looking for something fun to do. One of the things we liked doing was investigating new apartment buildings that were under construction. There were several in our neighborhood.

Barbara and I often volunteered to sing at weddings and funerals with the girls' church choir. One Saturday we sang at the wedding of the sister of one of our male classmates. Our classmate told us that his sister and her new husband had rented an apartment at the Terri Apartments building, which was at the end of the block where I lived. Barbara and I had explored the building several times as it was being built. That afternoon, having nothing better to do after singing at the wedding, we decided to check out the Terri Apartment Building.

This could be our last chance to explore the building if the apartments were already starting to be rented.

No one was around, and the door to the back of the building was unlocked. Once inside, we could see that there was a little more work to be done before the building was completed , because there were tools and other construction things still around on the first floor. We went up to the second floor and tried the doors to the individual apartments. None of them were locked. We entered a couple of them and looked around. They were completely empty of course. We had to settle for imagining how the apartments would look when fully furnished and decorated. Before leaving, we tried one more door and hit the jackpot. This apartment actually had furniture in it! We called out "Hello!" and got no answer, so we cautiously entered the apartment. Once inside, we noticed that there were casserole dishes and other items that looked like wedding gifts stacked on the kitchen table and countertops. We guessed that this was the newly-weds' apartment. We were looking at the gifts when we heard voices coming from somewhere inside the building. We had left the door slightly ajar, and quickly closed it so whoever was coming wouldn't see us. The voices got closer. It sounded like a man and a woman. Thinking it could possibly be the newly-weds, we ducked inside a closet and held our breath.

Sure enough! The newly-weds came into the apartment. From their conversation we gathered that they had just brought in another load of wedding gifts. My whole life flashed before me, and I'm sure Barbara was just as scared of being discovered as I was. I didn't know how long I could stay in the closet without needing to move around.

What would happen if one of us had to sneeze or cough? "Oh, God", I prayed, "Please don't let us be discovered."

Thankfully, the newly-weds didn't linger, didn't take time to unwrap anything and didn't decide to open the closet. One of the two said something to the effect that they were going down for another load, and out the door they went.

We waited a few seconds before coming out of the closet, out of the apartment and down the stairwell that led to the back entrance of the building. Luckily we didn't run into the newly-weds or anyone for that matter. We were so relieved to have escaped without being seen. We thanked God and probably asked him to "forgive us our trespasses". Did we ever trespass again? I'm not sure. If we didn't, it was only because there were no new apartment buildings available, because I am not one who learns lessons from narrow escapes.

My Crazy Dating Stories

First Date

My first date was embarrassing even before it got started. Maybe that's because of who it was with. His real name was Steve R., but it should have been "Unibrow". His hair was sort of dark, but he was definitely not tall or handsome. He had a very big nose for only being about five foot four, and he had one big, dark eyebrow that went from temple to temple. I didn't really like him all that much. He was Jack's friend. Jack was the really cute guy who my BFF Barbara was dating. Steve was just the leftover friend you'd settle for if you couldn't have Jack.

My parents required that my sister's and my dates come into the living room for a little inspection/interrogation session before we could go on our dates. My Dad, Mom and both sisters were in the living room ready to pounce on their prey. So I was nervous about the questions they might ask Steve. I had lied when my Dad had asked me if Steve was Catholic. I had told my Dad that Barbara and I had met Jack and Steve at a CYC (Catholic Youth Council) event. This was a partial truth. We had met them on a street corner while walking home from a CYC meeting. I did tell the truth when I told my Dad that Steve did not go to Catholic high school, and he had raised an eyebrow over that. I was more than a little nervous about what my family would ask Steve, how Steve would answer, and about how I looked, too.

At the appointed time, the doorbell rang. I took a deep breath and grabbed the door handle so hard that it came off in my hand! So there was no way to open our front door. In my usual tactful and discreet manner, I yelled out, "Go around the back. The door handle came off!" My Mom and sister Lois were laughing as I ran to the back door to let Steve in. I was still holding the door handle in my hand when I opened the back door. I said, "Hi" and without saying any more I led him through the dinette, kitchen, my parents' bedroom and into the living room where the Council of Wyoming Street was waiting to hold the Inquisition. I don't remember what was said or not said. I just know that I didn't really breathe until it was over and Steve and I were outside. Jack and Barbara were waiting out on the sidewalk.

It was very cold. It was January. Neither Steve nor Jack had a car, so we had to walk that evening. I'm not sure if they had even turned sixteen yet. I know I was fifteen, almost sixteen at the time. Even if they had been sixteen, I doubt that either one of them could have driven. They both came from low-income families. In my neighborhood, if a family even had a car, they usually didn't have more than one, and usually didn't let their sixteen year old boys use the family car for dates. So we walked, in the cold, for over a mile to the movie theatre. I don't remember what movie we saw, but I do remember Steve putting his arm around me and then holding my hand. It did make me feel grown up and a little flattered that a boy liked me, but I definitely wasn't in love or even close to it.

Several weeks later one of my friends threw me a "Sweet Sixteen" party and Steve was my date, but by the end of the party he was no longer my boyfriend. He had his eye on someone else at the party and made it very clear he was no longer my boyfriend. At first it hurt my feelings and I even wanted to cry, because according to Leslie Gore, it was my party and I could cry if I wanted to. Actually it was no big loss. He was my first boyfriend; the practice one.

My Second First Date

My second "first" date took place about nine years later. During those nine years, I had dated many boys, gotten engaged, been married, had two children and gotten divorced. It was time to get through that awkward first date again. This time I was pretty self-assured and not nervous at all. Again, I wasn't dating anyone I liked or was even mildly attracted to. I was just getting through the first one to get it over and done with. It was kind of like making pancakes. You know the first one never turns out good, so you're resigned to throwing it away!

I had met Jim D. at a "Parents without Partners" meeting that someone from work had dragged me to. It was my first and last PWP meeting. From the moment I signed in and put on my name tag I knew that this was just a "meat market" and not an organization dedicated to helping single parents. My first clue was a guy wearing a shirt that was open to his navel, and he had on a big gold cross with a heavy chain. I had just finished pinning my name tag onto my sweater when he rushed up, pulled on my name tag, presumably to see it up close. In doing so, he pulled my sweater away from my chest and was looking right down it! I don't remember exactly what I said, but I made it clear that I was not interested. I was dancing with my female friends from work when a nice looking man started dancing with me. When I say nice looking, I do not mean handsome or cute. I just mean that he looked like he was a nice person. I welcomed talking with someone who didn't seem like he was about to assault me. His name was Jim D. We danced and talked a little and I gave him my phone number. It was something I knew I had to do. I begged my friends to leave early, and checked "Go out to meet guys" off of the New Divorcee's Must Do List.

Much to my chagrin, Jim D. called me soon after and asked me if I wanted to go out for a drink. That seemed like something I could do without too much anxiety or too big of an investment in time. Jim picked me up at my place. I met him at the door instead of having him come upstairs. We went to a bar and grill not too far away, which felt safe. We had a drink and made some small talk. Actually I didn't talk. He did all the talking and I just listened and politely nodded my head. He went on and on about his postal route and how much his customers loved him, and how sad he was that he was divorced. He told me the divorce had been his wife's idea. "Gee, I wonder why she left *you*?" I thought sarcastically. "Could it be that you are so boring?" I must have seemed bored, because without my having to say anything, Jim suggested that we leave the bar after only one drink. It was still light outside and he said he would take me home. I was so happy that he didn't prolong my agony any further by suggesting dinner or going somewhere to talk. However, I wasn't out of the woods yet. The worst part of the date was yet to happen.

We got into his station wagon, and before he started the car, he told me that he had brought me a gift. "This is weird", I thought. "Who gives a gift on a first date?" Then he handed me an unwrapped, flat box; the kind that nylon stockings used to come in. "Oh, crap!" I thought. "The weirdo is giving me nylons!" I gingerly took the lid off and saw something white and crocheted. It was a tiny little crocheted baby gown that looked like it would fit a newborn. At the time my daughter Nancy was sixteen months old and Karen was three years old! I had told him their ages when we met. I was speechless. Then he said, "Could you use this for either of your kids?" I said, "Thanks, but I don't think it would fit either of them." I asked why he would have given me a baby gown, and he explained that one of the old ladies on his route just loved him and that she had made it for him. He insisted I take it, because he had no use for it. I said that maybe it would fit one of the girls' dolls or something". I took it, and then later gave it to charity. That was our last date, even though he bugged me with phone calls for about a year.

My Good, Bad and Ugly Prom Dates

Ron was a great dancer, but that's about the only good thing I can say about him. He was way too skinny, had droopy eyelids, horse teeth and had the manners of a wild boar. He asked me to dance one night at Teen Town. I was flattered because he really was the best Imperial dancer around. A group of his fan club stood around as Ron expertly led me. I felt so proud to be his dancing partner. After several dances it was time to go home and he offered to give me a ride. I gladly accepted, because I had just been dumped and was in need of a boyfriend. And Ron was so popular! On the way home he told me that he had recently broken up with his longtime girlfriend and that he had been "eyeing" me at Teen Town for a while. I fell for this hook, line and sinker. I really don't remember, but I guess we kissed. Then he asked me if I wanted to be his new girlfriend. I was so flattered. I said "yes", and we exchanged class rings to show that we were going steady. I liked the idea of him more than I liked him. I guess we were using one another. We both wanted to show everybody, especially our former steadies, we had moved on.

The next day at school I flashed his ring around to let everybody know that I had a boyfriend again. Ron and I didn't really date even though we were going steady. He called me a few times and asked me to come over to his house when his parents were gone, but I refused. I was not allowed to ever be at someone's house without their parents being there, and besides I wasn't that kind of girl. If he had been cute and I had actually liked him, perhaps I may have been tempted to break the rules. I am so glad that he was about as handsome as an emaciated work horse, so I was never tempted to go astray.

One evening at Teen Town, after not hearing from Ron for over a week, I spotted him dancing with a girl and noticed he was not wearing my class ring. I went up to him and asked where my ring was and said I wanted it back since we weren't even dating. He said it was at home and that he would give it back soon. I gave him back his ring. I don't know how much time passed without hearing from him, so I called him and demanded that he come over with my ring. He made some excuse why he couldn't come over that evening. I waited and then called him again. I told him that my Dad was really mad at him for keeping my ring and that he had better get over to my house with that ring or else. He said he'd be right over. My Dad wasn't home from work yet when Ron arrived with my ring. He asked if he could come in for a minute. He said he had some bad news to give me before giving me my ring. He went on to explain that he and some friends had been goofing around in Chemistry class and that someone had dipped my ring in mercury! He then handed over the grayish coated ring. It was no longer shiny. It no longer looked gold plated. You could barely make out the red stone or the engraving. I couldn't believe my eyes. I was speechless. My ring was ruined. Just then my Dad came home from work and saw Ron in our living room. Ignoring Ron, he gruffly asked me if I had gotten my ring back. I held it up and my Dad saw red, and it wasn't the stone in my ring that he saw! I had never seen my Dad that angry before or any time after that. He lunged toward Ron and yelled at him to get out of our house! Ron slowly backed out of the front door, shaking. My Dad started to come after him threatening to throw Ron down the steps if he didn't get out. After Ron left, I tried to rub the coating off of my ring to no avail. I sadly put the ring in my jewelry box. That was in January of my senior year.

    Soon after that, I started seeing my old boyfriend again, but it was short-lived. And I dated a couple of other guys, but my heart wasn't in it. I was pining for my old boyfriend. Soon April rolled around and I had to find a date for the senior prom, which was in mid-May. I knew my old boyfriend wouldn't go with me. He had a new girlfriend. There was no one I wanted to ask. The one guy in my class that I would have gone with did not ask me. A couple of other guys did, but I did not want to go with them. I called another old boyfriend from a couple of years earlier and we got together one evening. I asked him if he would take me to my prom, just as friends, and he agreed. Then we drove to a park to "talk", and when he tried to put "the moves" on me, I told him I wanted to go home and that I did not want to see him again. I got out of the car, and before my slamming of the door cut off his voice, I heard him call me a witch, only he pronounced it wrong! I was really stuck. I just had to go to my senior prom. So I did something really, really stupid. I called Ron.

I didn't like him, and was still angry with him, but because of his being so popular and a fantastic dancer, I thought he'd make a good prom date. We'd be the center of attention on the dance floor and everybody would see that I had a boyfriend (something that was obviously very important to me), and then we'd go back to never seeing each other again. It was the least he could do for me after ruining my ring. Almost to my surprise he said he would take me.

I should have been worried when I did not hear from Ron for weeks after asking him to go to the prom with me, but I wasn't. After all, we both knew we were not and would never be in a relationship. I needed a date and he owed me a big favor. It was really just a business deal. But the morning of the prom when I had not heard from Ron, I did start to worry a little. That afternoon a bunch of us girls went to a popular beauty shop to have our beehive hairdos lacquered into place, and there were girls from Ron's school there. Apparently Ron's school's prom was on the same night. But I wasn't really worried, because he had told me he was going to mine. I did want to confirm what time he was picking me up that evening, so as soon as I got home from the beauty shop I called his house. His Dad answered and said Ron was out getting his car washed for me. I had never met Ron's Dad, but he acted like he had known me forever, calling me "honey". He asked if I wanted Ron to call me and I said yes.

Apparently Ron was going to be a good date after all, if he was getting his car washed just for me and had told his Dad about taking me to the prom. Over an hour went by with no call from Ron. I was getting nervous. I had to start getting dressed soon and I still didn't know for sure what time Ron would be there to pick me up. Barbara and her date were going to meet us at my house and drive to the prom together, and she needed to know when they should be there. I called Ron's house again, and this time he answered. When I asked what time he was going to be at my house, he started stammering and explained that he could not go to the prom with me after all. He said his Dad had had a heart attack and was in the hospital, and that he had to go there right away! I told Ron that I had just talked to his Dad less than two hours ago. He stammered again and told me that it had just happened. I didn't believe him, but there was nothing I could do. I hung up the phone and started to cry. My sister Lois told me that her fiancé Don would be happy take me. I could borrow him for the night. She said she also had a corsage in the refrigerator left over from a banquet she had attended five days ago. I could borrow it, too. I cried even harder. I didn't want to go to my senior prom with someone who was practically my brother and with a rotting corsage to boot! I called my BFF Barbara and cried my heart out. She didn't know what to do, she said, but she would call me right back.

A few minutes later she called back with a plan. Her mom knew a handsome young man who rode the bus with her every day. Apparently she had introduced him to Barbara's older brother and they had become friends. Barbara's Mom called him and asked if he would take me to the prom, and he agreed. Bruce didn't have a lot of money, and neither did Barbara's Mom, but she said that she would pay for a corsage for me and pay for our after-prom dinner at an expensive steak house. What a lifesaver she was! I have never forgotten that sweet lady's extraordinary generosity! Barbara assured me that Bruce was very handsome and that I would like him. Bruce was a little older- twenty- I think, but he would play the part of my boyfriend very well. He wouldn't be wearing a tux, but he did have a nice suit to wear. Bruce would be with Barbara and her date when they arrived at my house in just about an hour. I dried my tears, splashed cold water on my red, splotched face and put on my make-up and my beautiful turquoise dress. It was going to be alright.

I was nervous of course, but when they arrived I was glad to see how handsome Bruce was and how nice he looked. He gave me a beautiful white corsage and I gave him the boutonniere meant for Ole Horse Face, and off we went. I hadn't told that many people who I was bringing to the prom as my date, so very few even noticed that I had switched dates at the last minute. Only Barbara and a few other close friends knew I had been stood up. Bruce was just a tad shorter than me in my two-inch heels. (I was wearing the two inch heels, not Bruce, just in case you are wondering.) A few years ago I came across the picture of Bruce and me at the Hawaiian Luau themed prom. We're posed in front of a grass hut and we look good together. But as nice as Bruce was and as hard as I tried to act like I was having fun, it was still kind of awkward. I was ashamed of having been stood up.

A bunch of my classmates all went to the Crest House, an expensive steakhouse downtown, after the prom. The Crest House was *the* place to go after prom. It was packed that night. I felt very self-conscious because I was not used to eating at fancy restaurants. I didn't really know how to cut steak. Luckily no one was looking when I attempted to cut mine. I sawed at it awkwardly and much to my horror, it fell off of my plate and onto the carpet! I casually bent over, picked it up and plopped it back on my plate with no one the wiser. I just wanted the night to be over. This prom thing was just not what it was cracked up to be, at least not for me. Oh, but it would get worse!

I happened to look up from the table when a group of high school kids walked in, and who did I see? None other than Ole Horse Face! I recognized the girl he was with, too. It was his longtime girlfriend, the one whom he had wanted to make jealous by wearing my class ring! They were back together and probably had been for some time, like since I saw them at Teen Town together in January. It was all making sense. Ron's Dad, whom I had never met, had been so friendly to me on the phone and even called me "honey" like he had known me for a long time, because he thought I was her! When he referred to Ron getting the car washed for me, his Dad had thought he was talking to Ron's girlfriend! And, it was no wonder Ron hadn't called me back. His Dad had probably told him to call the girlfriend back. Maybe Ron had forgotten that he had agreed to take me to the prom, or more likely, he just didn't care. I was tempted to go up to Ron and ask how his Dad was, but I was too chicken. I just kept it to myself that I had just seen the jerk that had stood me up!

After the restaurant we went to a small party at a classmate's house, which made me very uncomfortable. I didn't want to answer any questions about Bruce, so I just kind of stayed in a corner and was quiet. I had to leave the party early, because my Dad had given me a stricter curfew than anyone else had. When I was dropped off at my house, Bruce kissed me, but I didn't really kiss him back. I was very grateful that he had been my date on such an important occasion, but my humiliation over being stood up outweighed any feelings I could have had for him if I had given him even the slightest chance. I never saw Bruce again. His only fault was that he was too nice.

The next time I saw Ron, it was four years and a marriage later. And it was in Germany. My husband Terry was in the Army and stationed in Germany. We were on a weekend R and R at a military resort in Garmisch, Germany. We were eating lunch in a sparsely populated cafeteria when I spotted a skinny, droopy-eyed, horse-toothed scoundrel in an Air Force uniform, sitting alone at a table in the corner. I pointed Ron out to Terry and explained who he was, and right away Terry wanted to go over and confront him. I told Terry not to say or do anything. Now I kind of wish I would have had the guts to confront him. He had certainly caused me a lot of heartache.

Now that I've told the story, you know that the good prom date in the title of this story was Bruce, and that the bad and the ugly both were Ron, or Ole Horse Face as I like to call him.

By the way, the mercury eventually wore off of my class ring and I proudly wore it on my pinky to my 50th class reunion last summer. The only thing that remains tarnished is the memory of my senior prom.

My Third First (and Last) Date

It was my first date since entering widowhood seven years before.

I won't say much about what I believe was my last date ever, except to say it was a disappointment. It was about four years ago. I met D. on one of those "senior match" sites, and after months of emailing (his emails were pretty boring) and just a couple of phone calls, we went on our one and only date. I hardly talked during dinner, which tells you something if you know me. When I'm not talking I am either "madder than a wet hen" or am very "down in the dumps". It was the latter. We had no chemistry whatsoever. I didn't care for his looks, I thought his life was about as interesting as a monk's, he didn't get my humor and he was certainly no Jerry (the love of my life, who had left me a widow). I knew that I was not interested in pursuing any type of a relationship with him, but couldn't say no when he suggested we go to the movies sometime.

On the day of the movie date D. called me to say he had been puking all day and that he had diarrhea, too. That did it for me! Whenever I pictured D. it wasn't that good anyway, and this new visual was about as close to being attractive as seeing a horse take a dump on the racetrack!

After thinking how I could tell D. that I just wanted to be friends, I finally realized that this was an unfair expectation. How do a man and woman, who went out on a date presumably to meet someone for a relationship, become "just friends"? I sent him a very nice email explaining that I wasn't ready to date and that I did not feel comfortable in any relationship at this time. He responded kindly, and I honestly think we were both relieved.

And that, folks, concludes my dating stories and probably my dating experience for the rest of my life!

My Crazy Eating Stories

Donuts are a big part of my life. My Aunt Ann T. got me started on donuts. Whenever she visited she brought us bags of fresh donuts, and they have been one of my biggest downfalls ever since. My Mom died the summer I was seventeen. I was put in charge of the petty cash my Mom used to keep in her dresser drawer. My Dad always put a few dollars in the drawer in case we ran out of something and had to go to the grocery store before the weekly big shopping trip. I used the money to support my sweets addiction. I went to Zelch's bakery a couple of times a week and bought a dozen donuts each time. I started eating them on the way home. When I got home, I told my little sister Linda not to tell Dad that I had bought donuts, and offered her ONE if she would promise to keep her mouth shut. Some of the time Linda took a donut, but sometimes the pleasure of a donut didn't compare to the pleasure of seeing me get into trouble.

My BFF Barbara had a thing for jelly donuts until something awful happened to her while eating some. Here are some donut stories that may have begun with donuts, but ended in something not so sweet and satisfying.

Roaches in the Jelly Donuts!

Now, before I get into my first donut story, please allow me to give you a little background. My BFF Barbara and I had joined a parish organization called the Legion of Mary as eighth graders, even though the usual minimum age to join this organization was high school age. We were good kids, a little misguided perhaps, but we always meant well. One of the things that we did as Legion of Mary members is to try to encourage devotion to Mary, the Mother of God. We were sent to homes in our parish where the families were not active church goers. We were supposed to talk to them about coming back to the Church and then leave a brochure about Mary. We had a list of families we were supposed to visit that we checked off and turned in, along with any leftover brochures. Sometimes we got bored with this mission or became discouraged because many people would not answer their doors. So we changed the mission a little.

We went to the homes where boys that we liked lived. I don't know what we intended to say when the boy came to the door, but it really doesn't matter, because none of them ever did. Usually their mothers answered the door. After identifying ourselves as classmates of their sons, they usually told us that their sons weren't at home. I suppose they didn't appreciate girls coming to their homes looking for their sons. That was considered too aggressive in those days. Sometimes, a mother would call out to her son that Barbara and Marilyn from school were at the door, and then we would hear "I can't come to the door", "Tell them I'm sleeping" or something else that told us they did not want to see us.

On the day that this first donut story occurred, we were on a different (legitimate) mission for the Legion of Mary: collecting money for the missions. We weren't having much luck with getting people to answer their doors on a Sunday morning, and when they did, the contributions were usually just small change. We had collected a few dollars, but we were short of our goal, and we had run out of names on our list. So we decided to do the "boys-we-liked" mission. Not one boy came to the door. We were pretty discouraged, so who would blame us for what we did next? We needed a little "pick-me-up". We decided to "borrow" the money that we had collected for the missions to buy ourselves some treats at one of the confectionaries in the neighborhood. I bought a Nestles Crunch Bar and some corn curls and Barbara bought a bagful of her beloved jelly donuts.

We were walking down Utah Street happily eating our treats, when I looked over at Barbara, who had just taken a bite out of one of her jelly donuts. At first I thought I saw a big blob of jelly on her cheek, but then I saw the blob move. I yelled out, "A roach! There are roaches in your donuts!" As much as she loved her jelly donuts, she screamed bloody murder and then threw the whole bag in someone's trash can. I don't know why we didn't go back to the confectionary so she could get some roach-less donuts or her money back. Maybe Barbara was so horrified that she couldn't bring herself to even go back to the store. I think it was many years before she could bring herself to eat jelly donuts again, and I've never felt quite the same about them since. Don't get me wrong. I still eat them, but just don't enjoy them as much.

Take the Donuts Home to Your Kids

I was pregnant with Amy and eating a lot. I craved carbs and gained way too much weight during this pregnancy. One time when I went to the doctor I asked him what those big chunks of fat above where my hipbones used to be were called. The doctor said he didn't know what they were called, because I wasn't supposed to have them! He said I had to cut down on the eating. He (correctly) said that I was probably the type of person who gave the kids peanut butter and jelly sandwiches and thought I should make one for myself while I was at it. He went on to say that when my kids asked for cookies or ice cream, I probably had to have some, too. He was right, but he didn't even know the extent of how bad my lack of willpower had become.

I worked in the Bank's Executive Financial Center at the time. All of our customers had to have a minimum of $100,000 on deposit with us, so we dealt with a lot of people who were well off (by the standards of the 1970's), who owned their own businesses, etc. One of my customers owned a flour company. He came in every other Thursday and dropped off two or three big boxes of donuts on my desk. I used to put the donuts out for the rest of the department to eat. They usually disappeared very fast, because they were some of the best donuts you could ever imagine. One time there were a lot of donuts left at the end of the day - at least twenty - and someone urged me to take them home to my kids. "Sure, I'll take them home to the kids!" I said.

My kids didn't see a one. I started eating them as I drove home. I wasn't even out of downtown before at least four had been devoured. I took the long way home that night, so as not to have to eat while driving on the highway. At each stop sign, I grabbed another donut. By the time I was within a couple of miles of home, I looked into the boxes and realized that there were only a few donuts left. I reasoned that there weren't enough to bring to my two daughters and husband. Why there weren't even enough donuts left so that each of them could have two! And who can eat just one donut? So I did them a favor and ate the last few. I had indigestion by this time, but what's a mother to do? I took one for the team. Actually I took about five for the team. I stopped at a grocery store parking lot and disposed of the empty boxes. I carefully wiped off my sugar-ridden lips with Kleenex before entering the house to kiss my family hello. I told my family that I wasn't cooking that night because my tummy wasn't feeling too good, so my husband went to White Castle. I could smell the grease while they were eating, and actually got kind of hungry for some Whitey's, but I resisted. After all, it would have been rude of me to take food away from my precious babies, wouldn't it?

And that wasn't the last time I ate so many donuts in one sitting. My stomach can comfortably hold at least a dozen at a time. If I have to eat more, I have to give myself a little time in between each dozen.

My late husband Jerry used to love donuts as much as I do. We never bought less than eighteen at a time. Jerry would eat about six donuts and be done. He would tell me that the rest were mine. He probably expected me to take a couple of days to finish them, but it never took me that long. One time I woke up in the middle of the night in a cold sweat. I knew there were donuts in the kitchen and I knew they had to be eaten before the sun came up! I snuck into the kitchen and was as quiet as a mouse as I lifted the lid off of the box and removed one donut at a time, being careful not to rustle the tissue paper.

The next morning Jerry was incredulous that the donuts were gone. He really hadn't wanted any more, but he was surprised that they were all gone. I told him the awful truth; that while he was in a deep sleep, a horrible man had broken in, drug me into the kitchen and held me down while he force-fed me all of the donuts. I whimpered about how awful it had been! At least Jerry had a great sense of humor. He never scolded me about my eating binges or made me feel bad about eating more than my share of anything.

The $100 Scone

This next story sounds too crazy to be true, but I swear, it is. This took place not that many years ago.

Amy and I were both hooked on cinnamon chip scones from a local restaurant-bakery. One evening I gave her the money and asked her to get us each a scone. I devoured mine as soon as she got back with them, but she said she was saving hers for later. Knowing her scone was there started to drive me crazy. It's hard for me to eat just one of anything that I really like, and I really like scones. I kept glancing at the bag on the kitchen counter and getting more and more anxious. I get a weird anxiety about food, especially sweets, being in the house. I can't concentrate on anything else until the item is gone. I started hinting that I sure would love another scone. Amy just smiled. Then I came right out and begged Amy for her scone. She still just smiled. I got more intense as the minutes went by. I offered to pay her for the scone. Amy continued to just smile. She finally asked me how much it was worth to me, and I said "One hundred dollars!" Amy started laughing and said, "Really? One hundred dollars?" This gave me hope. I knew Amy never had enough money and also that she did not have a sweet tooth like her mother did. I got up and grabbed my checkbook. I was prepared to write

Amy a check in the amount of one hundred dollars, as crazy as that sounded even to me. I had placed the pen on a check when Amy told me that maybe I should look into the bag before I wrote the check. I went to the kitchen and opened the bag, thinking that she was just teasing me and making me wait longer for my scone. Actually she was being very decent about the whole thing, because there in the bag sat a great big delicious NOTHING! She had eaten the scone before I had started bargaining for it. Amy may be quiet and seem innocent, but she can really fool me sometimes. (See my story "Locked Out on New Year's Eve" in My Crazy Insane Stories section)

My Crazy Famous Stories

I call these stories my crazy famous stories because they are all about the few years when I worked at Famous-Barr Department Store that most people just called Famous, and because these stories are famous in my family. I have told them "ad nauseam" over the years. I only worked for Famous for about three years, but for such a short period in my life, I sure have a lot of memories about working there.

I worked part time, usually only a few times per week, and usually for four-hour shifts. I made $1.25 an hour. Sometimes I worked for eight hours on Saturdays, so that made for a fat paycheck. I usually spent all of my money on clothes purchased at Famous. I was an "extra" as they called it. It meant that I was a floater, placed in any department that needed me. A few times I was assigned to a department for an extended period, like when I was assigned to the Swimwear Department for an entire summer and to the Sunglasses Department for the last several months that I worked there.

Famous had many more departments than department stores have now days. At the Southtown store where I worked they had a Hardware Department, a Scout Department, an Infant Department and even a Pet Department. I worked in every department except in the highly sales-commissioned departments like the Furniture or Lawn and Garden Departments. For some reason, I never worked in the Candy Department. (Perhaps they knew about my sweet tooth and were afraid I would eat all the profits).

Shoes on the Customers' Heads!

This is my most famous Famous story. I was on winter break from college, so they assigned me to a weeklong project during the daytime. It was in the Bargain Shoe Department in the basement. This was the only assignment I ever had that was behind the scenes and didn't involve any customer (or even any co-worker) contact. It drove me crazy. I am a "people" person and do not like to work behind the scenes. So putting me in a back room to work for forty hours without any human contact was torture for me. As they said in the movie Dirty Dancing, "Nobody puts Baby in a corner!"

To make matters worse, the work itself was mindless and repetitive. It involved matching up shoes according to style and size and then attaching the left and right shoes to each other with a plastic "thingy" that shot out of a gun. The pairs would later be piled on bargain tables for customers to rummage through. Each day I started with huge piles of a certain size; left shoes on one side of my chair and the matching right shoes in a pile on my right. At first it was mildly interesting, but soon I got really bored. After I matched and attached a pair of shoes, I would throw it into a pile a few yards away. To make my job interesting, I would throw the shoes as hard as I could, and aiming just so, eventually creating a huge pyramid. As I threw the shoes, I yelled out "Woo!" for added oomph.

I noticed that the wall did not quite meet the ceiling. Because the pile was so high by Friday, some of the shoes started to spill over into (what I thought was) another storage room. I was happy to have an added dimension to my shoe-throwing. I threw the shoes even harder so they would land in the second storage room. I was almost having fun. I kept yelling "Woo!" and hurling the paired shoes as hard as I could.

All of a sudden I heard a man's voice yell out, "Hey! Who's throwing shoes on the customers' heads?!"

I can only imagine the customers, sitting on the long leather bench against the outside of the wall separating the store from the back room, trying on shoes, getting bombarded with more shoes and hearing some idiot in the back room yelling "Woo!". Maybe they thought it was a marketing gimmick like "It's raining shoes at Famous this week!" I never got any backlash from my antics; in fact, I don't even remember anyone coming back into the storeroom to yell at me. I just stopped throwing the shoes so hard and refrained from yelling out "Woo!" for the rest of the day.

Help Yourself, Kid!

The one time I worked in the Pet Department was one of my most memorable assignments. It was a Saturday evening, when the shopping was kind of slow. It was toward the end of my four hour shift when I got my first customer of the evening, a boy about twelve years old. At first I didn't pay him much attention, because I thought he was probably just looking while his parents shopped in another department. Besides, I was busy talking to a cute boy who was working in the adjoining department. After a while, the kid came up to me and asked for help. He said he wanted to buy a lizard. He had a wad of money in his hand, so I knew he was a serious customer. As we approached the glass case that held the lizard he wanted, I started to freak out. No one had told me how to retrieve a lizard from the case. Did I use a net like you use to retrieve fish from an aquarium? Were there gloves I could wear, because I knew that I was not going to touch that thing! And what was I supposed to put the disgusting reptile in?

There was a lot of tension in the air as the little boy and I stood in front of his future pet. The boy pointed to his lizard with eager anticipation, while I shivered with disgust. Then I handed him one of those white cartons that looked like a Chinese take-out container and said "Help yourself, kid. I ain't touchin' that thing!"

I unlocked the case and let the kid scoop up the lizard. I had chills running down my spine as I rang up the purchase. In fact, as I write this, I have the chills. I hate reptiles. I couldn't wait for that damned kid and his revolting little friend to get out of the department. I told Miss Schweppman (spelling?), the lady in the personnel office who assigned the "extra's" their jobs, never to put me in the Pet Department again!

I'll Meet You on the Other Side!
One day I was assigned to Men's Work Clothes in the basement. It was where they sold the men's work pants, jeans, and casual shirts and pants. I enjoyed working in that department, because I loved folding clothes, helping customers find their sizes and keeping the shelves neatly stocked. I also loved using the cash register, counting out change and bagging the purchases. I was really good at that part

of it, but I had no experience whatsoever with measuring a man for a pair of pants. I had seen the other lady working in the department do it, so I knew what to do, but I certainly didn't want to get that intimate with any of the customers. The other lady was busy with another customer or maybe she was at lunch. I do not remember. All I do remember is being the only one available to measure a fat man for pants. I was so embarrassed. The first thing I did was measure his waist. That seemed pretty innocuous until I actually started to do it. I started with holding one end of the tape at the center of his waist in front with the intention of wrapping the tape around his waist until it reached the beginning of the tape. Because his waist was so big, our bodies would actually have to touch, like I was giving him a great big bear hug. I definitely did not want to have my body touching his, so I asked him to hold the tape measure in place in the front. I told him I'd meet him around the other side with the rest of the tape. In a sing-song voice I said "I'll meet ya 'round the other side!" as I skipped around him in a circle! His wife was with him, and she did not look amused at all. The fat man seemed okay with the way I did it, though. Personally, I thought it was a fun way to measure his waist.

Then it was time for measuring his inseam. I couldn't think of any way I could do that part without dying of embarrassment, so I simply handed the fat man the tape measure and told him I didn't do inseams! He looked at me with confusion while his wife snatched the tape measure out of his hands and said "I'll do it!" She stuck her hand up into his crotch with one end of the tape measure. I felt a little creepy watching such an intimate moment. How I got away with that terrible customer service, I'll never know. They never registered a complaint about my measuring techniques.

Wrapping It All Up!

One day I was working in what I think was called the Ladies Sportswear Department on the first floor. I don't remember the brand names anymore, but I remember that this department sold relatively expensive popular brand name skirts, pants and shirts; clothing that I myself could not afford. A very handsome, well-dressed man was shopping there one day. He selected numerous items and told me they were a surprise for his wife. I thought how lucky his wife was, to not only have such a handsome husband, but one who bought her clothes!

Famous Barr was a very nice department store, and back then we didn't just stuff purchased clothing items into a plastic bag; we boxed them. This meant constructing the box, lining it with two pieces of tissue paper, folding the items "just so", and then placing the box in a paper bag. If there were multiple boxes, we stacked them and tied them together with string.

Now keep in mind, this man was very handsome and had spent a lot of money on this purchase, so I was really trying to impress him. He watched me intently as I went through each step of carefully packaging everything. Since this man had bought so many items, even though I put more than one item in each box, I ended up with a huge stack of boxes.

I was a little self-conscious because the man was watching me so intently, there was a long line of customers behind him and it wasn't so easy trying to tie six or seven boxes together. (In hindsight, I should have made two stacks of boxes). The man saw me struggling and offered to help, but I refused. I wanted to show him how competent I was and to treat him to the best possible customer service, since he had spent so much money. I sensed that the man and the customers standing behind him were getting a little impatient, but I was determined to expertly tie these boxes together. I finally managed to secure the string around the huge stack of boxes and even tie a bow at the top. I proudly handed the stack to my handsome customer. He started to walk away with the tower of boxes when I noticed that I had somehow tangled the telephone cord in with the string. I called out in horror, "Sir, the phone!" just as the telephone crashed loudly to the floor. He and I both looked embarrassed (he for me and I for myself) and the restless customers in line just looked at me like I was from outer space.

My Black Swimsuit Fetish!

One of my favorite assignments was when I was assigned to the Swimwear Department from April until the end of the summer. I always worked alone in that department, which I didn't mind, because I filled my down time with looking at the cute swimsuits. There were so many! One Saturday evening, when it was unusually slow, I decided to try some on. I was not supposed to leave the department except for a fifteen minute break when someone from another department relieved me, but I decided to take a chance. I was in one of the fitting rooms stripped down to my birthday suit when I heard a man's voice yelling "Miss Linkul?" It was my boss, Mr. Clark. He was in charge of several departments and had an office in the back room right next to the fitting rooms. I panicked. I knew he could come back into the area at any time. I certainly didn't want him coming back there, so I yelled out "I'll be right there, Mr. Clark. I'm just clearing out the fitting rooms." I scrambled to get dressed and came out with an armful of suits and hangers. Mr. Clark looked at me like he knew what I had been doing. He even asked me if I had been trying on suits. I lied and told him "no", but I think my flushed face had a guilty look on it. I never did try on suits while I was on duty after that. Mr. Clark was pretty creepy. One day he ran his finger up the back of my leg to make sure I was wearing hose. It made me all the more resolved never to try on swimsuits while on duty again!

It was fun to work in that department because lots of girls my age came in to try on suits and I had fun helping them with their selections. And I got to play music to add to the fun atmosphere. The only record we had was Simon and Garfunkel's album, the soundtrack from the movie "The Graduate", which I played over and over every time I worked in the Ladies Swimwear Department that summer. I knew the album by heart. I can't listen to "Parsley, Sage, Rosemary and Thyme" (or whatever that song's called), "Bridge over Troubled Water" or "Mrs. Robinson" without thinking of that summer. Except for Mr. Clark, it was my favorite assignment.

Besides almost getting caught trying on suits, the only really weird thing I did while working in that department was to tell a woman that I had a fetish for black swimsuits. I had just heard someone use the word "fetish" and thought it was a word that I should try to use in conversation at some time. Unbeknownst to me, I had the wrong idea about what it meant. I mistakenly thought if someone had a fetish about something it meant that he or she had an aversion to it.

One evening a rather plump woman was trying on swimsuits, and she kept coming out of the fitting room area to model them and ask for my opinion. She came out with an all-black suit and asked me if it made her look slimmer. I told her that contrary to popular belief prints were actually more slimming than solid black suits. I explained that when you wear a black suit, the eye tends to go from the boring black color of the suit to the skin areas; whereas, if you wear a print suit, the eye just keeps looking at the pattern of the suit and not at the surrounding skin. The fat lady seemed to be thinking about what I said, when I added "Besides, I have a fetish for black swimsuits!" She looked at me oddly and quickly told me that she had decided against the black suit. I remember feeling proud that I had known what I was talking about, and for using a fancy word (fetish) that I had just learned.

Shortly after this, when I heard someone else use the word fetish I gathered that it meant that you had a sexual desire for something. I thought back to the swim suit encounter when I had told the plump lady that I had a fetish for black swim suits. No wonder she bought the floral print. She probably thought I had a fetish for women and that I was trying to come on to her because of that black swimsuit!

I'm in Men's Underwear!

One of the departments that I was most often assigned to in my three years of working at Famous was in the Men's Underwear Department. I liked telling people I was in Men's Underwear, and I actually liked working in that department. I liked dealing with men much better than dealing with women customers. Men were straightforward and knew what they wanted. Women customers were demanding, complaining and never seemed to be able to make up their minds.

I sold hundreds of pairs of Gold Toe socks and packages of Fruit of the Loom undershirts. I love the feel of men's undershirts. They remind me of my Dad. I loved refolding the undershirts and putting them back into the packaging as if they had never been taken out. I was good at that. I also loved the challenge of stacking the slippery plastic packages into neat piles. I enjoyed helping my customers find the right size. Mainly, I just liked waiting on men.

As much as I loved being in Men's Underwear, there was one thing I longed for every time I worked in that department. It never happened until about the twentieth time I worked there. I was standing at the outside perimeter of the department watching the shoppers walk into the store. I liked to people-watch and I probably appeared to be eager to help, because many people stopped and asked me how to get to various departments. Finally, one evening, a man came up to me and asked the question I had been longing to hear for years. He asked, "Are you in Men's Underwear?" to which I replied without missing a beat, "Well, sir, that's a little personal!" Luckily he got it. We both laughed as I told him I had been waiting for years for someone to ask that question.

My Crazy Germany Stories

I lived in Germany for eight months, from December 9, 1969 until the first week of August, 1970. My husband Terry was in the Army when we got married in October, 1969. He had just finished boot camp and had to report to Bamberg, Germany a little over a week after our wedding. I didn't join him until December. I remember how excited I was when I arrived. There was snow on the ground and it looked like something out of a fairy tale. I guess you could say my eight months living in Germany was like living in a fairy tale. I had no real responsibilities and didn't ever feel like it was my real life. Everything was so different. It was my first experience of living away from my parents and it was in another country.

Terry and I never got to see much of Europe, or even much of Germany for that matter. Our two-year stint was cut short when he was sent to Viet Nam. We tried to take a trip to Northern Italy to see Terry's aunt, but the engine of our Volkswagen caught on fire when we were about ninety miles from home, so we had to be towed back home. I did get to visit Munich and Garmisch, though. And I got to see the outside of King Richard's castle, which was in the village of Litzendorf where we lived for most of the time we were in Germany. The short time I got to live in Germany was a wonderful experience. I made some lifelong friends, Dick and Judy, and got to experience a whole different world. I am so grateful for my time there, even though I would have loved to stay for the full two years. Of course, I had some crazy experiences while I was there. Here are the craziest stories.

The Big Move!

Our first apartment was in the city of Bamberg. I rarely ventured out, because I really didn't know very much German and I don't think Terry was too crazy about me walking around town by myself. After all, I was only twenty-one and not very experienced with life yet. We only lived in that apartment for a few weeks. The landlord raised the rent immediately when the second month's rent was due. I remember I was baking a cake one day when Terry called me from the base and told me that he had found us an apartment in the village of Litzendorf, and that I should get everything packed and ready to go right away. He was coming to pick me up in a cab. I remember telling him that we couldn't move that fast; that I had a cake in the oven! I only had our clothing and toiletries to pack, and the cake, of course. I must have stolen one of the landlord's plates, because I remember walking out of the apartment with our suitcases and the damn cake that I just couldn't bear to leave behind. I didn't even have anything to cover the cake with. I'm surprised I didn't just eat the whole thing.

I was so mad at the landlord for raising our rent without warning that I wanted to tell the future tenants (who would surely be

Americans) not to be fooled by the reasonable rent, because it would surely be raised after thirty days. I was afraid to leave a note because the landlord might see it and destroy it, so I did what I thought was very clever. I wrote my warning to the new tenants on the toilet paper roll. I unrolled it a little before I wrote my note and then rolled it back so the landlord wouldn't see my message. I said something like "Beware of Mr. Alt (the landlord). He will raise your rent after the first 30 days!" I don't know what I thought my note would accomplish, but writing it made me feel better. I felt like Mr. Alt was being mean to us because we were Americans. I had heard that the Germans did not like us, even though they made money off of us. Before I had left the U.S., I was told that the movie "Town without Pity" had been a true story set in Bamberg, and showed how much Americans were disliked by the Germans. I have never seen the movie, but having heard this, I was defensive before I even arrived in Bamberg. The toilet paper warning was my little attempt at justice for Americans! Ironically, the cab that we took on moving out day was stopped for a long time (with the meter running, of course) because the street was blocked by a moving van. As we passed it, I noticed its sign. It was a van from the Alt Moving Company, which our landlord owned! It was as if he was trying to screw us again!

Our new home in the village of Litzendorf was a large apartment on the second floor over a farmer's house. The barn was in the same building right next to the Schmidt's (owners') quarters. There were two other apartments on the second floor. One was probably just one room, and it was where the family's Oma (Grandma) stayed. I never even saw the inside of Oma's room. I occasionally saw her come out of her room in the morning with a smelly bucket of "you know what", because apparently she was not allowed to use the second floor bathroom. She always said, "Gruss Godt!", a greeting meaning "God bless you", without ever looking up at me.

The apartment at the other end of the second floor was also rented to Americans, Dick and Judy, who became lifelong friends. There was a refrigerator in the hallway just outside of our apartment's kitchen entrance. We would have to share it with Dick and Judy, whom I hadn't met yet. We also had to share the bathroom that was across from Oma's room. It had a glass door. It wasn't clear glass, so you couldn't see details, but you could see shadows. I didn't feel comfortable sharing a bathroom with strangers, much less knowing that if someone looked hard enough they could see the outline of my body while I was sitting on the toilet or taking a bath. Our bedroom had two twin beds, which we pushed together to make a double, but there were wooden frames on the beds, so there was a small strip of wood running right down the middle of our bed. As if these things weren't enough to get used to, the kicker was that the place was heated by oil burning heaters that required us to go down to the barn, pump some oil into a container, carry it up to our apartment, pour the oil into the heater and then light a strip of litmus paper to get it fired up. Terry seemed to love the new place right away, but I had some misgivings about sharing the refrigerator and bathroom with strangers, but since we became fast friends with Dick and Judy, it worked out just fine!

A Warm (actually hot) Welcome to Our New Home!
The day after we moved in, Terry left for his job as a clerk in an office on base, and I was left to fend for myself. He did get the

heater going for me, so I didn't have to fool with that on my first day. After he left I washed the breakfast dishes in the little sink. It was a bathroom sink, but it was in the kitchen, and ran cold water only. We didn't have an attached water heater like other Americans we knew had in their apartments, so I had to heat water on the stove in order to wash the dishes. There was no dish drainer, but there was a wooden table covered with a little woven braided throw rug right next to the little sink. That's where I used to stack the dishes after washing them. That little table was the only work space in the kitchen besides the small wooden table where we ate. It was kind of primitive, but I learned to make it work. At least there was a normal stove. I think it was electric, which I had never used before, but it worked. Thank God I didn't have to chop wood and cook over a fire.

After breakfast that first morning I went down to the bathroom and washed my hair in the sink. I wasn't brave enough to take a bath yet, since the tub was right near the glass door. So I quickly washed at the sink, which was further away from the semi see-through door. Since we were sharing the bathroom I didn't want to leave my wet towel there, so I brought it back to our apartment. I draped it over the oil heater to dry and decided to go downstairs and talk to the landlady about something I had just broken. I had been trying to open a beautiful antique armoire so I could hang our coats, and I turned the key too hard. It had broken off in the lock. Frau Schmidt knew a little English and I knew a little German, so we could communicate fairly well, but it took a lot of effort. She assured me that it was okay that I had broken the armoire and said she'd send her husband up to fix it after lunch. She kept talking and talking, and I started to get nervous. She just kept talking. All of a sudden a wave of anxiety swept over me, and I felt like I just had to get out of her place and back to my own apartment. I somehow managed to get away.

I climbed the stairs and walked into the kitchen just in time to see flames shooting out of the heater! The flames were an inch from the ceiling! The towel that I had draped over the top of the heater had made the fire more intense and it had caught fire. I quickly filled a bowl with water and doused the flames. But while that subdued the flames, it also caused parts of the blackened towel to stick to the heater. There was a lot of smoke. Just then Terry walked in the door. He was home for lunch. I don't remember if Herr and Frau Schmidt came upstairs when they had smelled the smoke, or if they just happened to come by to see about the armoire, but I remember them being in our apartment, too. I apologized profusely and was very close to tears. Terry couldn't believe that I didn't know that you can't completely cover the top of a heater when it's on. I still don't know what actually happens when you do that, but I now know that you shouldn't do it.

The next thing I remember is all of us being in the living/dining room of the apartment and I was talking while Herr Schmidt dug what remained of the key out of the armoire. Herr Schmidt looked very unhappy with me. Frau Schmidt just smiled. Apparently it was okay with her that I had started a fire and made a mess of the heater putting the fire out, and okay that I had broken the beautiful antique armoire, all on my first day! She really liked me for some reason.

Ashes from the Sky!

One day Frau Schmidt and I were outside in the front of the house just talking. That was the day she told me that someone had told her that Americans eat mice! I was horrified when she told me that. Surely she didn't really believe it. I kept telling her that we would never eat mice and she kept insisting that a former tenant (an American) had told her that Americans eat mice. Finally, after several minutes I realized that she was saying "Maize", her word for corn. In Germany people don't eat corn. It's considered pig food. We had a good laugh about our misunderstanding.

While we were chatting, I noticed some black flakes falling onto Frau Schmidt's head. At first there were just a couple of flakes, but then there were a lot more black flakes falling from the sky, and some of the pieces were bigger than flakes. Frau Schmidt didn't seem to notice at first. I looked up, and much to my horror, I saw a lot of black stuff shooting out of the chimney (or maybe it was some kind of vent on the roof). I immediately knew what was causing the black snow!

It was that damn heater again! We had run out of litmus paper and it was towards the end of the month, so we didn't have money to buy any. That morning, I pumped some oil as I did every morning, so I could start up the heater. Instead of lighting litmus paper, I used typing paper. I lit a couple of pieces of paper and threw it into the heater. The flame went out as soon as it hit the oil, so I kept lighting whole pieces of typing paper and throwing them in until a fire finally got going. I always felt kind of like a pioneer woman when I pumped oil and started a fire, and I felt pretty good about being so innovative that day.

Frau Schmidt finally noticed the black burnt paper flakes falling on both of us and looked up at the roof. She realized right away that it was the heater. She threw her arms up over her head, looked at me with exasperation as if to say, "What now, Frau Cima?" I told her I had put paper in the heater; a lot of it. We both raced into the open barn which was part of the house, up the stairs to the second floor and down the hall to our apartment. The heater was shaking and looked like it was about to blow. She turned it off, probably just in time. I remember she left, shaking her head and muttering "Oh, the Frau Cima!" But for some reason, she still liked me.

Sauerkraut for Breakfast, Sardines for Lunch and Spaghetti for Dinner!

As little as I knew about being a housewife, I knew even less about being pregnant. Every afternoon I got dizzy and nauseated. One afternoon I was standing in the hallway at one of my army wife friend's apartment (across the street) talking while we waited for "the boys" to come home for dinner. Suddenly I felt so dizzy I thought I was going to faint. I confided to her that I thought maybe I had a serious disease, because lately every afternoon I felt really bad, usually late in the afternoon. She got a knowing look on her face as I described my symptoms. Then she asked, "Did you ever think that you might be pregnant?" "No!" I exclaimed. That thought had not even crossed my mind. I had heard that when you are pregnant you get morning sickness, not late afternoon sickness. But the more I thought about it the more I thought that maybe I was pregnant. A visit to the infirmary on base confirmed that I was.

One Sunday I woke up feeling really nauseous. Terry was away on field maneuvers all week, so I was alone. It was about ten o'clock on Sunday morning and I was still in my night gown when I heard Frau Schmidt knocking at my door. I opened the door to see a smiling Frau Schmidt holding a big plateful of food. Being farmers, the Schmidts started their day at three o'clock in the morning, so by ten o'clock they were really hungry. That's when they had their big meal of the day. This being a Sunday, Frau Schmidt had cooked a special meal. As she handed me the plate, she described the food. It was meatloaf with a hard-boiled egg in the middle, sauerkraut (about a pound of it) topped with the biggest potato dumpling I have ever seen. Seriously, it was the size of a cantaloupe. The smell of the sauerkraut and the sight of all that food was enough to make me hurl, but I smiled and thanked Frau Schmidt, telling her that it looked delicious. Rather than just let me take the plate and close the door, Frau Schmidt followed me into the kitchen and told me to eat. I obediently sat down and took a bite of the dumpling. She beamed with pride as she watched me cut into her special meatloaf. She described how she had put the hard- boiled eggs in just the right place so that each slice of meatloaf had a little slice of egg in it. I took a tiny bite and told her it was delicious. Thankfully she was satisfied that I was enjoying her food and left before I was forced to eat sauerkraut. I can still remember how that food smelled and tasted. If I had it right now I'd be all over it, but being pregnant and nauseated, I couldn't enjoy it as good as it was. I tried really hard to eat more of it, but I just couldn't.

I didn't know what to do with the food. I knew from experience that I could not throw it in the trash, because the Schmidts went through our trash looking for food scraps that they could feed to their pigs. I certainly did not want to hurt Frau Schmidt's feelings. So I snuck the plateful of food into the bathroom. As I quickly scraped the food into the toilet, I prayed no one would come to the bathroom door and see what I was doing. I had to flush the toilet several times, because all that food, especially that five pound dumpling, wouldn't go down. I should have put small amounts of the food in the toilet, a little at a time, instead of dumping it all in at once, but I had been in a hurry. I was sweating bullets until at last it all disappeared. I could envision having to call Herr Schmidt upstairs to unclog the toilet, and having him see his wife's home cooked potato dumpling bobbing in toilet water. I planned to tell him that I had thrown up if it came to that, but luckily it didn't. That was one time I dodged a bullet while I lived there!

On that Thursday I decided to treat myself to a really good lunch. I went grocery shopping at the PX and came home with canned sardines in mustard sauce, barbecue flavored Fritos and chocolate ice cream. I made myself a chocolate shake and sat down to a lunch of sardines and BBQ Fritos. I had gone to the library on base so I had a good book to read while I ate my lunch. Eating something really good, while reading a really good book is one of my favorite pastimes. Knowing that I had nothing else to do all day made this scenario about as good as it could be. I don't know how I didn't get sick that day.

The next evening I actually did get violently ill. I had eaten way too much spaghetti. I also had salad with Wish-Bone Italian dressing on it. To this day I cannot eat that dressing. I didn't even make it to the toilet. I puked in the tub, which was closer to the bathroom door than the toilet was. I remember there was lettuce hanging out of my nose, which grossed me out so much that I puked some more. I kept gagging and heaving and praying to die as I tried to pick up the spaghetti and lettuce that wouldn't go down the drain of the tub. (I'm sorry. I hope you're not eating as you read this part. Oh wait. You probably wouldn't be eating while you read *this* book, because most people like to read a really *good* book while they are eating.)

They're Selling Like Hotcakes!

One day Judy and I were shopping in the PX on the first of the month, which was pay day. The PX was always crowded on pay day. While Judy and I were standing in line by the cash registers, I saw a large bin of something they called "Prophylactics", a word I had never heard nor seen. It seemed like every shopper, especially the guys, were picking up several packages of these mysterious items. I was intrigued. Finally I said in a really loud voice "I don't know what they are, but they're selling like hotcakes!" Everybody laughed. Judy blushed and whispered that they were rubbers. I learned a new word that day and will never forget it.

Inspection Day Disaster!

I tried my best to be a good Army Wife, but I was new to being a wife, much less an Army Wife. I didn't realize how important it was to keep my husband's uniforms in tip-top condition. Luckily Terry had his uniforms laundered on base, so I didn't have to worry about starching and ironing them just so.

One day Terry told me that there was going to be an inspection the next day. He told me that his uniform had to be perfect. He said that they would pull on every button, and not one had better come off. So he asked me to re-sew each one. I didn't like to sew and was not very good at it. I had trouble threading needles even though I had excellent eye-sight. It usually took me a few minutes to thread a needle, which was frustrating. To avoid having to thread it so many times, I usually made the thread way too long, which makes sewing very awkward. The thread always gets all tangled up. I usually stick myself many times while sewing, and often somehow end up sewing the garment I am mending to the clothes I am wearing. I did the best I could to sew those buttons on good. There were a lot of them, and I'm sure I got tired of sewing very quickly.

When Terry came home for lunch the next day, he was not very happy. He told me that the inspector had pulled on his buttons and every one of them had come off. There were buttons flying everywhere! He had been the laughing stock of his entire company. I was not a very good Army Wife. I told Terry that next time he should probably sew his own buttons on.

My Crazy Holy Stories

Don't let the title of this chapter fool you. There's not much holiness in the stories I'm about to share. Actually I used to be holy; from first grade until sixth grade, that is. That's when my focus went more towards the Twelve Cutest Boys in My Class rather than on the Twelve Apostles.

Don't Drink the Holy Water!

I was very holy in the first grade. I received three Sacraments for the first time within one week: First Confession, First Holy Communion and Confirmation. I was raised in a very Catholic family and went to Catholic grade school and high school where I was taught mostly by sisters. I was especially holy during the summer after fifth grade. It was 1959, the year before the world was going to end, according to the sisters who taught me at Holy Family School in South St. Louis (now Marian Middle School). Not only were we kids scared to death when we had to go through atomic bomb drills once every month, but the sisters told us that in 1960 the Pope was supposed to read the letter that Our Lady of Fatima had given the three children to whom she appeared in 1917. The letter supposedly said something about the end of the world. The sisters didn't want us kids to be unprepared for our final judgment, so they urged us to sign up for a holy hour each week during the summer of 1959. I still remember my holy hour. It was on Thursdays between 10:00 and 11:00. I was alone in the church during that time, which I liked. I prayed for most of the hour, but sometimes I got a little restless and started to walk around the church looking for ways to become even holier.

One day after praying for a long while, I wandered into the back of the church where there was a statue of the Blessed Virgin, and found a whole stack of Legion of Mary sign-up cards. The Legion of Mary was a lay organization devoted to Mary. It was for adults. One of the things they did was go door-to-door passing out leaflets that urged Catholics to pray to Mary. I guess I didn't realize that I was signing up for the Legion of Mary when I filled out a whole bunch of their cards. I just loved filling out forms. One evening a group of adults rang our doorbell. My Mom answered the door. They told her they were there to talk to a Marilyn Linkul. I was in my bedroom at the back of the house and I heard them asking if I was home. I also heard them tell my Mom that I had signed up for the Legion of Mary, not once, but several times. Oops! And I heard my Mom tell them that I was just a kid. She didn't sound too happy. She made me come out of my room and apologize for making these nice people come to our house thinking that they were getting a new Legion of Mary member. When I told them that I hadn't known what I was doing when I had filled out the cards, they laughed and seemed to take it pretty well. I didn't really get into trouble, but my Mom did explain to me that I better not do anything like that again; that she was embarrassed. As I am writing this I am wondering why they didn't ask themselves what adult who was serious about joining the Legion of Mary would fill out that many cards? And couldn't they tell by my handwriting that I was just a kid? I'm sorry, but those Legionnaires were holy alright. Holey in the head!

Another time, I wanted to feel what it was like to be up near the altar. In those days, women were not allowed in the sacristy (up by the altar). We weren't allowed to be servers either. Since no one was around, and I was sure God wouldn't mind, I went into the forbidden zone. I didn't stay too long, because I didn't want to get caught. I didn't want to get kicked out of my holy hour. But before I left the altar, there was one more thing I just had to do. On special feast days, the priest would sometimes lie prone on the floor in front of the altar. I always thought that was pretty cool. So I looked around and then quickly dropped into position. It felt good to act like a priest, even though I could never be one. I didn't think this was fair, but I thought the holiest vocation I could ever hope for was to be a sister. I kind of wanted to be one. At the time I did not know that marriage or committed single life are also Church-recognized "holy" vocations.

With each holy hour under my belt, I felt a little holier. One day I wanted to feel holier yet, so I decided to drink some holy water. I thought it would purify my soul. I dipped my cupped hand into the fountain and lapped it up. I can still remember what it was like. A thin film of scum had formed on the holy water, and I could feel little particles of scum on the inside of my mouth. And it tasted really bad. Years later, when I had my first taste of gin, I remembered how the holy water had tasted that day. Unless my church was also a bootleg gin distillery, that holy water tasted a lot like gin.

In addition to praying for an hour in church each week, in 1959 the sisters also asked us to go to Mass every day during that summer, with the promise of a prize for the child who went to the most daily Masses. Each time we went to a Mass other than on Sundays, one of the sisters would give us a punch on a card. That summer I went to Mass every single day, and sometimes twice. I remember going to funerals of people I didn't even know just to get an extra punch. I sang at a few weddings, too. I did whatever it took to win, and I did. I had over one-hundred punches by the end of the summer. My prize was a rosary. I was so proud of winning! And I did feel very holy.

Look at Our Little Nun!

When 1960 came and we were all still here, I soon forgot about trying to be so holy. But even though I no longer went to daily Mass during the summer or kept a holy hour in church, I did still pray a lot.

One Sunday, when I was in the sixth grade, one of the sisters asked me if I would please come to the convent with her after Mass. She explained that her order of nuns was changing their habits to be less restrictive and more modern. They had a sample veil that they wanted me to try on. I guess one of the sisters couldn't model it, because they could not appear in public (or maybe even outside of their rooms) without their veils, which at the time covered their entire heads and even a portion of their faces.

I was only too glad to be the model. One of the sisters gently placed the veil on my head and the other twelve or so sisters who were standing around me in a circle exclaimed their "oohs" and "ahs". I was in my glory as the center of attention. I felt holy, too. All was fine until one sister said, "Look at our little nun!" I had wanted to be a nun when I was in fourth grade, but that desire was fading. It was then that I noticed that the sisters seemed to be tightening the circle around me and I started to feel feverish and dizzy. I thought I heard them all say in unison "Don't let our little nun get away. She is one of us. She is ours now!" I grabbed the veil, flung it off and said, "I have to go!" I got out of the convent as fast as I could and ran all of the way home. That was the end of my dream of being Sister Theresa Rose*, and kind of the end of my holy years, too.

*Theresa Rose was the name I had given to a mission baby that I had adopted for $5.00 of my own money when I was in the fourth grade. My $5.00 paid for her baptism. I wonder what ever happened to little Theresa Rose in Bolivia. I hope she is a good Catholic. Theresa Rose, if you are reading this, because I'm sure my book will be translated into Spanish and many other languages and be sold all over the world, please pray for my soul!

A Bad Confession

Even though I tried to be a good Catholic, I sometimes failed, like the time I lied in Confession to minimize the fact that I had sort of stolen a bicycle.

A kid named Tommy lived across the street. I liked his sisters, but didn't like him too much. He was always trying to pick fights and was a general nuisance to his sisters and their friends. One day he bragged about his brand new bike. It was just a small two-wheeler with training wheels, but I was jealous. I did not have a bike yet. I didn't get one until my tenth birthday. I was about seven at the time Tommy got his new bike, and he was younger than I was, so I guess I was doubly jealous. He just kept bragging and saying stuff like "Neener, neener, neener. I got a bike and you don't!" I pretended to ignore him, but I saw him out of the corner of my eye, riding his stupid little bike back and forth right in view of my side yard. When his mother yelled at him to come home for lunch, he just dropped his bike to the sidewalk and ran home. I guess his Mom was pretty strict and had told him that he better come right away when she called.

When I saw him just drop his brand new bike on the sidewalk like it didn't even matter to him, I got kind of mad. We never got brand new bikes in my family. We got used ones. I didn't even have mine yet and wouldn't get one for three more years. And I was sure that when I did get my bike, even though it wouldn't be new, I wouldn't be careless enough to just drop it on the sidewalk and leave it. Somebody had better teach that Tommy a lesson. I felt like it was supposed to be me. So I grabbed the bike and walked it over to my back yard. I wanted to hide it so that when Tommy came back outside he wouldn't know where his bike was. I would let him sweat it out for a little while and then tell him where it was, just to teach him a lesson. There wasn't really a place to hide it in my backyard, and besides, I didn't want anyone in my family to see Tommy's bike in our yard, so I decided the perfect spot would be in the alley behind our ash pit. (For those of you who don't know what an ash pit is, it's an open, square cement structure about five feet tall and was used to burn trash and leaves.) No one really used ash pits anymore by that time, but every yard in my neighborhood still had one in the back yard at the alley line. If you didn't know what an ash pit was before I told you, you also might not know that back in the 1950's, when this story took place, there used to be "trash pickers" who would come around on trash day before the trash trucks came by, and they would rummage through the trash cans for stuff they thought was worth having. Once you set your trash can out in the alley, or any big items that didn't fit in the can, your stuff became fair game for the "trash pickers".

Well, that day was a Friday and it was trash day. About half an hour after Tommy went home for lunch, he returned to the place on the sidewalk where he had left his bike, and saw that it was gone. I was in my yard innocently playing by myself and listening to Tommy screaming and crying about his missing bike. After a few minutes he ran home to get his Mom. I decided this was a good time to retrieve the bike from the alley and return it to the sidewalk. Not only would I have taught Tommy a lesson about taking better care of his bike, but maybe I'd even make him look like a fool for dragging his Mom out of the house for no reason. Bonus points for me! But my sense of satisfaction didn't last long.

When I went to the alley to get Tommy's bike from behind the ash pit, it was gone! While I had gone inside for lunch the "trash pickers" must have driven down my alley and taken Tommy's bike! I felt terrible! I had certainly not meant for this to happen. Tommy's Mom yelled at him when she found out that Tommy's brand new bike was missing, but I was too heartsick to enjoy hearing Tommy get bawled out.

I couldn't wait until three o'clock the next day, because that's when confessions were heard at my church. I was first in line. After rattling off my usual sins of talking back to my parents and fighting with my sister (always exactly three times), I took a deep breath and told Father that I had stolen a little bike (with emphasis on the word *little*). Father asked, "So it was a little bike?" I said, "Yes, Father, an eensy-teensy bike". (I mean, Tommy was only five and kind of short. His bike was little. It was a beginner's bike with training wheels, not a full size bike). Father said, "Do you mean a bike like one of those little charms? A charm bike? Why that's not so bad!" I breathed a sigh of relief and said, "Thank you, Father!" I congratulated myself for having chosen the "right" description for Tommy's bike. Father gave me a penance commensurate with stealing a little charm, and I skipped home with a lighter heart.

And what do you think I saw in front of Tommy's house? You guessed it. His bike! I asked Tommy how he had gotten his bike back, and he told me that some mean, older kid who lived about a block away had taken his bike. Tommy had seen him riding it around yesterday afternoon. Tommy's Mom had confronted the kid and Tommy got his bike back. Darn it! I had been sick to my stomach for a whole day, had lost sleep that night, and worst of all, had kind of lied to a priest! I had not been responsible for somebody taking Tommy's bike after all! I wonder if it's too late to confess my little lie?

Willful Wilfred

When I was in eighth grade, I was asked to tutor the third graders in reading once a week and to sit with the third graders when they went to daily Mass if their teacher couldn't be there. I also monitored this class on the playground every day after lunch. So, these kids were pretty used to me being in charge.

Our school went to daily Mass. One day I was asked to sit with the third graders, because their teacher couldn't be there. There was one kid in that class named Wilfred who was a real handful! The third grade sat in the front few pews on one side of the church. I felt that all eyes were on me during Mass, which made me very nervous. The sisters would be watching to see how well I kept the third graders in line. I sat second from the end of the pew and had Wilfred sit on the end, right next to the aisle. That way he was next to me, but separated from any of his classmates. I thought this was a good way to keep him from getting distracted. Wilfred was fidgeting around during Mass and I told him several times to be still and to pay attention to the Mass. I was starting to feel embarrassed because it probably looked like I couldn't control Wilfred's behavior. So I whispered through my teeth in my most threatening voice, "Look at the altar!" and nudged him really hard; so hard that he fell out of the pew and into the aisle! The whole school saw it! I was so embarrassed! Kids started laughing, and I could hear some of the sisters nearby loudly whispering to their classes to be still. Wilfred was enjoying the disturbance he had caused. I'm sure my face was beet red. I was so scared I would get bawled out for pushing Wilfred out of the pew, but that didn't happen, thank God.

Apparently Wilfred enjoyed causing a scene in church, but I did not. As a kid, I used to have a recurring nightmare about walking up the aisle in church towards the altar and bumping into every pew as I walked. In this dream, I was so humiliated, because the entire congregation was staring at me. The Wilfred incident was kind of like my nightmare, making a spectacle of myself in church.

What had happened in church another time was even more like my nightmare than the Wilfred incident was. One day during Mass, I started to feel faint. It was very hot in church and I had an empty stomach because we had to fast after midnight in order to take Communion back then. I was seeing spots and felt like I was going to fall. I had to get out of there and into the fresh air. I don't know why I didn't walk out of the door that was closest, and was behind everyone, but I guess I was panicky. I staggered up the center aisle towards a door to the front and left of the altar; and just like in my recurring nightmare, I loudly bumped into a couple of pews on my way out. When I got to the side door in front of the whole congregation of school kids, I crashed loudly into a covered radiator! It made a loud noise. A sister came up behind me and guided me out of the door. I kind of collapsed in her arms just outside of the door. Again, I was humiliated. My nightmare had come true.

Until recently, I could not be in the front pew of a church without feeling a little lightheaded. I remember I felt like I was going to faint at my wedding as we knelt in front of the altar in front of everyone. Years later, when I sang in the choir with my sister Lois, we stood kind of sideways in front of the entire congregation. I always made Lois stand on the end closest to the congregation to create a protective barrier between the rest of the church and me. Having the recurring nightmare certainly set me up to feel vulnerable in church, but I think it was mostly Willful Wilfred's fault!

Shaking the Pillar of the Church!

When I was thirty years old I got married for the second time and moved with my new husband and two kids to a place very near to where my sister Lois lived. In fact we were in the same parish. Now, Lois and I had many, many things in common; however, she was a "pillar of the church" type of person and I was more of a "black sheep". One of the first times I went to our new parish for Mass, Lois and her two kids Carolyn and Larry, were also there. I had my two kids. (Amy wasn't born yet). The six of us sat in a pew together. It felt good to be in church with my sister, just like when we were growing up.

I was always more mischievous than Lois. She was the more serious one, but I could make her laugh fairly easily. There was a kid sitting in the pew right in front of us who had a square head. One of my kids pointed this out and I started laughing. I pointed the kid out to Lois and she started laughing. All of our kids were already laughing, but when they saw us join in, their laughter got out of control. Soon all six of us were laughing so hard that we shook the whole pew! One of my daughters was sitting next to me, and I kind of nudged her to be quiet because the most sacred part of the Mass was about to take place. The rest of us kind of calmed down, but for some reason she couldn't get it under control. When I nudged her, she let out a yelp! That started all of us laughing again. We just couldn't stop. Lois' face was getting red. I didn't know anybody in the church, but as a "pillar of the church", Lois did. We all sort of stopped laughing long enough to go up for Communion, thank God, but then I got us all started again when I pointed out that one of the women walking back from Communion looked like she was wearing a bathmat around her shoulders! Lois and I often reminisced about that incident. She always said she was surprised I didn't get her "drummed out" of the parish!

My Crazy Insane Stories

"They're coming to take me away, ha-ha…they're coming to take me away!" I hope by my telling these "insane" stories that someone doesn't call "the men in white coats" on me.

Shatter Proof!

It was 1979. I was a newly-wed. Steve, my new husband, was away on a business trip. Pepsi had just come out with shatter-proof, two-liter soda bottles. I was intrigued by the television commercials. I had taken my two daughters to the grocery store where I saw the new shatter proof bottles and bought one. I couldn't wait to get home to test it! I remember holding the coveted shatter-proof bottle up in the air and saying, "Look kids, shatter-proof bottles!" Then I threw the bottle down on the floor as hard as I could! They were right; the bottle was shatter-proof, but it wasn't explosion-proof! There was soda everywhere! It was all over the ceiling and dripping down on my head from the light fixture. I was standing there, slightly in shock when the phone rang. With soda dripping from the receiver, I answered the phone with a wary "hello?" It was Steve. He could tell by my voice that something was wrong. I explained what I had just done. He didn't laugh. He simply asked, "Why?" I think he was a little surprised that I had done something so idiotic. He really didn't know me that well yet. I cleaned up what I could. When Steve got back from his trip, he saw the stains on the ceiling and shook his head in disbelief. He asked me to never do anything that foolish again. That was asking an awful lot of me, because I am the queen of foolishness!

Flinging Hot Dogs!

In the first story ignorance had made me "insane", but in this story, I chose to act insanely. I was in my early forties and working as a telephone banking manager. I didn't get out much in those days, except for working and going to my kids' sporting events, so maybe I was a little socially repressed. We'll go with that as a partial explanation of why I acted so insanely that night.

I had led a big telemarketing campaign that evening, which lasted until 8:00 PM. I had started working at 7:00 AM that day, so I was a little crazy-tired. I always tried to make the evening outbound telemarketing campaigns as much fun as possible for our staff, because I knew they did not enjoy working such a long day. That time I had brought in picnic food including a big crock pot full of hot dogs in BBQ sauce. I always brought way too much food in, so there were many hot dogs left over. I remember coming out of the bank building with some of my staff that evening and laughing hysterically about something. I got into my car still laughing. I couldn't stop. I felt like I was drunk.

As I drove through the streets of the well-to-do neighborhood near the bank, I saw a man dressed in running gear jogging next to the curb. In my crazy-tired "drunken" state, I suddenly got the urge to do something insane. I rolled down my window, reached into the crockpot on the floor of my car, pulled out a dripping hot dog and flung it at the runner. It hit him smack in the face! I drove away, tires squealing, laughing like a lunatic. I decided that since he was probably running for his health that he might also be a vegetarian. How ironic that would be if my horrible, processed meat hot dog had hit a vegetarian. It was the ultimate slap in the face! I was laughing my head off as I drove through the quiet, darkened neighborhood.

I decided it would be fun to fling more hot dogs. I could just imagine how the next day someone would see hot dogs in BBQ sauce and wonder how in the heck they had gotten there. So I flung them out of my window, one by one, laughing the entire time, without even giving it a thought how I would explain myself if a policeman would have happened to see me. I laughed myself sick all the rest of the way home. The next day I told a co-worker what I had done and she didn't believe me. So Debbie drove to the street where I had thrown the hot dogs. When she returned to work, she told me the hot dogs were still there. For some reason that made me feel good.

As I write this story I realize how repressed and angry of a person I had become when this incident took place. My life was filled with a lot of stress during this time of my life. And so when I saw this man who apparently had control of his life, running and eating healthily, I was reminded that my life was a mess. I don't excuse my behavior that night, but in recalling it, I better understand the woman that I was back then, and celebrate the fact that I have done much healing and growing since those days.

To the man who got slapped in the face with a hot dog slathered in BBQ sauce, I sincerely apologize for my insane behavior. I hope that you didn't get a taste of the hot dog and abandon your healthy lifestyle in favor of becoming a couch potato who now eats processed meat with fillers. And I hope you didn't take it personally. And most of all, I am so glad you didn't get my license plate number!

Locked Out on New Year's Eve

In this story, I was not insane, not even temporarily. I just looked it. It was a few years after I had lost my husband Jerry. I had no plans for New Year's Eve, so my lovely daughter Amy was keeping me company. We played Scrabble and had a few snacks. No alcohol. All of a sudden, Amy looked up as though she was looking at the clock and exclaimed that it was already midnight! I remember thinking that the time had passed awfully quickly, but I believed her. I was in my pajamas, but I threw on my coat and a pair of purple ear muffs, grabbed a heavy pot lid and a big spoon and went out the front door, thinking Amy would follow. The door closed behind me and I thought Amy just didn't want to join me in welcoming in the New Year. I banged the big spoon on the pot lid and yelled out "Happy New Year!" over and over, until I realized that no one else was making any noise. The neighborhood was silent. There were no fireworks as there are every year at midnight on New Year's Eve. There were no gunshots, no anything. Then I got it. Amy had played a trick on me by telling me it was midnight already. I turned around to go into the house to give Amy a piece of my mind, just in time to hear the lock click. "Amy, I'm going to get you!" echoed through the otherwise silent night. She let me stay out on the porch a little longer before unlocking the door. We laughed so hard at how stupid I must have looked and sounded. None of my neighbors have ever said anything to me about that night. I guess they just thought it was business as usual for Insane Marilyn.

What Did You Do This Time, Grandma?

It was a Thursday evening in January, and it was the coldest day we had experienced in years. My grandson needed a ride from his hockey practice a few miles away from my house, so I agreed to pick him up and take him to his house. On the way, while I was stopped at a busy intersection, I looked over at the dairy store on the opposite side of the street and saw a sign that advertised "Buy 3 Get 1 Free". "What a great idea!" I thought. I'd stop by and pick up some ice cream for Justin and me to enjoy after I took him home. I'd take two pints home with me and leave two at my daughter's house.

I know that most people do not think of eating ice cream when it's cold outside, but I have always craved ice cream in the winter, especially if it's snowing. I picked out four different flavors of ice cream, including my favorite, cinnamon. (I found out only recently that Justin had not liked any of the flavors I had selected.) I was excited to be getting one pint free and looking forward to having a big bowl of cinnamon ice cream in a few minutes. I noticed I was running a little behind due to my ice cream detour, but I would only be a little late. I don't like being late, even if it is for a good cause, so I was a little anxious.

It's almost impossible to make a left turn out of the dairy parking lot onto the road that I had to take. So, I decided to make the easier right turn out of the parking lot, make another quick right, turn around, and then make a left turn to get me back on track towards the Rec Plex. After making the two quick right turns, I suddenly panicked because I didn't know exactly where I would turn around, and I wanted to do it quickly because I was running late. It was then that I noticed a "No U-Turn" sign. I hadn't intended to make a U-turn, because it was a very busy two-lane road, but the sign gave me the idea. Not seeing what else I could do quickly, I decided to make a U-turn. Oncoming traffic was far enough away that I could make the U-turn safely, or so I thought. It was dark, I was concentrating on traffic, and I was preoccupied with trying to not be any later than I had to be, so I didn't notice that there was a high median right in front of the "No U-turn sign. The coast was clear and I made a fast U-turn right over the median! I hit it hard; really hard. My car lifted up and thudded to the street! I feared that the whole bottom of my car had been broken to pieces. I was very shaken up and wasn't thinking clearly. I was stopped at a red light. When it turned green I could think of nothing else to do but make my left turn. I was on another busy two-lane road, so it was very difficult to pull over to the side. I was surprised my car was still running, but it was. I thought that maybe I had somehow come out of this fiasco with my car intact. I thanked God and just kept driving. I was looking for a way to pull over to the side of the road to catch my breath and check the car, without having an accident, but the traffic was pretty heavy and I was in the left lane. My car kept going, so I kept going. After several blocks, I had finally managed to get into the right lane, but I just kept driving. I had a waiting grandson and four pints of ice cream to worry about! Suddenly the car just quit. I was sitting in the right-hand lane blocking traffic. I panicked and just sat there wondering what to do. I couldn't remember if I had roadside assistance or not; and even if I did, I didn't have the presence of mind to even figure out what their number was. So I just called 911.

A patrol car came promptly. A woman officer came up to my window and asked what had happened. I explained that I had made an illegal U-turn, for which I was really sorry, but felt it had been necessary because I had stopped for ice cream and was running late to pick up my grandson. I told her that the "No U-turn" sign had actually given me the idea to make the U-turn, implying that it was the sign's fault and not my bad judgment that had caused the fiasco. I went on to explain that I had hit the median while making the U-turn, and that the bottom of my car was probably ready to fall out, because it had just stopped working. I was close to tears at this point, and asked her if there was any way she could take me to pick up my grandson. She explained that we couldn't just leave my car in the road blocking traffic and said that I would have to call a tow truck. By this time I was so upset that I could not think logically at all. I told the officer that I had to get to my grandson. He was only ten years old and was probably standing out in the cold all by himself in the dark and scared to death!

The officer said she would call a tow truck for me, but that I would have to tell the driver where to tow it. I had a hard time remembering the name of the auto repair shop that I had used in the past, but somehow I did. When the tow truck arrived, because I was so shaken, she explained to the driver where to tow my car, and then she asked me if there was anything in my car that I needed to take out. I practically screamed, "My ice cream!" I explained again that I had gotten into this whole mess because of the ice cream, and I sure wasn't going to let it melt! I opened the car and grabbed at the bag like I was snatching a baby out of harm's way. I held it close to my chest and thanked the officer for reminding me that it was in my car.

I got into the patrol car clutching my precious ice cream and chattered nervously to the officer all the way to the Rec Plex. She said things to try to calm me down, but I didn't know what to expect when we arrived at the Rec Plex. Would Justin even still be there? As we pulled up to the rear where I was supposed to pick Justin up, I noticed the building was dark. Much to my relief, I saw Justin standing at the curb with a man. It was his coach. The patrol car pulled up and I rolled the window down and meekly waved at Justin. I was about to say how sorry I was when Justin blurted out "What did you do this time, Grandma?" Justin's matter-of-fact statement was the comic relief I needed in the wake of all that had just happened. The patrol officer was nice enough to drive Justin, me and the precious ice cream home. Of course I thanked her, but I wish now that I would have offered her one of the cartons of ice cream.

It's been ten years since the ice cream incident. I don't remember exactly how much the car repair bill was, but I do remember doing the math at the time and figuring out that each of the four pints of ice cream had cost me over $100. So, my "Buy 3 Get 1 Free" deal hadn't really been that great of a deal after all!

My Crazy Jerry Stories

Crazy in Love!

    My Jerry stories aren't really crazy at all, unless you consider how crazy we were about each other from the first moment our eyes met! How we met is my favorite story to tell. It all began on September 23, 1966. It was my first week of college at the University of Missouri-St. Louis (UMSL). I had gone from a small high school of around five-hundred students in total to this large school where I had a Psychology class in an auditorium with five hundred students! I only knew a handful of students on that first day, so when I saw Joe H. in the cafeteria area I made a bee-line for him. Joe and I had gone to grade school together. We went to different high schools and I had only seen him a few times since grade school, but that day he was my best friend. Joe and I were sitting there chatting and taking in the sea of students that we didn't know when Joe started waving to someone he had gone to high school with. I followed Joe's gaze and my eyes landed on a boy with the biggest, brightest smile I have ever seen. It was Jerry! Jerry was waving back at Joe, but his eyes were locked into mine. Jerry joined us, Joe introduced us and I met the love of my life, all in under a minute! Years later, Jerry and I both recalled that first moment of seeing each other. I remembered his infamous smile, and he remembered my wide-eyed (as he described it) look and even what I was wearing that day!

I was so enamored with Jerry that when it came time for him to go to his first class, I quickly looked at my schedule and told him that I was in the same class. Jerry smiled and offered to walk with me. I don't remember what we talked about, but I do remember really liking him already. We entered the lecture hall/auditorium where the Psychology class was held and took seats together near the back. The professor walked in and introduced himself. Then he announced the name of the class and the section number. I looked at my schedule and realized that I was in the right place but at the wrong time. I was enrolled in Psych I, but in a different section, at a different time and with a different professor. I was so embarrassed, but I knew that if I stayed, I'd miss my own class; the one that I was really scheduled for at that time. So I whispered to Jerry that I was in the wrong class and had to go. I quickly left, looking and feeling quite flustered. I don't remember exactly when or how I ran into Jerry after that, but it was later that same day. We continued our earlier conversation, with the usual details about where we lived, how many brothers and sisters we each had, and all of the things two people talk about when they first meet. We started hanging out in the student lounge in between classes and before too much time had passed, Jerry invited me out to lunch one day.

We went to Steak 'n Shake in Jennings and Jerry introduced me to eating a steak burger with double Thousand Island dressing on it. I was a POM (pickle, onion and mustard) steak burger eater, but I agreed to try his favorite, and it was really good! I already liked him so much that I would have eaten my burger with tar on it if he recommended it. We went to Steak 'n Shake for lunch often during those first weeks of college. We fell in love pretty quickly and started dating. I remember one day at Steak 'n Shake, the Turtles' song "So Happy Together" was playing on the radio and Jerry declared it as "our song". Another of our songs was "Reach Out (I'll Be There) by the Four Tops. I can't hear either of those songs without going back in time and falling in love with Jerry all over again!

Jerry and I "went steady" from October 1966 until he left to go to college in a different part of the state in the fall of 1967. I won't go into detail, but we broke up after trying to maintain a long distance relationship. We both married other people, but I never forgot about how happy he had made me right when I needed someone in my life after my Mom had died and my Dad had remarried. I always thought God had sent him to me to help me when my whole life had seemed to be turned upside down.

It was September 23, 1995, exactly twenty-nine years from the day I first met Jerry when our lives collided through a series of coincidences. Actually I don't believe in coincidences. I believe it was finally "in the stars" for us to be together. Neither of us was happy with our lives. For a while we tried to be just friends, but eventually it was obvious that we had never stopped loving one another. We struggled with our feelings and situations. Somehow we made it through the turmoil and moved forward with our new life together in 1997. We got married on our special date, September 23rd. It was thirty-one years to the day after we first met. That boy with the smile and that wide-eyed lost girl were together at last!

Jerry and I had only been married for a little over eight years, when he was called to Heaven. He gave me more love in that short time than I had ever had in all those years since my Mom had died. He helped me find myself again. He was so good for me and my whole family. He taught me so much about loving, living and dying. I can't wait to see that big, bright smile again when it's my turn to leave this earth! I'll probably be wide-eyed and kind of lost at first, and Jerry will be there with that great big smile to lead the way!

Man of Excess

Jerry was a man of excess. He never did anything little. One Thanksgiving my daughter Karen asked that Jerry and I bring the pies to the gathering at her house. There were about seventeen people coming, but some of them were little kids. Now if you were asked to bring pies to feed this many people, how many would you bring? I have asked this question to many people over the years and I don't even mention that some of them were kids. Almost everyone says they'd bring three pies. A few have said three to four. When I came home from work the day before Thanksgiving, I saw two pies sitting on the dining room table. I said, "Oh, you baked two pies?" I had thought he would bake a couple more. He told me that there were more in the kitchen. I walked into the kitchen and saw four more. I thought six pies were too many, but that we could always bring some back home and freeze them. Then I saw two more on the living room coffee table. I started laughing hysterically. Jerry was standing there with a proud look on his face. "There aren't any more, are there?" I asked. He directed me to our home office for the answer. There were two more in there. I couldn't believe Jerry had baked ten pies that day, some pumpkin and some Dutch apple with streusel topping. I think we brought eight pies to Karen's. Some of the people who were supposed to be there couldn't make it. We had enough pies for every adult to have his/her own pie. And there was another dessert besides Jerry's pies. As some of the people left, Jerry thrust one of his pies into their arms. They thought it was great to get a whole pie to take home.

One summer my three girls and their families and Jerry and I all went on a Florida vacation together. We rented a condo. To save money, we decided to eat breakfast and lunch in the condo. Jerry wasn't much for sitting out on the beach all day, and he liked going grocery shopping, so he volunteered to stock the kitchen. When we came in from the beach and saw all of the bags and bags of groceries he had bought, we all laughed. I thought we'd never eat that much. He had bought about forty-eight cans of soda, at least twelve rolls of toilet paper, a big plastic jar of candy, and I don't know how many dozens of eggs, plus bacon and several tubes of cinnamon rolls. He also bought chips, bread, lunch meat, peanut butter, fruit etc. for our lunches. Every morning Jerry got up and cooked eggs, bacon and cinnamon rolls for us. Some days we ended up going out to eat for lunch even though we had enough lunch food to last for a long time, and we were only there for one week! Jerry made a couple of little trips to the grocery store for things we hadn't thought of earlier. Two days before we were to leave Jerry decided that he needed to go grocery shopping again. He had become a regular at the local Winn-Dixie by that time. He had his own Winn-Dixie card. I couldn't believe my eyes when he came home from that shopping trip. He had bought three dozen eggs and six tubes of cinnamon rolls, a big plastic barrel of pretzel bites, more soda and another twelve rolls of toilet paper! I told him he had gone overboard since we were only going to be there for two more days, and he assured me that we would use everything up. Well, he was right, we consumed almost everything, only it took a while. We brought a lot of groceries home with us. We had many cans of an off brand soda stored in our garage for years. We laughed when we finally threw them out. Karen made us a scrapbook of our vacation. Among the pictures she included Jerry's Winn-Dixie card. They really should have renamed the store "Winka-Dixie" in honor of its biggest beach customer ever!

Whispering Sweet Wehrenbergs in My Ear!

Jerry and I loved going to the movies. Almost every Saturday we would go, sometimes seeing two or even three movies in a row. Jerry taught me how to sneak into a second or third show. After the first show, you go to the refreshment stand and when you re-enter the theatre section you just "return" to a different movie. Jerry always told me that if he got caught he was going to feign having dementia. Who would kick out a poor confused old man? One time after seeing one movie, Jerry walked into a different theatre and sent me out to get refreshments. My hands were full with two sodas and a big tub of popcorn as I returned to the theatre section. When the usher asked to see my ticket stub, I held up the sodas and popcorn to emphasize that my hands were full, and I made a face and told the usher my ticket stub was in my pocket. "Do I really need to dig it out of my pocket?" I asked. The kid just waved me on. It was a narrow escape, but I was all ready to ask "Where am I? Who am I?" if the usher had busted me.

If any of you have gone to a Wehrenberg movie theatre in the last couple of decades you are probably familiar with their opening song right before the main feature starts. They sing "Bop bop bop bop…bop bop bop bop…Wehrenberg Theatres!" Then a man's voice loudly whispers "Wehrenberg" a few times before it gradually fades to silence. The split second that the man stopped whispering "Wehrenberg" Jerry would say it out loud, not even bothering to whisper. This always cracked me up. Then he started saying it more than once. Sometimes people would laugh, and sometimes they would look around while trying to decide if it was coming from the speakers or from somewhere out in the audience. Soon I started doing it, too. Now, every time I go to the movies at a Wehrenberg theatre, I loudly whisper "Wehrenberg" in Jerry's honor. I even have my friends doing it now. Once I even loudly whispered "Wehrenberg" at another theatre chain. Jerry's legacy lives on! (After writing this story I learned that Wehrenberg Theatres have been bought out and sooner or later it will no longer use the name Wehrenberg. I will probably still loudly whisper it, though, in memory of Jerry.)

Cooking with Love

Jerry didn't work for the last few years of his life, so he was at home alone a lot during the day. That's why he was so excited to greet me when I got home from work. Sometimes I was not very bubbly after fighting rush hour traffic for forty minutes or longer, but Jerry quickly got me back on track. He would kiss me and sometimes he even did a little dance to show how happy he was to have me back home. He always had supper ready, too. I would quickly change my clothes and join him in the living room in front of the television for supper. We never ate at the table. For years we watched Seinfeld re-runs while we ate. We must have seen each episode at least five times, but we never tired of watching. As you may recall, there were always three story lines in every Seinfeld episode. We would always try to guess what stories were together in each episode. Watching Seinfeld while eating supper became one of "our things" to do together. I still eat in front of the television out of habit, but I can't bring myself to watch Seinfeld re-runs without Jerry.

Jerry always took such good care of me, physically and emotionally. He was very nurturing. I once told him that his love for me reminded me of my Mom's love. I felt so appreciated and cared for by both of them. He fussed over me like a mother hen sometimes. He was always so proud of the meals he made for me. Just like a mother, as soon as I entered the door after a long day at work, he would tell me that supper was ready and that I should hurry up and change my clothes (my Mom would have asked me to wash my hands). Usually I enjoyed what he made. He made everything with love, but sometimes he went overboard with some of the ingredients. One of the things he liked to make was tuna casserole. I would have enjoyed it if he would have kept it simple like the recipe my Mom used: canned tuna, cream of mushroom soup, a few peas and noodles. But Jerry wanted to make it even better. Sometimes he would add mayonnaise, which I don't really like. As long as he added just a touch it wasn't bad, but one time he must have put in a whole cup of mayo. I could barely finish my portion. Jerry was puzzled why I didn't have seconds, because I have always been a big eater, but I just pretended that I was full. Then he started adding a layer of canned French onions on top of his tuna casserole. I like French onions on some things, but not really on tuna casserole, especially if the casserole also contains mayo. He kept trying to perfect his tuna casserole, and I never complained or asked him to just make it like my Mom had made it, because I didn't want to hurt his feelings. He started adding shredded cheddar cheese to it, which doesn't sound bad, but he added way too much of it. Along with the mayo and fried onions, the excessive cheese made it way too rich. The last time he made tuna casserole for me, he proudly announced that in addition to all of his extras, he had buried a secret ingredient inside of the casserole. He knew I was going to love this version! I dug my fork into his masterpiece and it hit something rock hard. I pushed the other ingredients out of the way so I could see this newest ingredient. It was a great big piece of carrot and it was nearly raw. I laughed. I think I hurt his feelings. He never made tuna casserole for me again. I loved him for trying to perfect his tuna casserole, but was sort of relieved when he abandoned his efforts.

Jerry knew I loved key lime pie and cheesecake, so one year for my birthday he made me a key lime cheesecake from his own recipe. While we ate supper, he told me that he had a surprise for dessert. I suspected it might be a key lime pie, because whatever it was, it was in the refrigerator. When it was time for dessert, he proudly told me that he had created his own recipe for key lime cheesecake. I was almost afraid that I'd find an uncooked carrot or some mayonnaise in it. It turned out that he had taken a recipe for key lime pie and combined it with a recipe for cheesecake and then added green food coloring. When he presented it to me, I almost died. It was as green as green could be, and it was unnaturally bright! It was really good, if you didn't look at it. There was a lot of love poured into that pie…almost as much as there was green dye!

Jerry was a good baker. One of the cakes he loved to make was lamb cake that "normal" people make at Easter time. He had inherited the cake form from his Mom. One day, nowhere even close to Easter, he had the sudden urge to make a lamb cake. We didn't have a cake mix in the house and Jerry didn't feel like going to the store, so he decided to use a biscuit mix for the cake batter. He added some red and blue food coloring just to give it some color. That turned out to be his worst culinary creation ever. The dough was very dense, like biscuit dough, and it was gray. It didn't come out of the lamb form cleanly either. When I came home from work and saw it on the counter I asked what it was. He had made a thin glaze that was still dripping from the mounds of gray biscuit dough formed into a big clump. It no more looked like a lamb than I did. He told me I didn't have to eat any of it, but I did try a bite. All I can say is that lamb had been slaughtered!

The first thing I'm going to do when I get to that big café in the sky is order "Tuna Surprise", with grass-green pie and grey lamb cake for dessert. I can't wait to see that crazy chef!

Me and my sister Lois in our backyard, taken when I was three. Note the white picket gate in the background, put in just so I could easily visit my next door neighbor Mrs. K. several times a day

Me and my first paper, taken on the first day of first grade

Me and my new doll Rusty on my fourth birthday in Overland, MO, 1952

My big sister Lois, me, and my little sister Linda, summer of 1963

The Dancing Waitress at our Christmas dance recital around 1956

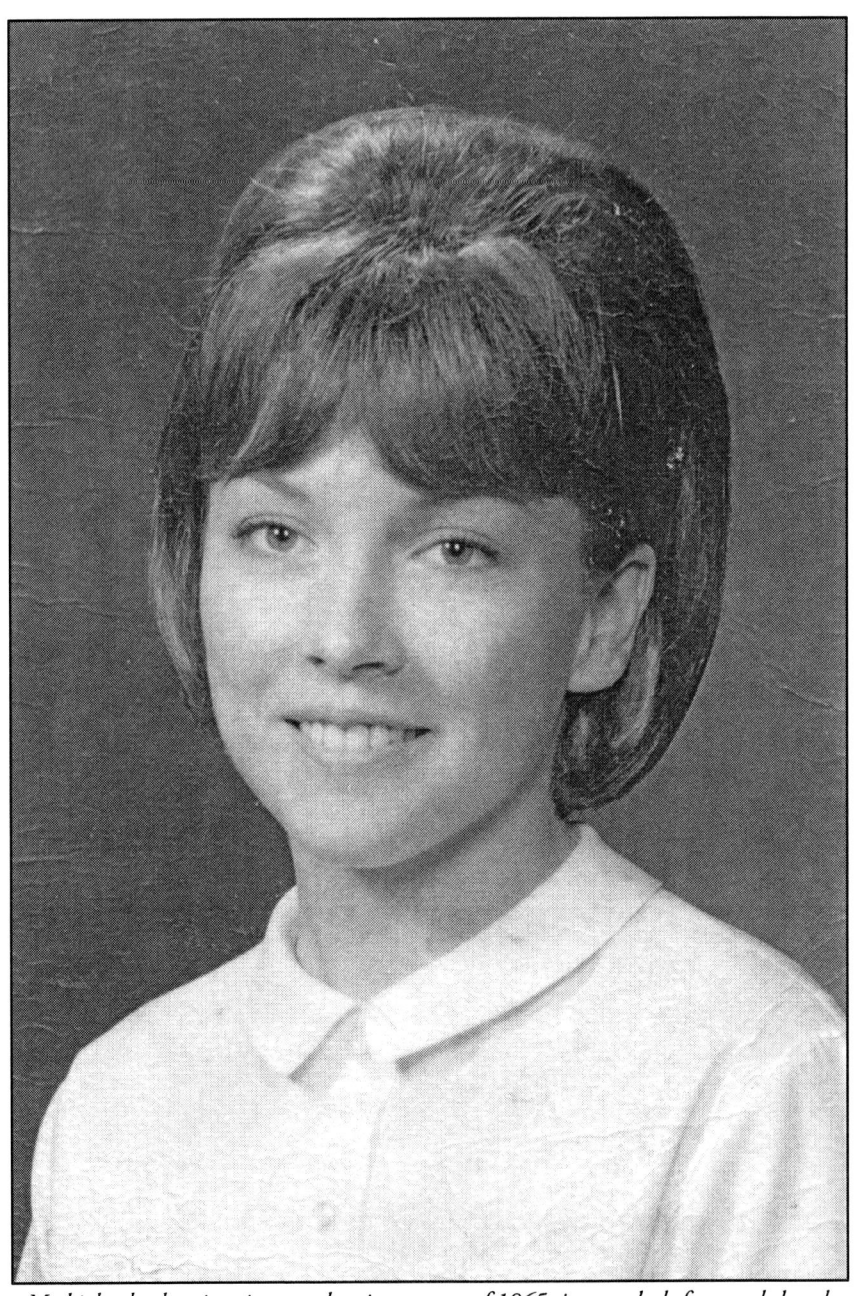

My high school senior picture taken in summer of 1965, just weeks before my beloved Mom passed away. Sadly, she never got to see this picture

My Crazy Kid Stories

My three girls are the most important people in my life! They've been with me through good times and bad times, always bringing me sunshine! I can't imagine my life without them. I am so proud of the wonderful women they have become, in spite of having me as their Mom. Sometimes I wonder who raised whom. I thank God that they accept me for who I am and that they forgive me for my mistakes. Life with me wasn't always ideal. I was immature (still am at times), a little crazy, selfish and inadequate, but I loved being their mother. I still do. I will always cherish the memories of my kids when they were little, even when they drove me crazy! I have so many precious memories of my three kids and their kids, but this book is about my "crazy" stories. So I will tell only the crazy stories and leave the serious stories for another book.

Karen Stories

Just like the oldest child has the most photos taken, Karen, my firstborn, has the most stories about her. Maybe that's because I have had her the longest.

Wop, Wop, Wop!!!

We were living on "The Hill", a St. Louis Italian neighborhood. One day when Karen was about two years old, we were out on the upstairs balcony. Karen was bouncing her brand new ball and saying "Wop, wop, wop", imitating the sound of her hand smacking the ball onto the concrete. I didn't think anything about what she was saying until an elderly Italian woman walked by and looked up at us with a strong look of distaste on her face. She was muttering something that I didn't understand, but I don't think she was saying how cute Karen was! It was then that I realized that what Karen was saying was a slang name for Italians. "Wop" stands for "without papers" and is a derogatory term that people used for Italian immigrants. I was so embarrassed. So much for trying to blend in and being accepted in the neighborhood!

That Lady Just Tooted!

Kids just say the truth, and sometimes what they say is so wrong, yet so right!

One day I took Karen to a grocery store. She was sitting in the seat of the cart being her cute little self, when she pointed to an elderly lady and loudly said, "Mommy, that lady just tooted!" I instinctively looked at the lady and she looked so embarrassed, like she had been caught in the act. I whispered to Karen to be quiet, but that made her say it again even louder "She tooted!" My mother-in-law had taught Karen to say "toots" instead of farts, and she was just applying her knowledge! It was a little embarrassing, but still very cute and funny.

The Hamburger

Another time that Karen embarrassed me was in a Wags restaurant, the restaurant in Walgreen's. We had just gone to see the pediatrician in the office next door. Karen was a little over two years old and hated going to the doctor, because she hated getting shots. She used to get so nervous going there that she broke out in hives. This visit had been for her new little sister Nancy to get shots, but I guess Karen was still upset about having to go to the office where she was usually the victim. I had very little money back then, so going out to eat, even at Wag's, was a luxury for us. I was probably pretty stressed out trying to take a newborn baby and a two-year-old out to eat. I ordered hamburgers for Karen and me. Karen loved hamburgers, but when our food arrived, Karen loudly announced that she didn't want hers. I was trying to eat while keeping Baby Nancy occupied and I had just spent money I didn't have, so I was probably pretty stern with Karen when I told her that she HAD to eat her hamburger. She stood up, her face red with anger, and said "No!" With that she threw the hamburger to the floor. I scolded Karen and told her to pick the hamburger off the floor and she refused. Everyone was looking at me like I was the worst mother ever. I paid the bill and got out of there as soon as possible. I didn't realize until now that Karen was probably still stressed out from having been at the doctor's, and maybe even trying to get some attention for herself, since she was still unsure of her place in the family since her new baby sister had arrived.

And Hurry Up!

Karen was always assertive, even as a little girl. One time her Daddy and I took her to a restaurant that had little speakers on the tables for calling in orders. When we sat down at our table we said we hoped our food wouldn't take too long to arrive because we were starving. Terry and I ordered our own food and coached Karen to say that she wanted a burger, fries and milk. She confidently took over and said, "Bunger, fwies and wilky!" We beamed with pride that our twenty-one month old daughter had placed her own order and hoped they could translate. Then we heard her add in no uncertain terms "And hurry up!"

It's the Screamer Again!

Karen was assertive when her new baby sister arrived, too. Karen was two years and two months old when Nancy was born and she was used to being the center of attention. She didn't know what to make of the new baby. The first couple of nights Nancy did not sleep very well at all. She cried a lot and woke Karen up several times. After getting woken up several times on the second night, I remember Karen yelling out in a thoroughly disgusted tone of voice "It's The Screamer again!" The next night when I got up to see what was wrong with Nancy, Karen threw up in her bed and looked over at me as if to say, "See? Now you have to take care of ME!" Smart kid!

I still cherish the time that I had with Karen as a stay-at-home mom. When she was a toddler and her Daddy had left for work in the morning, I used to bring her into my bed so I could sleep in just a little longer. Some days she would fall back asleep with me, but most days I couldn't get back to sleep because of the noises she made. She had a habit of sucking her thumb and rubbing her other thumb and index finger against the blanket while softly humming "Mmm, mmm, mmm". I would just about fall back asleep when her "Mmm, mmm, mmm" would get louder. I would love to go back to those days just once, and I wouldn't even care if I got back to sleep or not.

So Clean You Could Eat Off of It!

Kids can be so literal at times!

One day after cleaning my large kitchen floor to perfection, I beamed at it and declared in front of Karen that my kitchen floor was so clean you could eat off of it. With that, Karen opened the refrigerator, grabbed a slice of cheese, un-wrapped it and slapped it onto my clean floor. She was about to eat it, when I grabbed her and the cheese, and scolded her. If I had it to do over again, I would just watch Karen eat that cheese off the floor. What harm would it have caused? I was too serious sometimes.

Look What You Did to our Hats!

One Easter, my mother-in-law (actually ex mother-in-law by that time) bought Karen and Nancy matching blue and white pinstriped sundresses, white straw hats, white knee socks and white patent leather shoes. I so appreciated her buying my kids Easter outfits that year, because I certainly could not afford it. Mrs. C. was so proud of those outfits. Karen and Nancy looked so cute that Easter morning when we set out for Mass. I remember Karen complaining that she did not want to wear the hat, because it "itched" her head. I promised that if she wore it, once we got inside of church, she could take it off during Mass.

I proudly entered the church with my two little girls all decked out in their Easter finery. As promised, I let the girls take their hats off and put them on the bench of the pew. It was extremely crowded in Mass, being it was Easter Sunday, so people were squeezed together in the pews. There wasn't room for the kids to sit with their hats next to them, so when it came time to sit, I was going to grab their hats and hold them on my lap. But when it came time to sit, I forgot about the hats. I sat right on top of them! Karen, bless her heart, held up a flattened hat high in the air for all to see and yelled "Look what you did to our hats!" I actually heard some laughter out of the congregation that time.

After Mass there was an Easter egg hunt on the baseball field in Berra Park. Actually it was more of an Easter egg race than a hunt. Participants were grouped according to age, and at the sound of a whistle they ran across the dusty field to where the eggs were out in plain sight waiting to be grabbed up. Karen was old enough to participate, but not Nancy. This kind of event was right up my tomboy Karen's alley. She was fiercely competitive and could run fast! The whistle blew and Karen ran and skidded through the dustbowl, to the grassy area where the eggs were, like she was sliding into home plate. She scooped up most of the eggs before the other kids even got to the grass.

She came across the dusty field to where Nancy and I were waiting with the biggest grin on her face. She had a basket full of cracked eggs and dirt all over her white knee socks and dress. She even had dirt in her mouth! We were due to go over to Grandma and Grandpa C.'s house right away, with no time to change clothes. Grandma C. was anxiously waiting to see how nice her girls looked in the Easter outfits she had bought them. She couldn't believe her eyes when she saw how dirty Karen was. We had a big laugh over the "hat incident" that had occurred that morning in church and at Karen's appearance. Karen wanted to eat some of her eggs, but we had to throw them out, since they were cracked from the violence they had withstood when Karen pounced on them. The dust from the field had settled in all the cracks. I can still picture that little redheaded, freckled girl, grinning from ear to ear, a tooth missing and a mouth full of dirt, and dirt all over her girly outfit, topped off with a cock-eyed straw hat! I always told my kids that if they didn't come home dirty that meant they didn't have fun. Boy, did Karen have fun that Easter!

We're Getting Those Mrs. Beasley Paper Dolls!

It's true that kids say the darnedest things.

When Karen was seven years old and Nancy was five, I met Steve. One evening after the girls were asleep, he asked me to marry him and I said "yes". After he left, I went into the girls' bedroom and woke them up, because I was too excited to wait until the next morning to tell them my news. When Karen asked why I had awakened them, I asked her "What is the best news Mommy could tell you?" Without hesitation, Karen grinned and said to Nancy, "Hey Nancy, we're getting those Mrs. Beasley paper dolls!

Nancy Stories

Goo Mony!

When Nancy was four months old I had to go to work, so I didn't get to stay at home with her during her infant and toddler years like I did with Karen. Because I was so busy, I took a shortcut when it came to feeding Nancy some of her bottles. At night she would fall asleep holding her own bottle. I also gave her a bottle in her bed each morning so she could feed herself while I did other things to get us all ready to go. Years later I learned that having babies drink a bottle in bed is bad for their ears, but back then I didn't know that. If I had it to do over again, I would take the time to hold Nancy in my arms and take as long as she needed to finish her bottle. But there were a lot of things I didn't know back then.

I've always had a soft spot in my heart for Nancy because she didn't get to have the same "Mommy and Me" time at the beginning of her life that my other two girls did. But even though I was very stressed out from having to be a single parent, I remember holding her in my lap in the evenings and on weekends and giving her a little extra TLC. She would just sit there and look up at me with those great big eyes of hers as if to say "It's okay, Mommy, I know you're doing the best you can!"

Nancy always woke up so cheerfully. I would walk into the bedroom she shared with Karen, and when she was able to stand up on her own, she would get up and say "Goo mony!" (This was Nancy's version of "Good morning!"). This would awaken Karen, so I didn't have to. I would quickly change Nancy's diaper and give her a fresh "ba-ba", and she would be good as gold until it was time to get her up for her cereal and getting dressed. On weekends, Nancy would get up early as usual. I was two rooms away, but I could always tell when she awakened, because I could hear the sound of an empty plastic bottle from the night before hitting the floor. Her flinging of the empty bottle told me that I should get up and get her a new one. The next sounds I would hear were her "Goo Mony!" and then Karen's groans over being awakened.

Cold Peas for Breakfast?

I marvel now at the well-oiled machine that Karen, Nancy and I were. There was a lot to do to get ready in the mornings, but we always managed to get up and out of the door on time, usually without any trouble.

But one morning, when Nancy was maybe two or three years old, she didn't want anything that I offered her for breakfast. I offered cereal, eggs, waffles, toast and fruit and she said "No!" to all. Finally, in exasperation, I asked, "Well, what do you want? A cold can of peas?" Nancy's eyes lit up and she said "Yes!" She cried and cried when I told her she couldn't have that for breakfast.

If I had to do it all over again, I would have opened a can of peas, handed Nancy a spoon and let her eat her breakfast.

Thank God I'm a Country Boy!

I always took the kids to Mass with me on Sundays because I didn't have anyone to baby sit. They found it difficult to sit still and to not talk. It was a constant battle to try to keep them still and quiet, to the point where I should have just stayed home. No one, at least those sitting around us, got to do much praying.

One Sunday Nancy was having a particularly hard time keeping quiet. We were kneeling, and I had to keep telling her to stop fidgeting around, to stop talking and to stop looking all around. I guess I expected an awful lot of a three year-old. At one point I got frustrated and kind of poked her and reminded her that we were IN CHURCH and that we were there to THANK GOD! Nancy looked at me with those big beautiful eyes and smiled. Then she belted out a line from a John Denver song, "Thank God I'm a Country Boy!" I couldn't help but laugh.

I Was Going to Marry Him!

Nancy has always been very emotional and dramatic, like I am. When Elvis died, Nancy was only four-and-a-half. I remember we were in the car on the way home from the girls' daycare when I told Karen and Nancy that he had died that day. When we got home Nancy ran to her bedroom, threw herself across her bed and started sobbing uncontrollably. I asked her if she was crying about Elvis and she nodded. Then she sat up and sobbed, "I was going to marry him!"

Silk! Silk!

One Easter Sunday I wore what I thought was a very beautiful outfit to Mass. I remember it well. It was a yellow blouse and an eggshell white skirt, both in a very silky feeling material. And underneath the skirt I wore a nylon half-slip. While we were getting ready for church, Nancy had admired my outfit, rubbing her hands over my skirt over and over and exclaiming how silky it was. She kept saying "Silk! Silk!" I thought it was cute.

As usual I felt "on display" at church, because Karen and Nancy had acted up several times during Sunday Mass over the years, and we were probably known as "that woman and her two bratty girls". But Karen was now seven years old and Nancy was five. I wasn't worried about them misbehaving during Mass any more.

But while we were standing during the Mass, Nancy kept stroking my skirt and saying "Silk! Silk!" That didn't bother me too much. She wasn't saying it that loudly and like I said, I thought it was kind of cute. Cute, until she lifted my skirt really high to expose my slip, that is. I mean, she lifted my skirt really high and started stroking my slip saying "Silk! Silk!" Then, before I could stop her, she lifted up the slip, too, exposing my pantyhose and undies! She started to stroke my pantyhose. I managed to pull my slip and skirt down, but not before I had really been "on display"!

Karen and Nancy Together!

Charlie the Fly

We didn't have much money when it was just Karen, Nancy and me, but I tried to make everything we did as much fun as I could. One day on the way home from daycare a fly got into our car. I don't know how long flies usually live, but the next morning Charlie was still in our car. He stayed alive all day in my car. When the kids saw him that afternoon, we decided that he must like us pretty much. The kids asked if we could name him, so we named him Charlie. We couldn't afford a "normal" pet, so Charlie the Fly would have to do. Not being a studier of nature, I didn't know that flies don't live very long. I figured if we were careful when we opened the door, he might stick around for a while. Somehow he lasted overnight again, but when I picked the kids up from daycare that evening, he was not in the car. I told them he had probably flown out when I opened the door, but that he would always be our "Charlie the Fly". Actually, as I write this, I wonder what kind of a whacko mother I was, encouraging my kids to adopt a fly as a pet!

We Love You, Betsy!

The time we spent in the car together every day was precious to me. We never drove in silence. We were always playing some kind of guessing game or singing. I have always named my cars. The unreliable, ugly grey car that I was driving back then was named "Betsy". If Betsy acted like she wasn't going to start, or if she started shaking because I had too many electrical things on at the same time, I'd say "C'mon, Betsy, don't give out on me. C'mon, girl, you can do it!" One day I decided that Betsy should have a song. I taught it to Karen and Nancy and we sang it often, especially when we thought Betsy might be thinking about conking out on us. Please feel free to sing along.

We love you, Betsy,
Oh yes we do!
We love your colors,
All grey and blue.
We lied about the blue,
But not the grey.

*Oh, Betsy, we love you
Every day!"*

Mommy's Dead!

I used to talk on the phone for long periods of time back then, and Karen and Nancy usually behaved themselves pretty well. They usually played quietly while I talked. Once in a while they acted up, doing something they shouldn't be doing. Rather than hang up or put the phone down to correct their behavior, I would take off one of my slippers and throw it at them. That usually did the trick. But after a while they caught on and stood just out of range!

One Saturday I was on the phone with a gabby aunt (actually my ex-husband's aunt). I dreaded her calls because they lasted for over an hour. She did all the talking and I pretended to listen to every word. Sometimes I would quietly set the phone down to do something out of the range of the telephone cord and just yell loudly across the room "Uh huh", "I see", or any other affirmative until I could get back to the phone. She never even noticed.

On this particular day, as the aunt droned on and on, Karen and Nancy were playing one room away from me on the enclosed back porch that was their playroom. It's also where my washer and dryer were. They had a little table and chair set, play kitchen appliances and a little desk with a compartment where they kept all of their story books. The phone call lasted a very long time, and I realized that Karen and Nancy had been in the playroom all that while, quiet as mice.

Finally the telephone conversation ended and I walked across the kitchen to the playroom to see what my little angels were so busy doing. Before I actually got to the room I smelled the strong scent of laundry detergent. I didn't think much of it. I kept a huge box of laundry detergent out there and I was doing laundry that day, so the smell of detergent was par for the course. And then I saw it! It looked like it had snowed all over! The smell burned my nostrils as I took in the sight of mounds of detergent covering the kids' little desk, their little table and chair set, their play kitchen appliances and the covered radiator. Karen was putting the finishing touches on their little table, emptying the huge box completely. They both grinned up at me, evidently so proud of their little winter wonderland, while I stared at it in disbelief. I'm sure I let out a few exclamations!

I was overwhelmed. How was I going to clean this all up? I was totally exasperated. I didn't know what to do. I went into the bathroom to calm down. I couldn't calm down, so not knowing what else to do, I threw myself on the bathroom floor and just lay there with my eyes closed. The kids came to the open bathroom door and saw me lying there. I pretended to be dead. I just couldn't deal with the situation. I could feel Karen and Nancy just staring at me. Then little Nancy, who was only about three years old at the time, said in a somber tone "I think she's dead!" to which Karen replied, "Okay, let's go play out on the balcony!" Nancy said "Okay!" and off they went. (They were not allowed to play out on the balcony without me, so I guess Karen thought that now that I was dead, all rules were disbanded). When I heard that, I jumped up and got mad all over again. "You don't even care that I was dead?" I screamed in utter disbelief. My little angels just looked at me like I was crazy, and I guess I was.

I don't remember how long it took, but I made the little angels help me clean up the mess. We vacuumed, swept and wiped until it was all gone. I "sneezed my head off" from the strong fumes. After it was all cleaned up, and I was calmed down, I was able to appreciate the artistry they had shown. How could I stay mad? They had kept themselves quietly busy while Mommy talked on the phone, just as I had asked them to do. They hadn't eaten any detergent, thank God! And I knew that should anything ever happen to me, they could fend for themselves. Apparently I wasn't all that necessary. LOL!

Mayhem in the Restroom!

Like I said in another story, being a single parent family, we couldn't afford to go out to eat that often. When we did, I ate every bite and expected the kids to do the same. One evening I took the girls to a pizza restaurant. It was a step above our usual Mc Donald's dinners out. I ordered a huge pizza and salad. Karen and Nancy ate enough to satisfy me. I was still eating when they told me they had to go to the restroom. I didn't want to leave the table to take them because I was afraid the waitress would think we had "dined and dashed", and I was even more afraid that she would take my food away. Karen was about five years old and Nancy was three. I told them that I could not go with them, but that I expected them to behave, not to talk to anyone, to wash their hands and get right back to the table. I continued to eat. After a couple of minutes had passed, I started to worry. I wanted to get the waitress' attention so I could tell her to box the rest of the food and that I had to get my kids out of the restroom. We were in a back room (where they probably sat me on purpose when they saw that I had two kids) and the waitress was nowhere around. There were no other diners in that room, so there was no one to tell. I didn't know what to do.

What was keeping Karen and Nancy? Maybe there was a problem. Just then I heard extremely loud, gleeful screaming coming from the restroom. It was so loud that I was embarrassed, even though I was alone in the back dining room. What were they doing in there? I had no choice but to leave the table (and my food) and go see what was going on in the restroom. As I got closer, the screaming got even louder. I opened the door and saw a red-faced and sweaty Karen running from stall to stall opening the doors, flushing the toilets and banging the doors shut while laughing and screaming like a Banshee! There was toilet paper hanging from all of the stalls. All of the water faucets were running! Nancy was at one of the sinks splashing water all over the place and laughing like a crazed hyena! I'll never forget that sight. It makes me laugh hysterically to remember the mayhem those two little girls managed to create in just a few minutes! Thank God no one was in the back dining room with us. I grabbed the kids and got back to the table just in time to ask for the bill and a box for the leftover pizza.

This remains as one of my funniest memories of Karen's and Nancy's antics.

Two Old Biddies

One Sunday after Mass I was walking home with the kids. We only lived a block from church, so it was a short walk. I was probably busy talking with them at first, so I couldn't hear what two old biddies walking behind us were saying. And then I did. One of them said, "She always brings those kids to church and they never behave!"

The other one agreed and made a "tsk-tsk" sound. I turned around and pointed at the two old ladies one at a time and asked, "Which one of you wants to baby-sit next Sunday?" They just stared at me in response. I said "I thought so!", and continued walking home with my two little girls.

Let the Little Children Come to Me!

On another Sunday morning there was a visiting missionary nun at the Mass. After the priest gave the sermon he invited her to say a few words to the congregation. She asked for contributions in order for her and her sisters to continue their mission work in a foreign country. The kids were really getting restless. They had already sat through a lengthy sermon. They were shifting in their seats and talking. I was getting nervous, because while the nun was speaking, the other nuns from her order were sitting near us. I thought maybe they would be upset because my kids were distracting the congregation during their sister's pitch. But when I looked over at them they were smiling. But all of a sudden an usher came up to our pew, leaned over and asked me to please leave the church! If he would have just asked me to try to keep the girls quiet, it wouldn't have bothered me. But to ask us to leave the church was out of line in my opinion. I grabbed the kids, walked to the door, turned around and loudly said to the usher, who was practically walking on my heels, "Why don't you read the bible?…the part that says let the little children come to me!" And with that I turned around and walked out with my little children, slamming the heavy door as loudly as I could! I did not feel ashamed at all.

Weekends with my Girls

I do cherish the times that I let my kids do things that my own mother would never let me do. When it was just the three of us, on Saturday evenings Karen, Nancy and I always had TV dinners. It was a big deal. The kids always had the ones that came with fried chicken, fries, corn and a brownie. The brownie never baked all the way through and inevitably, there was a kernel of corn in it, but they loved that meal anyway. It was a special treat. In nice weather I would put their little table and chairs out on the balcony and we had a picnic. I sat on a lawn chair eating my "international' TV dinner while they ate their corn-studded brownie dinners. One Saturday night, several balloons from Forest Park's annual balloon race floated right over us as we ate. They were so close we could hear them talking. That was our best dinner ever.

On Friday nights I always let the kids stay up late with me to watch TV. I would fall asleep on the couch and wake up at some time after midnight. Sometimes I would put the kids in their beds and then go to my own, but most of the time I just let them sleep on the floor. They would wake up on Saturday mornings with their little legs in between the spindles of my wooden stereo stand. For some reason they loved propping up their feet on that stand while watching TV. And the dirty dishes from the snacks we had the night before would be on the floor. I used to think how horrified my parents would be if they knew that I let my kids eat in the living room and then fall asleep on the floor. It didn't hurt us any and it was a lot of fun!

Happy New Year! (Say It Don't Spray It, Karen!)

To celebrate New Year's Eve in 1975, when my daughters Karen and Nancy were five and three years old respectively, I planned a little New Year's Eve party for just the three of us. I made some fancy hors d'oeuvres (Ritz crackers with pimiento cheese and a pickle on top) and we had most of a large punchbowl full of red Koolaid (registered brand name) left over from Nancy's birthday party earlier that day. (I probably had my "Cocktails for Two", the brand name for little bottles of cocktails in a two-serving bottle that they used to sell at the grocery store. I used to buy a bottle each week for my Saturday night television watching marathons. Saturday night television watching was great in the late 70's with The Bob Newhart Show, The Mary Tyler Moore Show, The Carol Burnett Show and Saturday Night Live). I told Karen and Nancy that we would all stay up until midnight when we would bang pots and pans and party like animals!

I usually ended up falling asleep on the couch, especially if I had my "Cocktails for Two", and I really wanted to stay awake to celebrate at midnight. So I took some "Nodoz" (pronounced like what they were supposed to do; i.e. no doze), a popular over-the-counter pill that helped keep you awake if you had to stay up to study or something. I took two pills for good measure, because I really did not want to disappoint Karen and Nancy. Instead of staying awake, though, the Nodoz made me feel drowsy. I remember really fighting to stay awake. I'm not sure how long I actually made it before I succumbed to a really deep sleep.

The television was on and I could hear the kids saying. "Wake up, Mommy, it's almost midnight!" but I just couldn't get myself awake. I drifted in and out of a very deep sleep. It felt like I was trying to come out of a coma, but couldn't quite get there. (At least that's how I imagine it would feel).

They were making celebratory noises on the TV, which helped draw me out of my deep sleep. After really struggling, I managed to open my eyes half-way and lift my head a little just in time to see Karen with red Koolaid shooting out in an arc out of her nose and across the room, as she and little Nancy exclaimed "Happy New Year!" I looked over at the punch bowl, which had been more than halfway full when I had last seen it. It now had only maybe a cup of Koolaid left in it. I asked Karen if she had drunk all that Koolaid by herself, and she proudly said "Yep!"

I can't remember a better New Year's Eve. Two sweet little girls celebrating New Year's Eve the best way they knew how while their Mommy lay on the couch in a "drunk-on-Nodoz" stupor. Any fireworks I may have seen on subsequent New Year's Eves were not nearly as colorful or better timed than Karen's red fountain spewing out of her little freckled nose and across the room at the stroke of midnight!

Amy Stories

Amy simply didn't ever misbehave, so I don't have as many "crazy" stories about her. I honestly can't think of one crazy thing Amy ever did as a child, except the time she threw our kitten Sam way up high in the air. (See Cats Fly, Don't They?)

By the time Amy came along, I was remarried and Karen and Nancy were eight and six years old, so she didn't have a "partner in crime" like her sisters had in each other. What Amy did have were two parents to keep her in line. And, although I did go back to work when Amy was four months old, she did have me all to herself during the day during her first four months. And I was the parent who got up in the middle of the night to feed her, because her Daddy had to get up early to go to work the next day. I cherish the memory of those nights. I sat in my rocker and fed her and cherished my alone time with her. It was Amy and me with no interruptions, worries or stress. It was just a quiet time holding my baby and dreaming about how happy her life would be because she had a whole family to love her.

Cats Fly Don't They?

Amy didn't do it maliciously. She did it in all innocence. She was obsessed with Superman. She sat in our bedroom every Sunday morning wearing her Superman pajamas with a detachable cape watching the movie "Superman". We once calculated that she had watched it fifty-four times in one year (once a week every week plus two other times). One Sunday morning she decided to act it out. Only instead of trying to fly herself, she decided to let our cat Sam play the part of "Superman". She put the little cape on Sam and hurled him in the air as high as a four-year-old could throw a kitten, which was pretty high, while yelling "Su-u-u-per Man!" Luckily cats land on their feet. I can still picture it. It was so cute. I don't know how cute Sam thought it was, but the rest of us did.

Winnie-a-Pooh!

Karen and Nancy played a lot of sports, so I brought Amy with me to a lot of their games when she was a toddler. She sat there like a good girl and never got into any mischief. If she did get a little restless, she would stand behind me in the bleacher seats and sing

"Winnie-a-Pooh!" over and over, while blowing into the hair on the back of my head each time she said "Pooh". She would blow harder each time and then giggle. It's one of the precious memories I have of her as a toddler.

Saggy Baggy Elephant!

Even though Amy was very well behaved, quiet and shy, she sure could get an attitude on her if she didn't like something you said! Her Dad used to say "Who do you think you are?" to the kids when they did something wrong or talked back to him or me. Amy said that to me one day when she didn't like something I said. I remember her standing there with her hands on her hips and a very stern look on her little face, and in a quasi-British accent asking me "Who you finks you ah?"

One day after we came home from work and daycare, Amy was sitting with me on the side of my bed while I changed my clothes. I had just taken off my dress and was sitting there in my underwear. I don't know what she and I were talking about, but apparently I said something she didn't like. She shouted, "You, saggy, baggy elephant!" I was so taken aback. I didn't know that was the title for a children's book. Apparently she had heard the story at daycare that day. I thought she was remarking on the state of my body. I was just in my thirties, but thought maybe I had better start toning up a bit if my three year old had noticed I was starting to get saggy and baggy. I thought it was pretty clever of her to express her opinion of my body in that colorful way until I found out it wasn't her own expression.

And Then There Were Three

It was fun having three girls, except for one day when I was home on vacation when they were ages 14, 12 and 5. At different times throughout the day each of them had come to me and accused me of favoring or liking another one of them the best. Each one told me how unfair I was, because I liked a different one of them better. Finally I had had enough of the bickering and whining. I called all three of them into the kitchen and told them to line up against the wall facing me. Then I proceeded to recall how each of them had accused me of liking another one of them the best that day! Then I said, "The truth is, I don't like ANY of you! Now get out!"

One of the best memories I have of all three of my girls together was when Amy's Dad was out of town and I let all three girls get into bed with me. We ate Chinese food and watched the movie "Car Wash" that evening. The kids weren't normally allowed in our bedroom, much less in our bed, but when I was the sole parent in charge, all bets were off. I kept rewinding and replaying the vomit scene of "Car Wash". I'll bet we saw that scene a hundred times that night. We laughed so hard, we almost threw up, too! I had to change the sheets before my husband got home, because there was fried rice stuck on them. If only I could relive that night!

Grandkids Stories

It's almost more fun to be a Grandma, because when the kids act up, it's more of a reflection on their parents, and not on you. I can't recall ever being embarrassed about something my grandkids did. It's usually me who embarrasses them!

Alex Stories

My first grandchild, Alexandria Nicole, is twenty-one years old now. Alex has brought me so much joy over the years. She has always been a sassy girl and I love her for that. She always did melt my heart with that big bright smile and those huge ocean-blue eyes, and she still does!

Grandma, Are You Going to Pay for That?

Alex was a little over three years old when I had her for a whole week while my daughter Karen was between sitters. We had so much fun that week. I took Alex shopping with me at Target. It was around Easter and I saw the cutest pair of bunny ears for her. I let her put them on while we shopped. Now I don't know if she had heard tales about how Grandma Marilyn and Grandpa Jerry used to "reallocate" silverware from restaurants or not, but when we got to the check-out counter and I started putting things on the counter, Alex held the bunny ears up and loudly asked "Grandma, aren't you going to pay for these?" Actually I had forgotten all about them. I was a little embarrassed, probably from having a guilty conscience about the silverware.

Whizzer Da Boz!

Alex was obsessed with the story "Wizard of Oz" and made me read the book and watch the movie over and over that week. She pronounced it "Whizzer da Boz", which I thought was adorable of course. Several weeks later, she came to visit me one day and I took her to "my" pool across the street. Alex didn't ask me if I wanted to, but she TOLD me that we were going to play "Whizzer da Boz" in the pool. She loudly declared that she would be "Dorfy", and pointing to me, told me that I would be the witch. I can still hear her saying, "You be da witch!" For hours the witch chased Dorfy in the water. Dorfy screamed and screamed and the witch had to keep saying "I'll get you my little pretty one!" The lifeguard may have gotten tired of hearing this over and over, but the witch and Dorfy sure didn't. It's a precious memory now.

One day after the pool had closed for the season, Alex and I walked over to look at it and she asked me why my pool was closed. I told her that all pools were closed for the season. She asked if I could please unlock it because she wanted to go swimming. I told her I couldn't and she said, "Well, it's your pool, Grandma. You can open it!"

When Alex was about four years old, and the whole family was over at my house, she announced that we would all be playing school and that she would be the teacher. I remember that she demanded everyone's full attention. Her lesson was quite long. If anyone dared to look like they weren't paying attention, she would say firmly and loudly, "ALL EYES ON ME!"

These days I do not get to see Alex as often as I would like, but when we do get together we always have fun, sassily bantering back and forth. My little Dorfy is all grown up.

Justin Stories

My second-born grandchild is Justin, who is now eighteen. Justin is a sweet boy. He still likes to be hugged and gives great hugs to his Grandma. I think he and I bonded in a special way the night he spent his first sleepover at Grandpa Jerry's and Grandma Marilyn's.

Baby On Board!

Baby Justin was only a few weeks old when he spent the night with Jerry and me. He was very restless and cried a lot during the night. We fed him and rocked him, but he was inconsolable. We had changed him so many times that we ran out of diapers. Grandpa Jerry went out in the middle of the night to get more. When he got back, he saw that I was lying on the living room couch with Justin on my belly. Justin was quiet at last and was sound asleep. Grandpa Jerry suggested that I lay Justin down in his "pack 'n play" and come to bed. I whispered that I was fine just like I was. Grandpa Jerry went to bed and I laid there perfectly content. I had the sweetest baby lying on my belly. I could catch up on my sleep the next day. We lay like that for over an hour until I was afraid that I would fall asleep and Justin would roll off of me and get hurt. The image of sweet baby Justin lying so close to my heart reminds me that he will always be close to my heart, no matter how old he gets.

Why Does Grandpa Have Dog Balls?

My Dad was crazy about Justin. It must have been Justin's big blue eyes that twinkled just like his own that got to my Dad. One day Karen and her husband Jim brought the kids to see my Dad after he and my step-mom had recently moved into an assisted living home. My Dad had been diagnosed with Parkinson's disease and had started using a walker. The kids had never seen his walker. Justin, who was probably two years old at the time, took one look at my Dad's walker that had tennis balls on two of the wheels for stability, and innocently asked, "Why does Grandpa have dog balls?" There was dead silence. I was afraid to laugh out loud, because no one in my family had ever used the word balls to refer to anything but baseballs or golf balls. Finally, I couldn't keep it in. I don't know if my Dad had heard Justin, or would have even known the double meaning of the word "balls", but this goes down in history as one of the funniest things my grandkids have ever blurted out as far as I am concerned!

What'd You Do This Time, Grandma?

Another time that Justin said something so funny and so memorable was the time I pulled up as a passenger in a police car to pick him up from hockey practice, and he blurted out "What'd you do this time, Grandma?" You can read all about the events that led up to that remark in the "My Crazy Insane Stories" section.

Justice

My Dad used to say, "That Justice is a corker!" The Parkinson's caused my Dad to suffer from a little dementia, which manifested itself mostly in bizarre dreams. Sometimes my Dad wasn't sure if it was a dream he was remembering or an actual experience. He often dreamed of Justin, only he referred to him as "Justice". In his dreams Justice worked with my Dad and was always making my Dad laugh. Almost every time I visited my Dad, he would tell me about his latest dream of Justice and say, "That Justice is a corker!"

Jake Stories

Nancy's son Jake is super smart, but because he is so sweet and innocent, he can be gullible at times. He is taller than me now and is fifteen years old, but he is still as sweet as he was when he was about nine years old when this story took place.

Our Lady of Labor

Jake and Rachel were spending the night at my house. It was summer. We were at my subdivision pool with Aunt Amy. I have always loved playing tricks and teasing people, especially gullible little kids. The four of us were playing around in the water and I said to Amy that since the kids were being so good maybe we could take them to Orange Leaf (a frozen yogurt place) that evening. But instead of saying Orange Leaf, I said "O.L.", so it would be a surprise. Jake has always been very clever and he started taking guesses as to what "O. L." stood for. After many guesses I finally told him that "O. L." stood for Our Lady of Workers. I hadn't even thought about it, it just came out. So when he asked what Our Lady of Workers was, I had to think quickly. I am blessed with quick thinking (which is sometimes a gift and sometimes a curse) so I told him that it was a place where I volunteered. I went on to say that Our Lady's collected canned goods for the poor and that I had signed the four of us up to work there that evening. Jake was intrigued, so I went on to say that we had to count the cans and then stack them into piles. Then I got weird. I told him that we would have to be fast or else we'd be punished. I explained that the people who ran the operation were mean. If you didn't stack the cans fast enough they beat you. I told him that I had been beaten several times. As Jake asked questions I continued to give more details. I told him that it was actually fun at "O. L.'s" if you could work fast enough.

Later when we were preparing to leave for "O. L.'s", I expressed my concern about being fast enough. Jake balled up his fist and said so earnestly that it melted my heart. "Grandma, if they start to beat you, I'm gonna punch them square in the jaw!"

As we entered Orange Leaf, I explained that all of the work was done in the back and that if we did a good job counting cans, they would give us some frozen yogurt. Little Rachel, who was only about five, hadn't said much at all up to this point and now that we were there, she actually looked scared. So I knew I had to end the lie before she started crying. Amy and I started laughing. I explained that "O. L." stood for Orange Leaf and we were NOT going to be counting cans. We were just there for frozen yogurt. Then I said to Jake, "Well, I fooled you good, didn't I?" Jake claimed that he knew as soon as he saw the Orange Leaf sign on the door that I had lied about the whole thing. He still looked a little leery to me. I think both kids were glad when we got out of there without being beaten.

Rachel Stories

My beautiful dancer, Rachel, is starting to act more like a little lady these days, and I don't know how much longer she will appreciate my silliness. All of my grandkids have stopped laughing when I dance and sing outlandishly in the car. Instead of giggles like I used to hear, now I hear a desperate voice saying "Stop, Grandma!" Rachel is eleven, almost twelve now, so I don't know if I'll be able to get away with any more "crazy antics" or not.

Grandma's Got the Jo Jo's!

When Jake and Rachel spend the night during the summer, we usually end up going to a frozen yogurt place. There is another frozen yogurt place called Jo Jo's that we sometimes go to. Jo Jo's has little kid-sized plastic tables and chairs and provides erasable markers, too. Being the little kid that I still am, I always have to write something shocking on the back of the chairs, like "Oops, I farted!" Rachel especially gets a big kick out of that. When I asked for "crazy story" ideas, it was Rachel who reminded me that I always write something "bad" on the chairs at Jo Jo's. I wonder if I can still get away with doing stupid stuff like that this summer?

Chopped in the Pool!

One game Rachel still loves to play with me (at least as of last summer) is "Chopped". It's a game we created after the cable TV cooking show of the same name. We play it in the pool. Jake plays with us too, but mostly I now think of it as a Rachel game since we played it a lot last summer…just the two of us and whomever was in the pool with us at the time, even the lifeguard.

We take turns giving the participants four weird ingredients and then the participants have to describe what dishes they would prepare and exactly how they would prepare them. Rachel has been quite good at this game since we started playing years ago. Apparently watching "Chopped" was a favorite in her house. She was only about four years old back when we started playing "Chopped" in the pool. Rachel always started out her description of how she'd prepare her dishes with "Wit da!" She'd say, for example, "Wit da turnips I'd make a puree…" Jake and I used to make fun of her for saying "Wit da", but I long for those days when she was little enough to talk that way. Rachel is eleven as I'm writing this story and I can only hope that she will still want to play "Chopped" with me this summer. I am so looking forward to going to the pool and playing special games "wit da" grandkids!

Do You Know Where Can I Park?

One day a couple of years ago I took Jake and Rachel to The Mills outlet Mall in North County to ride the go carts there. The Mills is currently only occupied by a couple of stores and was already starting to look like a ghost town back then. As I pulled up into the almost empty parking lot a guy was walking by. I stopped the car, rolled down my window and in a really whiny voice asked him "Do you know where I can park?" He looked at me like I must be blind if I couldn't see hundreds of empty parking spots, but kind of pointed to where there were a few cars parked. Of course, Jake and Rachel thought this was hilarious and I added another reason for them to call me their crazy grandma.

My Crazy Linkul Stories

"What's a Linkul?" you might be asking. Well it's a last name; my paternal family surname. There aren't very many of us left; in fact, there never were many of us, because Linkul is a shortened form of Linenkugel or perhaps Leinenkugel. Yes, we Linkuls could very well be descendants of the family of beer brewing fame, but they either do not know about us or would rather forget. The latter is more likely. We are an odd bunch by most people's standards, at least the St. Louis faction is.

William David Linkul and his wife Maude Loretto Steffen Linkul had five children: William (my father), Dorothy, Loretto, John and Frederick. Sadly, William and Maude and their five children are all now deceased.

When my Dad, Bill Linkul, was about twenty years old his father died. His mother was placed in the Chronic Hospital because of a nervous breakdown. I'm not sure if that was before or after his Dad died. Either way, when my Dad was pretty young, he was solely responsible for taking care of and educating his four siblings. My Dad and his four siblings had a total of twenty-two children, nineteen of whom are my cousins. I know that none of us cousins knew our Grandpa William, and I don't think any of the Linkul cousins ever knew our Grandma Maude either, because of her being in the chronic hospital way before any of us were born. A few of the older cousins may have visited her, but none of us really knew her. She died on Christmas Eve 1953 when I was five. My only memory of seeing her was at her wake. I have a picture of her out on the lawn of the hospital grounds, with me as a toddler in the foreground. So, I know I visited her at least once, but naturally I do not remember it. My Dad rarely talked about his parents. All I know is that he really admired his father and that his mother could play piano by ear. My Dad first told me this when I was a little girl, and even though I certainly know now what "playing by ear" means, I can't get the picture out of my head of my grandmother bent over a piano playing it with her left ear! Another time my Dad told me his mother had beautiful chestnut hair and said that the color of my hair was like hers.

The five siblings, spouses and their offspring, collectively known as "The Linkuls", began getting together every December for a family Christmas party. The first Linkul Christmas Party was held in 1952. It was held at my Uncle Fred and Aunt Ann's apartment. We used to draw names at the family Labor Day picnic for the exchange of small gifts at the Christmas party. I remember I got a ladies brooch at one of the first parties. I was very disappointed, because I was only four or five, but my Mom whispered to me that she would buy it from me and then get me a coloring book instead. The limit on the amount that one could spend on these gifts started at 25 cents in 1952 and gradually increased over the years to one dollar. The limit was never indexed to inflation and remained at one dollar all the way until the last Linkul Christmas Party in 2010. Some people obviously spent more than the limit, but the gifts were always very small and of very little monetary value. Sometimes they were gag gifts, but mostly just little tokens to express holiday cheer.

The Linkul Family was made up of simple and down to earth people getting together to have fun. For years we got together just three times a year, unless there was a funeral or wedding during the year. Besides the annual Linkul Christmas party, we got together for picnics on the Sundays before Memorial Day and Labor Day. We never really got to know each other in a way that some aunts, uncles and cousins get to know one another. We were such a large group that we reserved a room at the Florissant Civic Center for many of our Christmas parties, and the picnics were held at public parks rather than in someone's backyard. So, it was kind of an artificial relationship that we had with one another, since we usually only saw each other in public places and in a large group, but our times together were special and make up some of my best childhood memories. Here are highlights of the Linkul Christmas parties and picnics and the dearly beloved characters that made them so special.

My Dad, aka Uncle Bill / Uncle Weets / Bullwinkle

My Dad was the patriarch of the family. He was usually a very serious man, but when he got together with his siblings, he cut loose. We always played music at the Christmas parties and we invariably ended up dancing in a big circle, taking turns with one person at a time dancing in the middle. Of course, we tried to out-do one another with silly dance moves. My Dad worked at a meat packing plant and sometimes the guys at work started cutting up (pardon the pun) and imitating the cattle. So my Dad developed a really good cattle call. When it was his turn to dance in the middle of the circle, he always did a crazy little dance with his hands on either side of his head mimicking bull horns and yelled out "Ma-a-h-h!" It was so out of character for him that all of us delighted in seeing him having so much fun. He would get red in the face and start laughing until he had tears rolling down his face. He had so much fun when he was with his siblings. When I think of the many faces I saw on my Dad during my lifetime, his face at the Linkul Christmas parties as he danced is the most precious one! This is for you, Dad. Ma-a-h-h! My Dad and his brothers all loved to play golf. My Dad also liked to do his cattle call just as one of his brothers was about to tee off on the golf course!

My cousins, especially Aunt Dorothy's kids, used to call my Dad "Uncle Weets". I once asked my Dad why Aunt Dorothy's family called him "Weets". He told me that when he was a boy his aunts and uncles used to exclaim how much he had grown each time they saw him, saying that he was growing like weeds. So his nickname became Weeds. But somewhere along the line someone (maybe Aunt Dorothy) thought it was "Weets". Therefore, Aunt Dorothy started calling him "Weets" and passed that name along to her family. I used to love hearing my cousins call my Dad "Uncle Weets". It was a term of endearment. I knew that my Aunt Dorothy loved my Dad so much and that she had instilled that fondness in her family.

My Dad's youngest brother, Fred, sometimes called my Dad "Bullwinkle" after the popular cartoon character. He had mentioned to one of his friends that he had a brother named Bill, and that friend had said, "Hmmm. Bill Linkul. That sounds like Bullwinkle". So that became one of Uncle Fred's nicknames for my Dad.

One time as an adult I called my Dad "Sweet William" because I had just planted some of those flowers, and he told me that Aunt Dorothy used to call him that, too. My Dad's siblings all loved him so, because he stepped up at the age of fifteen, giving up his own education, to get a job so he could help out with the family finances.

I don't remember if Uncle Jack or Aunt Loretta had nicknames for my Dad, but I know they loved and admired their oldest brother, too. And my cousins all respected my Dad. Things were never the same at the parties or picnics after we lost Dad/Uncle Bill/Uncle Weets/Bullwinkle.

Our Beloved Aunt Dorothy aka Red

One year we did the limbo dance at the Christmas party. That was the year we discovered that Aunt Dorothy didn't wear underwear! When confronted, she laughed and said in her husky smoker's voice "I only wear it when I go to the doctor!" I guess she wore it then so she had something to take off when the medical assistant instructed her to take off her underwear and put the paper gown on.

Every year Aunt Dorothy called my sister Lois about a week before the party and asked for my sister's recipe for fudge. My sister always wondered why Aunt Dorothy didn't write the recipe down so she wouldn't have to call every year, but Lois came to expect and even enjoy that yearly call. Lois would answer the phone and immediately know it was Aunt Dorothy, because the conversation always started with a husky-voiced and frantic "Lois!" followed by "What's that fudge recipe?"

Aunt Dorothy was the life of the party. Besides that famous voice of hers, she was known for her red hair. Her nickname was "Red". As my Dad would say, Red was a "corker". I always thought he meant that she was funny; comical and thought maybe the term corker refers to Irish people who come from County Cork; that maybe they are all funny. Even though Linkul (derived from Linenkugel) is a German name, our family does have a lot of Irish in it. We do have ancestors who lived in County Cork. (There will be more about our Irish heritage when I talk about my Uncle Fred). But I just "Googled" the term "corker" and learned that it is a slang word meaning a remarkable or astounding person or thing.

Aunt Dorothy got her glasses broken at one of the Linkul Christmas parties when we had "The Gong Show" as the theme. Aunt Dorothy was practicing her "wheelbarrow" act. Yes, Aunt Dorothy was indeed a corker. Her whole family was actually the life of the party. Her husband Ed liked to hog the microphone at the parties. He played the part of emcee, filled in lag time with corny jokes and even sang. Sometimes if another family member had something to say to the crowd, such as leading us in a prayer before the meal, that person would have to wrestle the mike away from Uncle Ed. The parties were never the same after Uncle Ed passed away. Aunt Dorothy and Uncle Ed had four children. Sadly two of them, Dave and Bob, have passed away. For years, the three brothers used to perform to Ray Charles' "Tell Me What I Say". They danced really well and took turns using the microphone *if* they could get it away from their Dad.

Aunt Dorothy had diabetes and was supposed to really watch what she ate. My sister Lois and I visited her during her last year when she was a widow. Lois, Aunt Dorothy and I all lived near one another and went to the same church. We thought it would be nice to bring her fish from the church fish fry. Knowing she was supposed to limit her fried food intake, Lois got baked fish for all of us, even though I would have really preferred the fried. When we showed Aunt Dorothy her dinner, she said "I don't want baked fish. I can't stand that stuff!" She pouted the whole time we were eating. We also noticed that there was big cake in the middle of Aunt Dorothy's table when we got there. There was a big hunk missing. We asked if she was supposed to have cake. She looked like she had been caught in the act and said "Oh, I just keep that for company." I remarked that she must have had company recently. She acted like she didn't hear me.

Once when she was in the hospital, Lois and I visited her. She complained that she hadn't liked what they had given her for dinner and asked us if we could get something for her to eat. We asked the nurse on duty and soon they brought Aunt Dorothy a tuna sandwich. She looked at the tuna sandwich with total disgust. Then she spotted a teenage boy coming into the room that she shared with another patient. He was coming to see his grandmother. Without even saying "hi" to him, she yelled out "Kid! Go get me something from Mc Donald's". Before he could even answer, she was pulling dollars out of her bedside drawer and waving them at him. Lois and I were laughing so hard. I must have inherited the same genes that Aunt Dorothy had, because I'll do almost anything for food, too.

Yep, Aunt Dorothy was a corker!

Aunt Loretta aka/Lo (short for locomotive)

My Aunt Loretta (actual name, Loretto, after Our Lady of Loretto) was a single mother for as long back as I can remember. She didn't have a car, so my Dad always picked her and her three girls up for the picnics and Christmas parties. One of my best childhood memories is of the time when I was about five or six. Our family of four at the time picked up Aunt Loretta and my cousin Cathy to go to the family picnic. Aunt Loretta and Cathy sat up front with my Dad and my Mom sat in the back with my sister and me. My Aunt's nickname was Lo, short for Loretta of course, but also for locomotive, because according to her brothers, her mouth ran as fast as a locomotive. I used to love hearing my aunt's stories as we took the long drive to the picnics. My Aunt Loretta was a smoker. She talked and talked and smoked and smoked all the way there. Later my Mom told my Dad that she would sit in the front seat on the way home, because Aunt Loretta's ashes kept flying in my Mom's face on the way there.

I liked it when Aunt Loretta and Cathy sat in the back seat with me, so I could hear Aunt Loretta's stories better. I remember her as being very pretty and funny. She turned ordinary events into funny stories. Maybe some of that rubbed off on me. She was an elevator operator at a department store and told us how she often got so busy talking that she passed up her passengers' floors and that she sometimes announced the wrong floors. One time she said "Ladies Lingerie" for every floor just to get reactions. At least elevator rides with her wouldn't have been boring.

My Dad used to tell a story about how when he got his first car, he took Aunt Loretta out for a spin. He took a corner way too fast, the door flew open and Aunt Loretta fell out in the street. My Dad said she got so mad that she shook her fist and yelled "Oh, you nut!" to my Dad. I think it's hilarious that this is all she said! I chuckle at the image of her picking herself up from the street, shaking her fist and saying "Oh, you nut!" as my Dad drove on, laughing.

Aunt Loretta died way too young. She was around forty-nine or fifty years old. Although it's been many decades, I can still picture her three- room flat on Gibson Avenue with the iron fence in the front yard. The rides to and from the Linkul Family events helped me get to know Aunt Loretta a little better than I knew my other Linkul Family aunts.

I wish I could have had Aunt Loretta in my life when I was a single parent. She would have been very supportive I'm sure.

Uncle Jack

Uncle Jack worked as a salesman for the meat packing plant where my Dad worked. Since his sales territory was near our house, Uncle Jack would drop by our house for lunch once in a while. That was always a treat, because we didn't have company very often, and when we did it was mainly my Mom's side of the family. Like I said earlier, the Linkuls usually got together in large groups and only three times a year. We didn't really get to know each another that well as individuals. I remember my Uncle Jack had a sense of humor like all of my Dad's siblings and that he admired my Dad a lot. They loved rattling one another at the golf tee.

When I was fairly young, my Uncle Jack built an extension to their house out on Highway 21, which back in those days was way out in the country for us city folk. On Saturdays, my Dad, Uncle Ed

(Aunt Dorothy's husband) and Uncle Fred would load their families into their cars and drive out to help Uncle Jack build the added rooms. All of us cousins played, the women gabbed and cooked and the men worked. It was like a big picnic. I loved those times. The men used to send me and another cousin into the house for cold beers. I remember taking a swig out of each bottle. One time Uncle Jack noticed I had taken quite a big swig out of his and he laughed and told my Dad that he'd better watch me. My Dad just laughed. He already knew I liked beer. Every Saturday night while he watched "Gun Smoke" my Dad had a beer, and he always poured an inch or two into a fruit juice glass for me. That was one way I bonded with my Dad. I would sit right up next to him drinking "our" beer. Sometimes he would reach over and wrench the skin on my wrists (Indian burn) to see if he could make me yell, but I never did. I pretended it didn't hurt. Then I would pull the hair on his arm real hard, and boy did he yell!

One year Uncle Jack built a tiny wooden stage so my sister Lois and I could perform a tap dance at the Christmas party. This was when Lois and I were in our forties. We had performed a tap dance to "Singin' in the Rain" in a church talent show, and our relatives commanded a repeat performance at the party. Lois and I laughed so hard when we saw how little the stage was, but were so touched that Uncle Jack had built it just for our dance. I think this may have been Uncle Jack's last Christmas party. We decided that the stage was just too little for both of us to fit on it, so we tap danced on the carpeted floor while my cousin Susan (one of Uncle Jack's daughters) banged tap shoes on the stairs. She did a pretty good job keeping in time with our foot movements. Lois and I could hardly dance, we were laughing so hard. Then right in the middle of the dance, Uncle Jack came up to Lois and me in all seriousness, while we were dancing, and handed us each a Christmas card. In our family, instead of mailing Christmas cards, we just handed them out at the Linkul Family Christmas parties. I guess Uncle Jack didn't realize we were in the middle of our performance. Lois and I just took the cards from him and told him he'd get ours in a minute, and we just kept on doing the "soft shoe" while Cousin Susan wildly banged tap shoes on the steps!

Uncle Fred

Uncle Fred was especially proud of the Irish part of our ancestry. In fact, he seemed to have forgotten that our many of our ancestors came from Alsace-Lorraine. But he celebrated the O'Neill and Maloney branches of our family tree. Uncle Fred loved his beer and he loved telling corny jokes. With his red hair, blue eyes and that Irish spark in his eyes, you would have thought his last name was O'Linkul, especially when he wore his Kelly green blazer and sang "Danny Boy" at family funerals, changing Danny to the deceased's first name.

Uncle Fred liked to have fun. He was always among the first, if not *the* very first, to arrive at the family picnics. He always brought hot dogs to be grilled for the second meal of the picnic, and he often brought a portable TV so he wouldn't miss any important televised sports events. He was an avid talk-radio caller and became famous, at least locally. He was known as "Fred from Florissant".

Uncle Fred just recently passed away in 2016, and oh, how he is missed! It's like the flame that dwindled with each passing Linkul sibling was finally snuffed out. Our family will never be the same. Uncle Fred absolutely adored my Dad and instilled this into his family. At Uncle Fred's funeral Mass, his oldest son, my cousin Larry, gave a beautiful eulogy. He talked about how much his father loved and appreciated my father. He told about how my Dad stopped his own education so his siblings could continue with school instead of going to work like he had to. My Dad and Uncle Fred were very close; the oldest son looking out for his little brother and the little brother looking up to his big brother and being forever grateful. It was a beautiful relationship. When my Dad was in a nursing home, Uncle Fred and Aunt Ann visited him often. My Dad's eyes always lit up when Uncle Fred came around. My Dad generally didn't like talking on the phone (I guess that'd where I get it from), but when Uncle Fred called they talked for at least an hour.

The Three Amigos

My Dad and his two brothers were all very close and loved to play golf, cut up, dance and even sing together. Somewhere along the line, at every Christmas party they donned sombreros and sang a song called "Three Amigos". Uncle Fred could sing very well, but my Dad, not so much. He sang too loud and a little flat. Uncle Jack fell somewhere in between, or maybe he sang so quietly I couldn't really hear him as much. They actually sounded worse every year, but the "Three Amigos" became a staple at the Linkul Family Christmas parties. At one point, my cousin Dave joined in, maybe when Uncle Jack passed away. Sadly all four of the "Three Amigos" are gone now. But if you listen really hard, on the first Sunday of December, you might just hear a song that includes a very loud and flat "Aye Carumba!" coming down through the clouds. I know I'll be listening.

Don Johnson and the Hams

In 1977 the Linkul Family held its twenty-fifth annual Christmas Party. One of our relatives called in to a local television station and they sent a popular news anchor named Don Johnson and his camera crew to film a few scenes. The family was all a buzz. Our family was going to be on TV! Almost everyone in the family was a frustrated star, so this was right up Linkul Alley!

We had no clue when Don Johnson and crew would arrive, so we tried to carry on with our party as if we didn't know he was coming, even though everyone was a little anxious about it. One of my cousins, Jeanne, in her attempt to keep us all from acting like idiots, periodically went up to the microphone and reminded us to act natural. Soon it was time to eat. Jeanne led us in prayer. You could tell she was a little nervous, because even though we knew that she meant to lead us in a prayer for all of our dearly beloved relatives before we ate, she abruptly started the prayer. Without preamble, she picked up the microphone and solemnly said (almost yelled) "Prayer for the Dead!" I don't know why this struck me so funny, but my sisters and I could hardly pray, because we were laughing so hard. We hoped Don Johnson wouldn't arrive during the prayer and film the three of us with hands folded, laughing our heads off.

After we ate it was time for the entertainment. One of my cousins and her husband were in "black face" because they did a little skit where Al Jolson sang "Mammy" to Aunt Jemima. It was not meant to be disrespectful to black people. It was just meant to be entertainment. When Don Johnson arrived, several of us got a little nervous when the cousin in black face greeted him without a second thought as to her appearance. Luckily Don didn't seem to take offense.

Everybody started getting rattled when they actually started filming. Don wanted to get a shot of several couples dancing. Several aunts and uncles got out on the floor to do some ballroom dancing. The cousin with the microphone kept saying "Everybody act natural…act natural!" as the music played. I don't remember if I could hear her in the background or not when I watched us on the late night news that night. They showed my aunts and uncles dancing while they gave a nice narrative about how our family had been holding our annual Christmas parties for twenty-five years and it was still going strong. I remember the camera was focused on my Aunt Mary dancing with Uncle Jack. When the camera zoomed in on them you could read Aunt Mary's lips. She was saying through kind of a half-smile, half grimace, "Smile, Jack!"

After the filming everybody was fawning over Don and his crew and you could tell he just wanted to get out of there. Aunt Dorothy told him to take the leftover ham. She thrust the huge hunk of ham into his arms. He had a surprised look on his face when she did that. I still have the image of Don Johnson holding our ham under one arm and high-tailing it out of that crazy assignment.

We needn't have worried that Don took our ham; there were plenty of "hams" left!

The Gong Show Christmas

In 1978 we put on "The Gong Show" as the entertainment portion of the Annual Linkul Christmas Party. My cousin Pat invited a blind woman to the party as our honored guest. We welcomed our guest with open arms and wondered how she would like our loud, crazy family. The strange thing about this however, was that my cousin asked the blind woman to be a judge in our "Gong Show".

I was a newly-wed, and wondered how my new, conservative husband would like all of the craziness. He had been asked to provide the music, because I had told everyone that he had an extensive music collection. I remember my one cousin, knowing that my husband was from England and liked music, asked my husband if he knew the Beatles. That was his first clue that the evening was going to be "one for the books". Besides one family picnic and our wedding, this was only the third time my husband was with my crazy family, so I was a little worried. That's why I did not volunteer to be in the Gong Show.

My daughters Karen and Nancy had practiced their skate-dance routine to Olivia Newton-John's song "Xanadu" for weeks. When the lights were dimmed and their music came on, they looked a little scared, but soon really put on quite a show. I was so proud of them. They did not get gonged, because their act was actually normal, but many if not all of the rest of the acts were gonged.

Aunt Dorothy teamed up with my Cousin Pat's husband to do a wheelbarrow act. The act consisted of little Aunt Dorothy standing behind Ken, who was lying face down on the floor. The plan was that he would raise himself up on his arms and would kick his legs up behind him. Aunt Dorothy would catch him by the ankles and they would walk to music, wheelbarrow style. Unfortunately, while practicing right before the show, one of the lenses from Aunt Dorothy's glasses got kicked out. They tried their act without Aunt Dorothy wearing glasses and therefore not being able to see, and they got gonged right away.

My sister Linda and her husband John danced for their act. They danced with great enthusiasm and were so cute together. We all started throwing trash at them just to add to the craziness of the Gong Show theme. The blind woman "gonged" them, even though their dancing was good! She must have been influenced by the sound of trash being thrown at them.

Here Comes Santa Claus!

The funniest part of all of the Linkul Family Christmas parties was when Santa Claus arrived. Starting in 1952 or 1953, one of my aunt's brothers (not a Linkul) had access to a Santa Claus costume. Because he was not a Linkul, the kids did not recognize him, and really thought Santa Claus had arrived. As a kid, I remember feeling so privileged that Santa made a special trip to our family parties every year. Right before Santa arrived, the Master of Ceremonies (usually Uncle Ed) would lead us in the song "Here Comes Santa Claus". The song started out just fine. But after "right down Santa Claus Lane" nobody knew the rest of the words. You would think that somebody would have caught onto this and would have brought the words to the song to the next party, but no one ever did. At the last party that I attended, probably in 2009, we were still singing "Here comes Santa Claus. Here comes Santa Claus. Right down Santa Claus Lane.

Hmm, hmm, hmm, hmm. Hmm, hmm, hmm, hmm. Hmm, hmm, hmm, hmm, hmm!"

And you should have seen that Santa costume after thirty or so years. It looked pathetic! Santa was played by many men over the years, but the funniest Santa appeared in the late 70's or early 80's. He was a skinny old priest who was apparently a friend of one of my uncles, but the rest of us didn't know who he was. The costume was way too big for him and the pillow he had stuffed in his pants as his Santa belly had fallen down to his knees. He walked in all bent over like he was carrying a car on his back. But the funniest part was that the white wig that he wore under the Santa hat had become scraggly and moth-eaten over the years. And he wore these strands of matted hair over his face to disguise himself. My sisters and I laughed ourselves sick at the absurdity of it all. The really little kids who were supposed to enjoy Santa Claus actually ran away in fright that year!

We haven't had a Linkul Christmas party since 2010, just days before my sister Lois passed away. That was the first Linkul Christmas party she had ever missed in her life. She had been in charge of the menu for many years. A few people wanted to have the party the next year and asked me take over being in charge of the menu. I just couldn't do it. Now that we have lost Uncle Fred, the last living Linkul sibling of my Dad's generation, we just can't have any more Linkul Christmas parties. Many of the cousins have gone their separate ways and only two ladies from the older generation, wives of Linkul brothers, are still with us. The Linkul Family Christmas Party just wouldn't be the same without the true Linkul siblings!

But one thing I know is that the Linkul Family Christmas Parties are still going on, just not on this earth. No one has to rent a hall anymore. Aunt Dorothy doesn't have to worry about making fudge or even making sure she has underwear on. Lois doesn't have to worry about the menu. Uncle Jack doesn't have to build a bigger stage. And best of all "The Three Caballeros" sound better than ever, now that they have a choir of angels to back them up.

My Crazy Mom Stories

My Mom was a funny lady. Maybe I got my sense of humor from her. She did some spontaneous things just to be silly. I loved that about her.

Straight Ahead?

One Sunday as we were driving in the country we saw a man standing by the side of the road. Without explaining, my Mom asked my Dad to stop. She rolled down her window, pointed, and asked the man "Straight ahead?" The man looked slightly dazed and nodded "yes". My Mom rolled her window back up and told my Dad to resume speed. Then she laughed and laughed and told us that people are sometimes very suggestible and will answer "yes" anytime you ask them "Straight ahead?" without even knowing where you are trying to go. You ought to try this some time.

People Are Like Sheep

Another lesson my Mom taught us about human nature is that people will blindly follow you like sheep if you act like you know where you are going. We were walking in Forest Park on the way to Lindell Boulevard where the annual Veiled Prophet Parade would be passing that evening. We were in a very large cluster of people all walking toward the same spot. My Mom said "Watch this" and proceeded to walk towards her left for a few yards and then back towards her right, repeating the pattern several times. Everybody followed her. It was hilarious.

Look Up!

And one day when we were downtown shopping, walking on a crowded sidewalk, my Mom abruptly stopped walking, stared up at the sky, and then resumed walking. She asked us to quickly turn around and tell her how many people were looking up at the sky. They all were. Mom taught us again that people are suggestible, followers and plain funny sometimes.

Like Mother Like Daughter

I guess my Mom taught me well, because one of my favorite things to do in a crowd is to get everyone to follow me in laughing or clapping without a reason. One time I was visiting my BFF Barbara in Dallas. She took me to a large omni-theatre in Fort Worth where they were showing some kind of celestial show. At various times during the show I suddenly started clapping very loudly, and sure enough, the whole crowd joined in. I waited until there was hardly anything going on and then would erupt in thunderous clapping. Each time, the whole theatre followed my cue. It was a powerful feeling and quite amusing to me.

When I was about eleven or twelve years old I got kicked out of the movies for laughing when there was nothing funny happening on screen. It was during the movie "Parent Trap" starring Hayley Mills. This was around the time that my Mom had taught me that people follow like sheep. I was just trying to see if I could get everybody to laugh with me. I waited until nothing funny was happening in the movie and then let out a long, obnoxiously long bout of laughter. I kept it up and kept it up. A few people laughed, but I did not get the effect that I was going for. An usher came up and asked me to leave the theatre. It was towards the end of the movie and it was not the first time I had seen it, so I didn't put up much of a fight. I did say something to the effect that I had only been laughing and that it was a funny movie, implying that I was being treated unjustly. But I did leave.

The bad thing was that my Dad was picking Barbara and me up, and he had arrived early. He saw me standing out in front of the theatre, alone, and asked me where Barbara was. I couldn't tell him I had been kicked out of the theatre before the movie ended. I said, "Barbara had to go to the restroom." I guess he bought the story, but just then the movie let out and everyone came walking out. My Dad kind of looked at me and I just shrugged my shoulders and said, "I guess everybody else had to stop at the restroom on their way out, too!" But I couldn't continue the lie, so I admitted that I had gotten kicked out of the show for laughing too loudly. My Dad never said a word. He just kept on driving and slightly shaking his head. The next Monday at school everybody was talking about the movie "Parent Trap". Several kids said they had been at the same theatre at the time Barbara and I had been there. One of the boys said he thought he had heard someone laughing way too loudly and had thought it was me! Instead of being embarrassed, I was proud that I had made such an impression on him.

I suppose I shouldn't blame my Mom for my being obnoxious, but she did instill in me a love of being silly.

I loved the way my Mom used to dance with abandon in our living room, especially when American Bandstand was on television. She watched it with us every day and knew each of the featured kids' names. Even though she was old (in her forties) she loved to dance. One day she broke into this funny dance, really playing it up like she was on stage. I cracked up and often had her do that dance for me. It became her signature dance and I can still picture her doing it.

My Mom used to listen to the radio all day and knew all of the popular songs. When Lois and I couldn't make out all of the lyrics to a song, we would ask my Mom to write the lyrics down for us. She would stop her ironing or whatever she was doing and grab her pen and tablet when the particular song came on. She would write down parts of the lyrics as many times as it took her to get them all.

What a great Mom she was! I've had some pretty bad days in my life, but the very worst one was the day she died.

Biddle Street Blues

Like I said, my Mom encouraged me to act silly. One day in freshman year of high school I went to a friend's house after school instead of coming straight home like it was expected. I knew I had to call my Mom to tell her where I was. I decided to play a trick on her. She had often spoken of a street in downtown St. Louis, making it sound like the worst possible place you would ever want to be. It was

Biddle Street. When My Mom answered the phone, I pretended to be crying and really shaken up. I told her I had decided to take the bus home from school that day (which was unusual) and that I had apparently taken the wrong one. I had gotten off the bus in a strange neighborhood and didn't know where I was. In all seriousness my Mom asked if I could see a street sign. I then said in my most dramatic voice, "Yes, it says B-I-D-D-L-E". I heard my Mom scream out to my Dad "Oh no, Bill, Marilyn's on Biddle Street!" Then to me she said, "Stay calm. Your Dad will come get you." She sounded so scared for me that I didn't have the heart to keep up the prank. Besides my Dad would soon be on his way, and he would not think it was funny at all. So I told her I was just kidding. She was so relieved that she didn't yell at me, but she told me to get home. By the time I got there, she had calmed down and actually laughed about how I had fooled her.

Thrown Under the Bus at the Bus Stop

My Mom went to eight o'clock Mass nearly every morning, and as she passed by the bus stop at the end of our block, she usually saw Mrs. G. standing there. They briefly exchanged pleasantries every day because my Mom and Mrs. G. knew each other from the ladies group at church, and I was in the same class as Mrs. G.'s daughter. One day during the summer I had gone to eight o'clock Mass, but my Mom had not. When I came home from Mass I was very upset, because I mistakenly thought they had announced in church that we should pray for Mr. G. because he had passed away! When I told her, my Mom was in disbelief. Mr. G. was the picture of health and only in his thirties. My Mom always kept sympathy Mass cards in the house and quickly addressed one to Mrs. G. and put it in the mail.

The next morning as she walked to Mass my Mom was surprised to see Mrs. G. at the bus stop. She wondered how Mrs. G. could go to work when her husband had just died yesterday. She went up to Mrs. G., took her hand and said, "Oh, Mrs. G., I am so sorry to hear about your husband." Mrs. G. replied that it was okay; that he was getting better. My Mom asked what she meant, and Mrs. G. explained that he had something fairly minor and that he was going to be fine. She thanked my Mom for her concern. My Mom told Mrs. G. that she would be getting a card in the mail. She apologized profusely and then proceeded to "throw me under the bus" by saying that I had mistakenly heard in church that Mr. G. had died. Mrs. G. explained that she had asked for prayers because Mr. G. had undergone a medical test. My Mom later told me that she had been mortified, and that next time I had better pay better attention in church when they announced why parishioners needed prayers! That was one time when I thought I was pretty funny, but Mom really didn't. She once told me that every time she saw Mrs. G. after that, she was embarrassed.

Candy Bars in the Toilet Tank?

Besides inheriting my Mom's sense of humor, I also inherited her sweet tooth. We didn't have candy around the house when I was growing up. The only exception would have been on our birthdays and on holidays. We usually only had one package of cookies for the whole week, and those were for lunch time only. My sisters and I used to sneak into the pantry and take a few cookies when Mom wasn't looking, so we often ran out of cookies after only a couple of days. That left nothing for my Mom when she "got her sweet tooth". Sometimes she would eat jelly on toast to satisfy it, but I imagine there were many times when she just wanted something better, like a candy bar. She was usually stuck at home and didn't have extra spending money, so she couldn't easily go out and buy herself something sweet.

Unbeknownst to us, when I was in high school, she started buying a package of candy bars for herself when she went grocery shopping for the week, and she hid them from my sister Lois and me. I imagine she told herself that she deserved a treat once in a while. Lois and I could get candy at school, so it wasn't like she was being mean by hoarding candy bars for herself. She may have shared her candy with our little sister Linda and told her not to tell Lois and me.

One day she and my Dad were going out, and before she left she told us that she had bought herself some candy bars and hidden them and that they had all better be there when she got back. As soon as we heard the car doors close, we started frantically searching the house. We looked under beds, in our parents' dresser drawers, in the big walk-in coat and storage closet, on the highest shelf in the kitchen pantry where the seldom-used fancy dishes were kept. The candy bars were nowhere to be found. Desperate now, we started searching the bathroom, even looking through the dirty clothes in the hamper. Finally, we knew we had gone too far when I lifted the lid from the toilet and looked for the candy bars in the tank. I had seen Audrey on General Hospital tape a gun to the inside of a toilet tank and thought that would be the best place to hide candy bars, as long as they were wrapped in a tightly sealed bag. We started laughing hysterically at how desperate we had become! We finally did find them in the kitchen junk drawer and we each ate one. My Mom laughed as hard as we did when we told her that the minute the car doors had shut we had started tearing the house apart looking for the candy bars, and how we had even searched the toilet tank. She wasn't even mad that we had eaten two of them.

My Biggest Supporter

My Mom was so proud of me when I won the Junior-Senior Speech Meet in my junior year of high school. She had helped me practice my country accent and helped me put together a hilarious costume. I remember coming home from school and telling her that I had won. She cried with pride and joy. I was asked to come to the next St. John's PTA meeting to perform my speech. My Mom was very sick at the time. She was in and out of the hospital and back and forth to doctors for treatments for her breast cancer. But she promised that somehow she would make it to see my winning speech. Unfortunately she was way too sick to make it. I didn't know anyone in the audience that night and I sorely missed my biggest supporter. I didn't do well at all. I blanked out several times, because all I could think was that my Mom wasn't in the audience. She was so sick that she went back into the hospital shortly after that night. I remember going to see her in the hospital on my way to a dance and how she was so excited for me because I had met a cute boy and was going to the dance with him. I thought about how sick she must be, yet she continued to act like nothing was wrong. She never complained or let on how sick she was. She just kept on being a supportive and fun Mom.

My Mom and I spent her last summer playing double solitaire and drinking pitchers of iced tea every afternoon. It was just the two of us. I'll never forget that precious time. We had so much fun together. Sadly, her life ended on August 20, 1965. Not only did I lose the best Mom ever, I lost my biggest supporter and my best friend. I love and miss you so much, Mom! I know you're in Heaven and probably playing tricks on people. I wonder if when you entered the pearly gates you asked St. Peter, "Straight ahead?"

My Crazy Naughty Stories

It's Not Stealing if the Bag's Open!

One day when I was about six years old, my older sister Lois and I were in the snack food aisle of the grocery store, which back then consisted mainly of plain potato chips, pretzels and Planter's peanuts. Our parents were in another area of the store. Lois decided to use this time to teach me a lesson in grocery store etiquette. She taught me that it was okay to eat food right out of the bag if the bag was broken. She added that it was not considered a sin to do so. To demonstrate, Lois held up a bag of Old Vienna potato chips, our family's favorite brand, and pulled the bag really hard from each side until the bag burst open. Then she said, "This bag is open, so you're doing the store a favor by eating the chips before they start drawing roaches or rats!" With that she popped a chip into her mouth and gestured for me to follow suit. I felt a little funny about eating the chips, but since Lois was my big sister I figured she knew better than I did about what was a sin and what wasn't. A few years later, I taught my friend Judy H. the difference between stealing and helping the grocery store out by eating the food that was in broken packages.

Pizza and Taxis

In freshman year in high school my BFF Barbara and I were invited to spend the night at one of our classmate's house. Cathy had been excluded from another girl's PJ party and had invited Barbara and me over for a PJ party of our own. Cathy convinced us that we should help her get even with Jane (the girl who had excluded Cathy) by sending pizzas and taxi cabs to Jane's house. I had never heard of doing such a thing, but it sounded like great fun! I have always loved playing pranks.

We called every pizza delivery place and every taxi cab company in the area and sent them to Jane's. Jane lived just a couple of blocks away from Cathy's house. We walked over to Jane's block, hid between two houses and watched the drama unfold. There were already two pizza delivery men and a cab driver on Jane's front porch. We could see Jane's mother's face and her gestures as she tried to explain that no one from her house had ordered pizzas or a cab. Another cab pulled up. This was getting good! We could hear some of what Jane's mom was saying and we heard Cathy's name come up. We also heard her giving the cab driver Cathy's address. So, we high-tailed it back to Cathy's house, hoping to get there before the cab driver did. As we turned the corner, we saw that we were too late. We timidly walked up the steps to the front porch where Cathy's mom and the cab driver were talking. Neither one looked happy. Cathy's mom apologized to the cab driver. She knew by our faces (and probably from experience with her daughter) that we had called him. I think she paid the driver for his time. After he left, Cathy's mom told us how she was very unhappy with us, but I don't think Cathy got grounded or anything. Thankfully, Cathy's mom did not call Barbara's or my mom.

We went to the basement to resume our PJ party. We laughed about the pizzas and the taxi cabs showing up at Jane's house and swore we would never tell Jane that it was us who had called. (I guess I'm breaking girl code now by telling this story.) Then we decided to play a few phone pranks. I had never played them before except one time when two old ladies were talking on our party line. The one old lady said that she had just made roast beef and invited the other old lady over for dinner. I said, "Oh that sounds good. I'll be right over, too!" As I was hanging up I heard one old lady say "Who was that?"

After tiring of phone pranks (one where I scared a little old lady out of her wits pretending like there was a man in my house ready to attack me), we went out and stole a "For Sale" sign from a yard and placed it in front of another house, followed by throwing a rock at the window of the corner bar. Luckily we didn't break it.

It was a night of naughtiness all right. The next day I told my Mom how much I had missed her and that I was glad to be home. Even though I had had fun, I felt guilty about all of the naughty things we had done that night, and I had really been homesick for my Mom.

Don't Laugh, I Have Ringworm!

Over the next couple of years Barbara and I played many phone pranks. I think my best performance was when I called a beauty school. I told the poor girl who answered the phone that I had a huge hair problem. She told me to come on in and that she could fix any hair problem I might be having. I told her that it was my prom that night and I didn't know what to do. Then I started crying and told her that I had ringworm and that most of my hair had fallen out. (Is that even what happens when you have ringworm?) I told her there were just a few tufts left and asked if there was anything she could do to make my hair pretty for the prom. She told me to hold on for a minute. I heard her ask the other girls in the beauty school if they could think of anything. She mentioned I had ringworm, that my hair had fallen out and that I wanted to look pretty for the prom. I could hear them laughing in the background. When she came back to me, barely stifling her laughter, she suggested that maybe I could come in at 3:30 and that they would tie some pretty bows on the few strands of hair that I had left, but that's about all they could do. I started crying hysterically and screamed into the phone, "Stop laughing at me. It isn't funny! How would you like it if you had ringworm and had to go to your prom with stupid bows on your head?!" Then I reluctantly told her I'd be there at 3:30 and I hung up. I often wondered if they really believed me, and if they had been disappointed when a half-bald girl hadn't come in at 3:30.

I have played many phone pranks in my life, some better kept to myself. If only some moron hadn't invented caller ID. I'd still be in the phone prank business today!

Overdriven Heap

One night after the last performance of our church youth group play, several of us from the cast rode around the neighborhood looking to get into mischief. It was a Sunday night and we were all keyed up from our last performance. One of the girls was driving and her boyfriend was sitting next to her in the front seat. There were a few of us girls in the backseat. We parked for a while in Tower Grove Park and the boy passed a beer to us in the backseat. I guess the beer was supposed to amuse us girls while he and our friend made out in the front seat. Finally, we left the park after he gave the driver a hickey. With no ideas about what to do next, we headed to our homes.

There was a used car lot at the end of my street. Not wanting the evening to end, I announced that I had something I just had to do at the car lot. We were carrying a bucket of white paint and a paint brush, left over from when we had painted the scenery for our play. I grabbed the can of paint and the brush and told everyone to watch me. A car in the front row had "Overdrive Cheap" printed in white across the windshield. Armed with a paint brush and a couple of sips of beer, I added an "N" to the end of the first word and removed the "C" from the second word.

The next day I took the bus to school instead of walking like I usually did, because I wanted to sleep in a little after being out late the night before. I sat down on the bus and pointed out the window to the car lot and loudly exclaimed, "Look, everybody, the sign on that car says "Overdriven Heap! No wonder this car hasn't sold!" I expected everybody on the bus to laugh themselves sick, but I'm not sure anybody got the joke except me. To this day I am proud of my cleverness, even if no one else appreciated it. I still laugh when I think of Mr. Pickle wondering why the car wasn't selling, and eventually discovering how I had altered his sign. (See "My Crazy Childhood Stories" for other mentions of Mr. Pickle.)

Trespassing with Amy

Believe it or not, I usually follow rules, at least when they suit my purpose. I am mischievous, though, which is one of my Dad's words for me. I also do not like being told what to do. My Dad had a word for that, too. He said I was stubborn. When someone tells me I can't do something, I am determined to do it all the more. When I see "wet paint" signs, I just have to touch the paint. I am usually disappointed to find the paint has already dried. When I see a "no trespassing" sign, I take it as an invitation to come on in!

One day when Amy was about thirteen, we decided to explore our new neighborhood. We had just moved into a new house in unincorporated North County, down the road from a large, wooded area that led to the Missouri River. Right down the road from us there was a mansion belonging to the Mc Donnell family of Mc Donnell-Douglas fame. It was later used as a training site for the Boeing Corporation, but back then it was still a private home used not as a residence, but for gala events. There were "no trespassing" signs all over the place, but I was determined to get as close as possible to the windows so I could peer inside. I don't remember seeing any security personnel or guard dogs, but I felt like we were being watched. So I thought perhaps we should walk through the woods and approach the house from another angle.

We were walking in a thickly wooded area when we came across an old cabin or shack. (I don't remember exactly what it looked like). "How exciting" I thought when I saw it, thinking it was a great place to do some exploring. Then we heard an angry voice asking "Lady, can't you read?" I was all ready to say that I hadn't seen any "no trespassing" signs and that we were just taking a leisurely walk in the woods, when I looked up and saw a man with a shotgun pointed at us. I decided for once in my life not to smart back. I muttered something like "I'm sorry. I didn't see any signs!" when I almost ran into a big "no trespassing" sign tacked to a tree right next to us. I grabbed Amy by the arm and we walked faster than we would have if someone had announced there was free ice cream out on the road. Amy's dad wasn't too happy when he heard about our adventure in the woods, but it is a special memory to me.

It's Later than You Think!

Jerry and I married when we were both forty-eight years old, but we still acted like kids. He always let me be me, and he liked to do naughty things too. One night we went to Denny's. It was about eleven o'clock at night. While we were waiting to be seated and no one was looking, I changed the clock on the wall near the entrance to one o'clock. It was so much fun to hear people come into the restaurant and say, "Wow, it's much later than I thought!" Jerry and I started laughing harder and harder as each customer came in and made some remark about how late it was. On the way out of the restaurant I mentioned to the cashier that I had changed the clock as a prank and that she might want to change it back now that we had had our laughs. She said, "I know what you did. I saw you." She chuckled and changed the clock back. Maybe she wished I would have kept my mouth shut so she could have gotten off of work a couple of hours early!

I think being naughty keeps a person young. I plan to keep playing pranks and acting silly until the day I die, and I urge you to do the same!

My Crazy Obnoxious Stories

In my unending quest to be the center of attention and to make people laugh, I have done many things that "normal" or "emotionally mature" people would consider to be obnoxious. Well, all I have to say to those people is "I'm sorry." By that I do not mean that I am sorry for my behavior or sorry for offending you. I mean I am sorry that you aren't carefree and childlike enough to be able to do any of these things. It must be very confining and boring to be normal and emotionally mature.

Deadly Serious Cultural Event

When I was in my teens Father B. was the moderator of our Catholic Youth Conference (CYC) teen group at church. Fr. B. was a newly ordained priest and he really took an interest in us kids. I think he felt sorry for my BFF Barbara and me, because he knew no one would probably vote for us if the chairman spots were filled by an election, because we were a little crazy. Father B. appointed me as the Cultural Chairman of the group. He appointed Barbara as the Social Chairman. Barbara was the perfect person to be the Social Chairman, because she was and still is a very social person. I, on the other hand, was not, had never been and am still not a "cultured" person.

As Cultural Chairman I organized the monthly cultural events that had been tradition in our CYC, but added a few new ones of my own. One of the events that I planned had never been done in the history of the Maria Goretti Sodality (the name of our CYC group). It was a trip to the City Morgue. I don't know how I came up with that idea. Not that many kids signed up for this event, but it turned out to be very educational and even entertaining, thanks to Fr. B.

The tour began in the room with drawers of dead people. We saw the draped body of a man on a gurney. One of his feet was sticking out. I remember his toes were yellow and waxy looking and there was a tag on his big toe. I think I was as freaked out as the rest, but I had to maintain my composure. After all, I was the Cultural Chairman and had planned the event. I remember hoping and praying that the tour guide would not take the sheet off of the dead guy. To keep my mind off of that, I started thinking weird thoughts like how much fun it might be to pull on the dead man's big toe, but I couldn't bring myself to do it. And I probably chuckled to myself a little thinking of the scene that the dead man would make if he suddenly sat up!

Our little group was standing at the foot end of the gurney that had the cadaver on it, listening to the tour guide and feeling a little "creeped out" by it all, when Father B. suddenly poked me in the back. I jumped and made a semi-loud noise. He was lucky I didn't let out a blood curdling scream like I usually do when someone startles me. Father B. startling me was the comic relief we must have all needed. We all laughed, albeit nervously, and with that we were led out of the room and the tour concluded. I think that was the last time that the Maria Goretti Sodality ever toured the morgue.

A Cultural Night at the Municipal Opera

Another event I organized was a trip to the Municipal Opera (now commonly referred to as the Muny by St. Louisans). The Muny is an outdoor theatre in Forest Park, St. Louis' Crown Jewel. Seeing a Muny show is a must if you've never been there!

The show that we saw that night was "Westside Story". We had a bus load of kids for this event. Fr. B. was our only chaperone as I recall. We were all dressed up, as was the custom for attending the Muny back then. We were seated in the last couple of rows of paid seats, with just a couple of rows of "free seats" behind us. I had gotten us the cheapest seats available in other words.

Everyone was watching the show and behaving like cultured little teens, except for one obnoxious girl. She must have been bored or maybe she had undiagnosed Attention Deficit Disorder, because halfway through the show, even though she was enjoying it, she started fidgeting around. Then she had the zany idea to belch loudly into the ear of a woman sitting directly in front of her. This obnoxious girl "urped" loudly, in staccato, right into this woman's ear for about five minutes. Finally, the woman could stand it no more. She motioned to the usher, and the usher asked the girl to leave her seat immediately.

As Cultural Chairman and organizer of this event, I was so embarrassed to be escorted out of my seat and told to stand behind the "free seats" for the remainder of the show!

The Tale of the White Radish

When I was a sophomore in high school I had "study hall" every morning. I hated it, because you had to spend the entire period (close to an hour) in silence, and you were supposed to, of all things, study during that time! I have always had a hard time sitting still and I really hate it when I have to sit in silence and study by myself.

The monitor of the study hall was an old nun who was obviously very close to dementia. The poor dear was very obsessive and compulsive about certain things. My sister Lois, who went to the same high school a few years before me, had Sister in history class. Lois used to talk at the family dinner table about how Sister blamed everything on the Communists. She was supposed to be teaching about many other historical events, but all she talked about every day in class was about the Communists, and how they were bringing about the end of the world. So I was pre-disposed to judging Sister as a crazy old woman from these many dinner table tales.

My opinion of Sister was confirmed when I was assigned to her study hall. She went through a ritual at the beginning of every study hall of having us line up our desks precisely so that the left side of our desks sat exactly in line with the tiles on the floor. Kids being kids, we purposely scooted our desks out of line throughout the study hall period just to get a rise out of her. Moving the desks also provided me with a little reprieve from the prison time that I had to endure every day.

One day I brought a foot- long white radish to school. My next-door neighbor, Mr. Lindley, had grown it just for me. My Mom thought I was bringing the radish to school for lunch, but I secretly planned to whip it out during study hall and chomp on it to make everyone laugh. The classroom where we had study hall still had those old fashioned school desks with lids. Everyone was settled in, desks in perfect line with the tiles and studying their little hearts out, when I slowly lifted the lid of my desk. I raised it about halfway and hid behind it as I munched away. Looking over my shoulder at everyone to make sure I was the center of attention, I loudly chomped on my prize white radish. I was enjoying the laughs and attention immensely, when all of a sudden there was a hard tap on my shoulder. Sister had obviously spied me, stealthily came up from behind out of nowhere and attacked me! Maybe she had been studying espionage tactics to protect us from the Communists! I sheepishly grinned up at her and asked if she wanted a bite. That prompted gales of laughter from my audience, but only a severe (almost KGB-like) glare from Sister.

For my punishment I was assigned a two-hundred-fifty word essay on respecting teachers. I was told to turn in the paper at the end of the study hall period. I sat there for a minute, inwardly fuming at the unfairness of my punishment. I loved to write even back then, but I really didn't see how eating a radish in study hall constituted disrespect for a teacher! I thought that this assignment was just busy work to keep me from clowning around in study hall, and that no one would ever really read it. I started writing about the most horrible teacher imaginable; one who was not worthy of any respect at all. I furiously wrote about this generic teacher who wasted class time making her students line up their desks, and filling their heads with nonsense about the Communists instead of teaching history. I wrote about a teacher who must be crazy to think that eating a radish during study hall had anything to do with respect. I asked rhetorically how such a teacher could really be worthy of respect. I finished my masterpiece with a simple declarative sentence. "If the shoe fits, Sister, wear it!" When the bell rang to signal the end of study hall, I sullenly walked up to Sister, shoved the essay into her liver-spotted hands and marched out of her classroom, never dreaming she would actually read it.

At lunch, I passed around what was left of my prized radish to my friends and bragged how I had really let Sister have it in my essay. I confidently declared how it was too bad she wouldn't get to read what I had written, because it was a masterpiece. I just knew that she had torn it up and thrown the pieces away the minute I marched out of her room.

I was sitting in class that afternoon when the public address system came on. My heart stopped when I heard "Will Marilyn Linkul please report to the Principal's office immediately after dismissal!" I knew without a doubt that not only had Sister read my essay, but she had turned me in to the KGB! After my last class for the day, I gathered my belongings, said good-bye to my friends and slowly made my way to the Principal's office to meet my fate. Instead of meeting with the principal, I was soon under the stern gaze of my former homeroom and math teacher, Sr. Mary R. Sister Mary R. probably didn't like me too much, because I had not paid attention in her math class in freshman year, and I had disrupted several of her classes by laughing non-stop or by placing objects in the rat's nest hair of the girl who sat in front of me.

Sister Mary R. really let me have it for my outrageous essay. I humbly stood there accepting her harsh assessment of me. Inside I was wondering why Sister Mary R. was getting so riled up. The essay hadn't been about her! Then all of a sudden Sister Mary R. had herself so worked up that she raised her hand to slap me in the face! I waited for the sting, but it never came. Her hand was in mid-slap position as she started talking about what a good family I came from. Then, instead of slapping me, she used that hand to tenderly hold my face. With tears in her eyes, she gently said "Your mother is such a good woman, and your sister Lois is such a good girl. What happened to you?" I looked at her with tears in my own eyes and told Sister Mary R. that I was very sorry. I wasn't as sorry about being disrespectful to Sr. Mary Communist as I was sorry that I had disappointed my dear Mom, who had raised me to be better than that.

At the dinner table that night, my Mom asked how everybody at school had liked my foot-long white radish. I just kept my head down and mumbled, "Well, everybody except Sister liked it. I started eating it in study hall and she caught me." My Mom looked at me and smiled. She knew that Sr. Mary Communist was a little off her rocker, and she probably wasn't all that surprised that I had eaten the radish during study hall. After all, I was her mischievous daughter!

Girl Gang at Large!

I guess it's fair to say that I didn't respect people and I didn't respect property when I was a teenager. In freshman year of high school I experienced my first real Halloween trick-or-treating. Before then on Halloween I had dressed in a costume and gone door-to-door telling jokes and holding out my bag for candy or other treats. When I said "trick or treat" back then, I meant I'll do a trick, and then you'll give me a treat. Now that I was a high school teen, I had outgrown that lame version of trick-or-treating. When I said "trick or treat" I meant I'm going to play a trick on you and it will be such a treat for me to see (or imagine) your reaction.

My BFF Barbara and I were invited to hang around our new friends Cathy, Bettye and Linda for Halloween that year. They lived in the neighborhood around the high school, while Barbara and I lived three miles away. So, Barbara and I felt we could do whatever we wanted in their neighborhood, because no one in that neighborhood knew us. We were told to bring as many rolls of toilet paper as we could. Cathy, Bettye and Linda would provide the lipstick and the eggs. Boy was this going to be a night to remember! Barbara and I went to Cooks Market with a few dollars and bought as many rolls of toilet paper as we could afford. Back then a few dollars got you a whole lot of TP!

Cathy, Bettye and Linda didn't like a girl named B., who was also in our freshman class, because one of the sophomore boys who played in a band liked B. The rest of us were so jealous, especially Cathy and Linda. The five of us went to B.'s house and located her mother's car parked in front. Cathy and Linda used lipstick to write bad stuff about B. on the windshield while Bettye egged the car. Barbara and I just watched. It was kind of exciting to be a part of it all. The five of us fancied ourselves to be a tough gang. We even gave ourselves gang names. I don't remember anyone else's gang name, but mine was "Dink", short for Dinkle that rhymed with Linkul, my last name. I remember Linda gave me my name. She was so cool that I would have accepted any name she wanted me to have.

Next on the agenda was to TP the house of another classmate, a boy, who had not invited any of us to his Halloween party. To protect his identity, I'll call him Kip. Kip lived in a very nice house. One of Barbara's and my friends was his new girlfriend. She had told us about the party. Barbara and I had not been invited because we were known to hang around with Cathy, Bettye and Linda, who were probably thought to be unsuitable invitees by Kip's parents. We could hear music and laughter coming from the basement of Kip's house as we silently draped roll after roll of TP on several trees in Kip's big backyard. When we were finished I remember the five of us standing in the alley in awe of our handiwork. It looked like a winter wonderland!

Kip's Mom came outside just as we were about to leave. I remember there were no other sounds in the neighborhood except for Kip's Mom loudly exclaiming "Oh my God!" That was the pay-off for our hard work. We played the *trick* and Kip's Mom *treated* us to a big reaction!

The next Monday Kip was the first person I saw as I walked into our homeroom. I cheerfully said, "Good morning, Kip!" He just glowered at me and said, "I know it was you, Linkul, you and your friends!" I kept a straight face and innocently asked what he was talking about. He continued to glower at me and said, "You know." I met his steady gaze with one of my own and simply said, "I don't know what you're talking about, Kip. And by the way, how was your party?"

We *both* knew. I knew he had a party that I wasn't invited to and he knew who had TP'd his yard.

When Life Was a Playground!

For two summers I had a job as Playground Leader for the City of St. Louis Parks and Recreation Department. I was still a kid myself, a very immature one at that, so it was kind of funny that I was entrusted to take care of many children for eight hours a day.

On my first day, my Dad dropped me off at Gravois Park on his way to work, so I got there early. I let myself into the little building where the craft supplies and sports equipment were stored and pulled out the plastic strips used for making lanyards. I am not good at making things. I never have been. I was always the last one working on crafts in Girl Scouts and usually had to have a leader finish the project for me. I knew from orientation that I would be expected to know how to make a lanyard, a standard playground craft. I painstakingly wove the plastic strips together, but could not figure out how to end the lanyard. I saw that a little girl had arrived. I introduced myself, pulled her into the building and said, "Teach me how to make a lanyard and do not EVER tell anyone that I didn't know how to do it!" She looked like she was kind of afraid of me, but showed me how to finish the lanyard. Later, when it came time to make lanyards with the kids, I did not remember what she had showed me.

I was terrible at making every one of the crafts that we were expected to make with the kids. I tried to weave a basket. I soaked reeds in tubs of water so they would bend. I sort of knew how to weave the reeds to resemble a basket, but did not know how to make the borders. I just wasn't good at finishing woven projects. I had never been able to finish pot holders either. My Mom always finished mine for me. One day I attempted to make rugs with the kids. We used pot holder loops. Like I said, I could weave the loops, but did not know how to make the border. The rugs that we made curled up instead of lying flat.

One afternoon a woman came walking across the ball field towards me like she was on a mission. She held a half- finished lanyard, a curled up rug and a woven reed something-or-other. She asked if I was the playground leader and I said yes. Then she proceeded to hold up the craft projects one at a time, and asked "What is this sh*t?" I didn't care for her attitude at all and was not going to apologize for my lack of crafting skills, so I explained what each item was. I told her in my most confident voice that the lanyard was a rabbit leash, that the curled up rug was a toilet seat cover and that the woven reeds were meant to be used as a placemat. Then I looked at her and said "Do you have a problem with your son's crafts? She just stared at me for a moment and walked back home, shaking her head in disbelief. Her son never returned to the park after that.

I was really good with kids, maybe because I was one of them. They loved me. One day I played football with a group of ten-year-old boys. It turned into a free-for-all with the boys all piled on top of me on the dusty baseball field. It was a very hot day and I had been running and was out of breath. When the boys wouldn't get off of me right away I panicked. I really thought I was going to be smothered to death. I managed to get them off of me just before I was about to pass out. What a sight I must have been when I got to my feet. I was shaking and covered with dust and sweat. Except for almost dying, it was kind of fun.

There were four of us playground teachers and two shifts. George and I worked the 9:00 to 5:00 shift and Mary Jo and Ken worked the 1:00 to 9:00 shift. George was more serious than I was and spent all of his time coaching the kids in baseball and softball, while I took care of the crafts (ha ha!) and girls' volleyball. I can't say that I really coached volleyball, because I was no good at playing, nor did I really know the rules. But I was a good motivator. I made sure my team practiced a lot. And I taught them to look tough when they approached the net. My team actually won the city championship one summer.

My team consisted of girls at the upper end of the age requirement and they were tough kids. They lived in a pretty rough neighborhood and looked kind of intimidating. I remember bringing them to another playground for a game. As my team walked towards the net, the other team, which consisted of very little girls who were all at the lower end of the age bracket, you could hear the little girls murmuring in fear. I heard one little girl say "Oh, sh*t!" right before the coach announced that her team was forfeiting the game.

When Mary Jo and Ken joined George and me at 1:00 PM every day, that's when the fun began. George stayed busy coaching the boys, but Mary Jo and Ken and I joined the kids and played volleyball all afternoon. That's how our teams got so much experience, and I was relieved from having to make those darned crafts. We had so much fun together. We were college kids getting paid to play volleyball all afternoon. And as a bonus I got a fantastic tan!

One afternoon Mary Jo and I decided to take the girls on a little shopping trip to Woolworth's on Cherokee Street. She needed something for one of her craft projects. We were not supposed to take the kids out of the park unless we had cleared it with our Regional Director and had obtained permission slips signed by the parents. It was a spur of the moment idea to go to the store and we decided to forego the formalities and just go. After all, Cherokee Street was only a few blocks away and we wouldn't be gone long. We told the kids not to tell their parents. Counting Mary Jo and me, we were a group of about eight.

As we entered the store I happened to look over at the lunch counter and saw our Regional Director, Laverne, sitting there eating. We referred to Laverne as "The Turtle", because of her posture. She periodically visited the parks in her territory and we Playground Leaders were kind of intimidated by her. She was a no-nonsense kind of person and three out of four of us were nonsense kind of Playground Leaders. If Laverne had looked up into the mirror behind the counter she could have seen us in the reflection. She would have certainly recognized us and asked to see the permission slips. I whispered "Quick, girls. Hide. It's The Turtle!" as I pointed to Laverne. Mary Jo looked as alarmed as I felt upon seeing The Turtle. We quickly pushed the girls behind a turnstile of dress patterns and waited for a minute to regroup. We managed to get out of there undetected by The Turtle.

Sadly, at the end of my second summer as a Playground Leader at Gravois Park, I was asked not to return the next year. It wasn't because of that crazy field trip. It was because of an innocent free-for-all on the last day of the summer. Traditionally, the Playground Leaders at Gravois Park let the kids have a water balloon fight on the last day. Somebody, probably me, suggested that we surprise the kids and bring other stuff to attack each other with. I remember bringing cans of grape and tomato juice. Another person brought the eggs. After we had run out of water balloons, we brought out the good stuff. It was a free-for-all of epic proportions. When it was all over, my tee shirt was so drenched it hung down past my knees, and it had grape juice stains, tomato seeds and pieces of egg on it. My hair was purple-red and soaking wet, too. My face even had grape juice stains on it, and there was dirt and grass stuck in my teeth from being rolled in the dirt of the baseball field. I had never had so much fun in my life!

We Playground Leaders were due at a restaurant on Cherokee Street (actually a bar) for the traditional end-of-summer lunch with The Turtle. All of the Playground Leaders from her district were already there. We were running late because of our "water balloon" fight. I remember sitting alone with the kids on the steps of our little building (I think the other Playground Leaders were busy closing up the craft and storage building for the season or something) when the police came. I guess we had raised such a ruckus that someone from across the street must have called them. (I have always thought that it was the woman who had complained about the crafts, because she lived right across the street from the park and obviously didn't like us).

One of the policemen asked where the Playground Leader was. No one said a word (those kids were very loyal) until I spoke up and said, "We don't know, Officer. They just left us kids." I guess I did look like just another kid to the policemen, because they just dropped the whole matter and went back to their car.

A few minutes later the four of us Playground Leaders walked into the bar on Cherokee Street where The Turtle and all of the other

Playground Leaders were waiting. As we walked in with our stained, wet clothing we were greeted with some laughter, some judgmental looks and a great big turtle glare. That's when The Turtle said, "The four of you needn't come back next summer." I didn't really care, because I hadn't intended on returning anyway.

My Obnoxious Driving Episodes

My first crazy driving episode occurred when I was in the second grade at my school picnic at Chain-of-Rocks Amusement Park. I talked my Mom into letting me drive a race car around a real track. My Mom looked worried and even asked the attendant if he thought I was old enough to drive a car. No one was in line with me, so he probably didn't care if I could drive one of those cars or not. What harm could I do? So I got in and started driving slowly, getting a feel for driving. I gave my usual wave and smile every time I passed Mom and Lois. Then I got a little cocky. I started driving really fast. As usual, I was showing off, especially because Lois was almost four years older and was afraid to drive one of these cars. Then my car kind of went out of control and I crashed really hard into a stack of tires meant to cushion the impact of any crashes. A few of the tires fell off the stack—that's how hard I hit it! The attendant yelled at me to get out of the car! I heard him tell my Mom to keep me away from the track; that I was too wild of a driver!

My Dad didn't let me drive even after I turned sixteen, so I didn't learn to drive until I was about twenty-two years old. I was married and had a child already, but I had about as much business driving as I did launching a military rocket! My BFF Barbara picked me up and took me to Tower Grove Park one Saturday afternoon.

She told me to get into the driver's seat. I was so scared. I was babbling on about how scared I was and how I couldn't do it. Barbara was so patient with me. I was only driving about ten miles per hour and could barely manage that when a car came towards me. It was on its own side of the road and going as slowly as I was, but I panicked. I gripped the wheel and screamed as I passed it. My nerves were shot from that experience. I wanted to stop driving, but Barbara wouldn't let me. After a few more minutes, she allowed me to go back to being a passenger. I was so relieved. She drove me to my in-law's house where I was living with Baby Karen while my husband was in Viet Nam. When we drove down the alley that ran behind their house, Barbara got out and announced that I was going to drive into the drive-way and park the car. If I was scared to drive in the park, I was terrified of bringing her car into the driveway. Barbara assured me that I could do it. I assured her that I could not. Barbara doesn't take no for an answer, so I tried, but failed. The driveway was narrow, and there wasn't a lot of leeway for error on either side of it. I over-compensated to avoid hitting the house and ended up scraping up the side of Barbara's car against the gate. She didn't even get that upset with me. I think my in-laws gave her some money to have it repaired, but there was no amount of money or anything anybody could say to repair my nerves.

Barbara let me drive another time to get me ready for my driver's test. Our goal was to have me a licensed driver by the time Terry got home from Viet Nam. This time she made me drive on regular streets, even a couple of two lane roads. I was driving and she was directing me. She told me to go on a road that paralleled the highway. I thought she was tricking me into actually getting on the highway, so I started screaming, "No!" Barbara kept telling me I wasn't going on the highway, but I just kept screaming. I don't know how she put up with me, but thanks to her patience, I did learn enough that day to be able to eventually pass the driving test. But alas, I failed at my first two attempts, because I was too nervous.

During the first driving test I had made so many mistakes that I remember looking at the sky and actually seeing the letters F-A-I-L written in the sky! I was so busy looking at the imaginary letters that I ran a red light. When the instructor yelled out, I got so nervous that I stomped on the gas pedal and almost crashed into a Velvet Freeze store front. The instructor had no sense of humor whatsoever. I tried to explain that those huge letters in the sky had thrown me off, but he wasn't having any of it. I failed. I don't even remember the second test that I took and failed. Terry came home from Viet Nam and I didn't have my license like I had planned to surprise him with, but I did get it shortly thereafter.

On my third try I drove to the test site in my own car instead of borrowing someone else's like I had had to do for the previous tests. Terry had made me practice using the turn signals and we went over all of the dashboard and steering wheel stuff. I felt confident that I would pass this time. All was going well until the instructor asked me to work the signals. I yanked on the turn signal thing way too hard and the damned thing came off in my hand! I held it up with a "Lucy" look on my face, expecting him to laugh. He didn't. He just gruffly told me that I would have to take the test using hand signals. I had tears in my eyes when I asked if we could just skip using signals altogether since I hadn't practiced using hand signals. He told me in no uncertain terms that if I wanted to take the test, I would use hand signals. I drove the course using hand signals and following all of his instructions very well. When we approached the street that was set up with cones to test my parallel parking skills is when it all went downhill. The instructor told me to line my car up and parallel park it. I had practiced with real cars and had done pretty well, but using cones was too hard for me. The instructor said "You are so far off, lady, just go on. We're going to skip this part of the test!" I thought I had failed again, but I scored a 70 on the nose. I didn't drive that much in my first couple of years of being a licensed driver and was not a good driver at all.

I've done some pretty wild driving since then, like the time I made a fool of myself while driving a cart in a grocery store. I was recovering from one of my foot surgeries and still wearing a boot. Rather than just have Amy go grocery shopping for me, I decided to go along. I planned to sit on a bench while she shopped, but when I saw the electric carts just waiting for drivers, I decided to try my luck on the track there. I remember Amy laughing at me because I kept starting and stopping very suddenly. I really could not regulate the speed. And turning the corners in that thing? Forget about it! As I whipped around my first corner, I nearly crashed into a crabby man, stopping very abruptly within an inch of his heels. He turned around and loudly yelled "Hey, lady, watch where you're going. You almost hit me!" I didn't like his attitude so I gave him some back when I said "Yes, ALMOST!" Every time he saw me after that, he flinched and jumped out of my way. It was actually comical to see him react the way he did.

I almost hit a lot of shelves and I remember I had a hard time maneuvering around the egg case. People were watching me and laughing. I finally got to the front of the store. I didn't have any items in my basket, since I had only driven around with Amy to advise her if she needed it. (Actually she kind of separated from me after I had almost hit that old man). I was about to cut through an open cashier lane so I could return the cart when I hit a display rack, nearly knocking it over. I think an employee, or maybe Amy, told me they would get the cart back to where it belonged. I dread the day, if it ever comes, when I have to use a cart like that to shop.

No Time for Seatbelts, Kids!

A former co-worker recently reminded me that I used to tell this story when we worked together, and that he hoped it would be included in my book. Thanks for reminding me, Ryan! I think it belongs in "My Obnoxious Stories".

I was waiting for a parking spot in J. C. Penney's parking lot. I had my signal on. The car backed out and took off. Before I could pull in, a convertible coming from the wrong direction whipped in front of my car and took the spot. I sat there dumbfounded. Then I yelled "Hey, that was MY spot!" The family of three just looked at me with smirks on their faces. Boy did that make me mad!

I was seething as I herded the kids into JCP to the catalog pick-up counter. And who did we see waiting at the counter, but the Dad, the parking spot thief himself! I marched right up and stood next to him. I was so close I could hear him breathing. He had to know I was there, but he kept his eyes looking straight ahead and ignored me. I was breathing into his left ear, but he continued to ignore me. Then I noticed beads of sweat forming across his upper lip and forehead. I was making him nervous. Still, he looked straight ahead and ignored me. The counter lady came up and asked who was next. I said loudly enough for everyone in the crowded area to hear, "Oh, I'm sure he's next. He's always next. He makes sure he's first in line for everything!" His face turned beet red and sweat started streaming down his face. But that wasn't enough for me. He was winning, because he was not acknowledging me. This infuriated me.

I decided that I had to get revenge. I would leave the merchandise for pick-up at a later date. I grabbed my youngest daughter's hand and told the other two to come with me. I was running so fast that my daughter's feet flew off the floor and she was flying a couple of feet off of it! When we got to the convertible, I instructed all three of my kids to remove the chewing gum from their mouths and to smear it all over the leather back seat, so the smug little brat who had gloated at us would get in trouble and maybe get a spanking from his smug, gloating parents! I told the kids to hurry up. I looked up at the front door of JCP and the smug, gloating family was leaving the store. I grabbed the kids, pushed them into the back seat and yelled "No time for seatbelts!" as I took off at about 40 miles per hour! I explained to the kids that sometimes you have to teach bad people a lesson! I realize I'm not going to get the Mother of the Year award for my bad behavior, but in spite of the bad example I set for my kids, all three have turned out to be good, upstanding citizens who would never smear gum on anyone's leather seats, much less involve their children!

I drove home extra fast that evening, because I had a feeling the family saw us doing something to their car and were following us. When we got home, I decided to go bike riding with my older two girls. We liked to ride to a nearby cemetery that was on top of a hill and then drive at breakneck speed down the hill and onto a road that wasn't traveled very much. That evening as we sped down the hill and onto that road, we saw a convertible coming towards us. It was them! They probably saw us driving to our neighborhood and were looking for our car. As soon as I saw them, the girls and I took an abrupt detour through a park and through our across-the-street neighbor's yard to the safety of our home. I guess they didn't recognize us or didn't know which house was ours. Our car was out of sight, in the garage. The police never came knocking on our door and I never saw the smug, gloating family or their gum-stained leather-seated convertible again!

My Crazy Performance Stories

My first public performance occurred in Kindergarten. Each of us was called upon to come to the front of the class, stand on a chair, face the audience of fifty or so fellow Kindergarteners and sing. I don't remember the song, but I remember how I felt singing it. I was excited that all eyes and ears were on me. I reveled in the applause! I remember that my teacher, Miss Erna, said that I had a very good voice!

Since then I have sung, danced, acted and made presentations in front of crowds and audiences sometimes numbering in the hundreds, and have loved every single minute of it. Here are some of my favorite public performance memories.

My Lovely Blossoms Will Die!

My grade school had class plays for many years, but sadly, they discontinued them just when I was getting started. In Kindergarten, I was given the role of Spring Beauty in our class play of the same name. The play was about flowers, but I don't remember the plot. I do remember my costume and my only speaking line. My costume was a long pink dress that made me feel like I was a fairy princess rather than a flower. My line was "My lovely blossoms will die!" I milked it for all it was worth. There wasn't a dry eye in the crowd as I lamented what would happen to my lovely blossoms. (Well, at least my Mom may have had tears of pride and joy in her eyes). Acting was in my blood and it's been hard to keep me off of the stage since then.

Marilyn Had a Little Lamb!

In first grade, our class presented a play about nursery rhymes. I was cast in the role of Mary, as in Mary had a little lamb. Nick V. (I know his last name, but want to protect his reputation) played the part of the lamb. I remember in rehearsals that I had to pet Nick's head while reciting my lines. I must have been boy crazy even then, because I loved petting Nick's head. During the performance, Nick's head was covered with the head of his lamb costume, so I didn't get to feel his ginger colored crew cut as I pet him. Besides, I had white gloves on. I remember my costume. My Grandma, who was a great seamstress, made it. It consisted of a pink blouse and skirt in a crinkly material, a petticoat and an aqua apron, a brown corset with shoe string ties and an aqua floppy bonnet that tied over to one side under my chin. I remember that I had to dress myself at dress rehearsal, which was held during class time, so my Mom could not be there to help. I remember that she was worried that I wouldn't be able to tie all the ties, snap all the snaps and pin all the pins, but I did it! I know my Grandma Bertha loved seeing her grand-daughter perform as

Mary, and was probably just as proud to see her beautiful handiwork on stage.

Dancing Stories!

In second grade I started taking dance lessons. The Lee Carol Dance Studio was just three doors away. The studio was in the basement of the P. family home. The dance instructor, Carol Lee P., was only sixteen years old when she opened her own studio, and was a fantastic dancer. Her mother, Mrs. P., played the piano. My sister, Lois, and I were in the same class even though she was almost four years older than me. One Christmas, we had a little recital just for the parents in Carol's basement. I had a tap solo to "The Chipmunk Song". It was four reps of hop-shuffle-ball-change to "We can hardly stand the wait, please Christmas don't be late." My costume was my black leotard covered by a little red and white skirt that snapped at the waist, and a Santa hat. Midway through my routine, the skirt came undone and fell off! I kicked it aside and just kept dancing, even though I was embarrassed. Afterwards my Mom told me she had been so proud of me for not stopping. I have never forgotten that the show must go on!

My best friend from second to sixth grade was Judy H. We met in dancing school. The other girls in our class were older than we were, so Judy and I bonded right away. Judy and I were both good dancers. What we lacked in technique, we made up for in showmanship.

After our first recital, which I missed due to illness, while the costumes still fit and we could remember some of our routines, Judy and I decided to have a dance recital in her back yard. We passed out flyers around the neighborhood, and a couple of neighbors came, but it was mostly our families in the audience. Our dance teacher, her little sister and Mom also came.

We charged admission and sold popcorn and Koolaid from Judy's garage, which also served as our dressing room. As the crowd sat and waited on folding chairs in the grass, Judy suddenly started scratching her arms; a sure sign that she was nervous. Judy had eczema, and it always flared up when she got excited. It was time for the show to start and Judy was furiously scratching her arms and eating popcorn as fast as she could get it into her mouth. I knew the show had to go on, so I went out to the yard and made the announcement that the show would be slightly delayed. I remember saying "I'm sorry, folks, but you'll have to wait a few more minutes. Judy's eating!" Then I went back into the garage to wait with Judy until her nerves calmed down. After her bag of popcorn was gone, I decided that we had to start the show. Judy was still scratching and I was starting to get kind of nervous myself. Judy had a white, frilly umbrella for one of her numbers. I decided that I wouldn't be as nervous if I could hide behind her umbrella while I was performing, at least for my first number, so I asked Judy if I could borrow it. I went out to the sidewalk wishing the recital was over.

We didn't have any music to play, so we just hummed while we danced. I thought that once I got out on the sidewalk and started humming that my nerves would go away, but they didn't. Suddenly I couldn't even remember my routine. It was kind of difficult to hum the right notes, remember the right steps and concentrate on twirling the umbrella all at the same time. And my dance teacher was there! I felt so much pressure. I hid under the umbrella during the whole routine, humming, twirling and tapping the same steps over and over. Finally, when I was out of breath, I took a bow and ran back to the safety of the garage. Judy came out next and she hid behind the umbrella throughout her entire number, too. She came back into the garage and it was my turn again. I decided to use the umbrella in my next routine, too. It was less scary to dance behind it. I would somehow have to make it seem like the umbrella was part of this routine, too. What routine? I couldn't remember the steps to this one either. It was a disaster. Most of the show consisted of Judy and me taking turns coming out of the garage, hiding behind the umbrella, humming softly and doing the same few steps over and over, all on a narrow sidewalk stage. (I bet you're sorry you missed that recital!)

We did ditch the umbrella for each of our best routines. Judy wore a sailor outfit and performed to "I'm Gonna Sit Right Down and Write Myself a Letter". Her routine started with her sitting down on a little stool and pretending to write a letter. I can still to this day see that cute little blond girl in her red-white-and blue sequined costume singing and dancing to that song. In my best number, I wore a red checkered blouse, short turquoise overalls with a red kerchief sticking out of the back pocket and a straw hat. I danced to "Goofus". And I can still hear my "shuffle-hop-down-brush-step-close, shuffle-hop-brush-step-close-step" to "I was born on a farm down in I-o-way".

I Was Settin' on the Porch

In my junior year of high school I entered the annual speech contest. It was for juniors and seniors. My speech was about a teenaged country girl. I don't remember much about the story, except it began with the lines "I was settin' on the porch. It was a real hot day." I was dressed in a green and white polka dot dress, with knee socks and tennis shoes. My hair was in pigtails, and I had big freckles on my face, drawn on with eyebrow pencil. I don't know why I thought country people dressed like that, but I think I tried to model my character after Ellie Mae Clampett from the Beverly Hillbillies. I sounded pretty much like her. One of the nuns came up to congratulate me after they announced that I had won. She told me she laughed until she cried when I first came onto the stage with my chest all caved in, wearing that crazy dress that was way too big for me in the bust.

My Guy

My BFF Barbara and I used to sing all the time. One summer Barbara and I sang "My Guy" in a talent show. During our performance the microphone started sliding down. I squatted lower and lower to stay in line with it as it slid downward. We (me and the microphone) finished on the floor without me missing a note. Barbara stood there with a look of horror on her face, but she kept singing, too. The audience thought it was part of our act, and laughed and clapped. We didn't win the talent show, but we made the most of the technical glitch. Some people told us after the show that they had liked our comedy skit!

They didn't know that I was behaving just like I did when my skirt fell off in the middle of my dance routine several years earlier. I was following my two performance mantras: "Never let them see you sweat!" and "The show must go on!"

Hang on Sloopy

In the summer time, Barbara and I usually had nothing better to do with our afternoons and evenings than walk around our neighborhood looking for boys and singing. One of our favorite songs to sing was "Hang on Sloopy". I love to harmonize, and this song was perfect for that. Barbara and I each had good singing voices on our own, but we sounded even better when we sang together. Barbara used to say that she couldn't sing without me. She had trouble singing her part when we tried to harmonize, and always ended up singing mine. Just as much as Barbara sometimes needed me to guide her to the right notes, I sometimes needed the strength of her voice. We practiced "Hang on Sloopy" over and over during the summer before our senior year, until we harmonized perfectly.

One evening while we were walking around the neighborhood singing, a carload of boys stopped to chat. They told us that they had a band and were looking for a girl singer. We told them we came as a package deal and they agreed to let us audition, right there on the street! We sang "Hang on Sloopy" for them and they thought we were really good. They asked us to join their band in a "Battle of the Bands" to be held at a local church teen town. Barbara and I used to dress alike sometimes, and we had recently purchased the cutest dresses at Famous Barr. They were sleeveless "hip-hugger" dresses. The top was camel with a dropped waist; the pleated skirt was short and in a grey and camel hound's tooth pattern. There was a wide black belt worn low on the hips. They were great dancing dresses, because the short little pleated skirts swayed with our hips. Perfect dresses to wear in the "Battle of the Bands".

We practiced with the band a few times before the event. Neither Barbara nor I could read music, and we didn't know all of the words of many songs, so it was decided that "Hang on Sloopy" would be our only contribution to the performance. If the band won the battle, Barbara and I would be offered the position as "girl singer".

It was a dream- come- true night! I have always wanted to be the female singer in a rock band. It's still my dream job, and I will do it in my next life! As we sang our signature song, Barbara and I danced in unison, swaying in our short little hip-hugger dresses. The crowd went wild. The band, which really wasn't all that good, won the "Battle of the Bands", because of our singing perhaps, and partly because of our dancing and our dresses, I think. None of the other bands had girl singers. The main thing is that we won, and Barbara and I were on our way to becoming famous! Barbara and I each got $5 for our performance that night, which wasn't bad considering it was 1966 and we only had to sing one number. I couldn't wait to tell my Dad the good news. I was going to have a job and it was my dream job! But my excitement was short-lived. My Dad told me that he would not allow me to sing in a band, because of the late hours and the partying for which musicians were known. I was heart-broken, of course. My Dad was very protective of me and I didn't appreciate it at the time. I took a part-time job at Famous-Barr instead. I wore my "Hang on Sloopy" dress for a couple of years. It was always a favorite, especially for dancing.

Gladys Phipps

I was working at a downtown bank as a Personal Banking Officer. It was in the early 1980's. The bank was introducing a new senior citizen activity club called the Vista Club. I was asked if I could write a theme song that the new members could all sing together at the first meeting. I wrote a song that was a parody of "Ragtime Cowboy Joe".

I was then asked to write and star in a skit to introduce the benefits of belonging to the Vista Club to the other Personal Bankers who would have to sell the idea to our senior customers. Of course I jumped at the chance to use my creative writing skills, and more importantly, to have the starring role in the skit. I chose a co-worker named Dennis to play the role of the banker in my skit. I was told to tell Dennis that our skit was supposed to be serious, and that I had been forbidden to make it some kind of a comedy skit. Dennis believed me.

I created the character of Gladys Phipps, who looked a lot like Mama of "Mama's Family", the popular television show starring Vickie Lawrence. Gladys was a bank customer who complained to her Personal Banker that she was getting old and was lonely. Dennis, as her Personal Banker, was supposed to sell Gladys on the idea of becoming a member of the Vista Club.

Dennis knew I would look pretty funny in my Gladys get-up, and that he had to keep a straight face throughout the skit, but he was totally unprepared for my "Gladys Phipps" performance. I wore a gray wig, an old lady hat, glasses pushed down on my nose, a house dress, rolled down nylon stockings and some old lady shoes. Dennis struggled to keep a straight face when Gladys walked into his office. He suppressed a snicker when Gladys opened a pill container and they spilled all over his desk. She picked them up one at a time and popped them into her mouth like they were candy (they were really

M & M's) and said they were her "rheuma-tiz" pills. Dennis got through his lines very well considering that he had to look at Gladys the whole time without laughing. But when Gladys announced that she needed to use the bank's restroom right away, and then stood up and peed all over the floor, Dennis lost it. I had pinned a water balloon to my underwear. I made sure Gladys was sitting on a hard plastic chair, so when she pushed down to hoist herself up from the chair she caught the balloon and pressed down really hard, enough to break it. I had practiced this at home several times until I could do it effortlessly. The water poured out of the broken balloon as I (I mean, Gladys) stood up. It was genius, if I do say so myself. It really looked like Gladys had peed all over the floor. Everyone laughed and Dennis knew that he had been had when I had told him that we had to be serious during the skit!

After the meeting, which had been held bright and early before work, one of my supervisors came into the restroom where I was changing out of my costume to tell me how much she had enjoyed the skit. I remember telling her that I had forgotten to bring a dry slip to change into and that the dress I was wearing to work in that day was kind of see-through. So she took off her slip and lent it to me. This is one time that I actually wanted my boss to give me a "pink slip"!

The Dining Room

When I was thirty-nine years old, I quit working and went back to the University of Missouri-St. Louis (UMSL) as a full-time student in order to finally obtain my degree. The plan was to graduate within one year and then go to work in broadcasting. Most of the classes I took during that year were theatre and broadcasting classes. One of my theatre professors directed a play called "The Dining Room" by A. R. Gurney Jr. It has roles for six individuals, three of each gender. I was cast in the role of Actress #3, playing characters ranging in age from six to eighty-six: Sally, Girl, Ellie, Winkie, Old Lady, Helen, Meg, Bertha and Guest.

I have been in several plays as an adult, but none more fun than this one. One of my characters was a little girl named Winkie, who was celebrating her sixth birthday. I was married to someone else at the time, but how ironic that I would later marry someone with the last name of Winka! It was also ironic that one of the performances was on my fortieth birthday. There I was with a party hat, blowing a party horn into the face of another actor and talking in a high pitched voice about it being my birthday, when it really was!

If you ever get the chance to see this play or even to read a copy of the script, you'll know what I mean when I say it is such a fun play. Each scene is set in the same dining room. In one scene, I played a young woman who nervously tells her father that she is in love with another woman. The father, immersed in reading the newspaper, is hardly listening to his daughter. That part of the scene came naturally to me, since my own father often buried himself in the newspaper, thereby making himself unavailable to the rest of the family. When my character said "There's someone else, Dad" in a nervous voice, I sounded just like I had at times in the past when I had to tell my Dad some news I felt would not be good news to him, like the time told him I was re-marrying and that my fiancé was a non-Catholic. I sounded familiarly nervous talking to my stage Dad when I said, "It's not a man, Dad." (Pause). "It's a woman!" My real

Dad was in the audience for one of the performances and I wondered how he would react to this scene. After all, he was a very strict Catholic, and we had never talked about homosexuality, or even any kind of sexuality. I wasn't even sure he would "get" that in the play I was a lesbian.

In another scene my character is typing and keeps making mistakes. The script doesn't say this, but the director told me to say "Sh*t!" every time I made a mistake. (I think she threw that line in when she realized that I couldn't even "pretend type").

The morning after he saw the play my Dad called me to talk about it. I was all ready to accept his praise about how good of an actress I was, but I soon learned that this was not why he was calling. He cleared his throat like he always did when he was nervous, and said, "Your Mom (step mom) and I were wondering if it was really necessary for you to use that language." I asked if he was referring to the word I had said in the scene where I was typing. He said yes, that this was the scene to which he was referring. I explained that the director had told me to use that word and that it was not my idea to use it. My Dad said he thought I should have just told the director that I could not use that kind of language. I said, "Dad, you don't do that in acting!" He said that's all that he had wanted to discuss, and then ended the call. I was left feeling properly chastised and a little disappointed with the conversation until I realized the humor in it. Here I was, a forty-year-old woman, and I had been bawled out by my Dad for saying the word sh*t! And even funnier, he had not said one word about the conversation between the father and daughter in the scene where I told him I was in love with a woman! I wonder what he was thinking when my character declared this. Perhaps he had stopped paying attention to my lines after hearing me use the awful "S" word.

Yes, I did the best acting of my life in "The Dining Room". We had professional lighting, a professionally done set and we had a very talented costume designer. I had several costumes and they were all color-co-ordinated. Each of us actors had a different color palette. I remember my colors were camel and burgundy with a touch of salmon pink. I felt like I was in a Broadway production!

One of the girls in the ensemble went on to be a famous Hollywood entertainment lawyer and producer. Her friend, a famous and infamous football player, was actually in the audience at one of the Saturday evening performances. My cast mate pointed him out to me in the audience. She wanted to introduce him to all of us, but he ducked out right before the end of the play because he had to catch a flight back to LA. (Any guesses as to who this was?)

We were given a videotaped copy of the play, but unfortunately, I no longer have mine and do not know how to reach any of my cast-mates or the director to obtain one. Right after graduation I had registered with a local talent agent. She sent me to a photographer for an expensive head shot to add to my acting resume. She asked for a videotape that represented my acting abilities. The copy of "The Dining Room" was the only tape I had. I gave it to her thinking I would get it back soon, because she promised to make a copy that she could keep. Well, she kept the tape but didn't keep her promise to get me work in television commercials or to make a copy of my tape and return mine. After about a year her agency finally called me on a Saturday afternoon. They needed me to be Susan Sarandon's stand-in for the movie "White Palace" which was being filmed in St. Louis.

The "permed" hair-do on my head-shot did kind of make me look a little like Susan and they said I was about her height. Then they asked if I was still a size 10, because that was Susan's dress size. My acting resume stated that I was a size 12, which I had been when I had it printed it a year prior to this call. But by the time they called me I was a size fourteen. I told them the truth, which eliminated me as Susan's stand-in. I should have just lied, worn a girdle and hoped they wouldn't send me home when they realized I was not a size 10! Sometimes it doesn't pay to be honest, I guess.

Just think, I could have run lines with James Spader! Maybe I would have been discovered by the producer/director who was from St. Louis and happened to be one of my college professor's sons. I'm sure I would have told him that I knew his father if I had been given the opportunity to talk with him. Maybe I would have been given a small part in "White Palace" and would have been discovered by Hollywood and would be a famous star by now. Oh why, oh why had I eaten so much during the year I quit work and went to school? Forget the freshman fifteen. I had gained the senior sixteen and had eaten my way right out of Hollywood!

The Butler Did It

Shortly after performing in "The Dining Room", buoyed by my recent success, I auditioned for a community theatre play and got the lead! I had previously only performed in community theatre musicals, having only one line and being in the chorus. This was my first and last community theatre performance in a non-musical play, I'm sad to say. I have thought about auditioning for a few plays where they have older characters - believe me those parts are few and far between -

but, I am afraid I can no longer memorize lines. So I don't bother with auditioning any more.

The play was "The Butler Did It!" I played the lead, who was a "Miss Marple" type character, but do not remember my character's name. It was twenty-eight years ago, folks. Now you know why I am afraid of auditioning for a play if I would have more than a couple of lines.

I used the acting methods that I had just learned in college and developed a character profile. I knew my character inside and out before the read-through. I knew her middle name, her first pet's name and even how she made a sandwich. (She was the type who put all the ingredients away before eating a sandwich, by the way). Funny, how I once knew her intimately and now I don't even remember her name!

I had to speak with a British accent. I thought my accent was pretty good, but my British husband didn't think it was very authentic. I remember that I had a lot of lines. It was in May and classes had just ended, so I spent hours every single day memorizing my lines. Even so, I still struggled. I do not know how professional actors memorize their lines. I think I had to concentrate so hard to say the right lines and to say them with the British accent that my acting suffered. I guess I did alright, and was even nominated for the theater group's best actress award that year (I didn't win); but it was not my best performance.

Actually, I did something horrible during that play. I was so busy chatting and acting goofy behind stage during one performance that I missed my cue and left another actress looking like a fool on stage. She kept dusting the same spot over and over and saying something like "She'll be here any minute now…yes, she's on her way…she should be here any second now…"

This reminds me of another time when I was in a play for this same theatre group. I wanted to become well-rounded in theatre so I could perhaps someday try my hand at directing, so I signed up to work props. This was like a punishment for me, because I was not seen by the audience, and I do not do well when the job requires that I pay strict attention, and when it leaves no margin for error. I was goofing off so much behind stage that more than once the stage manager had to tell me to be quiet. I was too busy cracking jokes to pay attention. In the most crucial scene of the play, the main character shoots another character and kills him. I was supposed to have the gun ready for the main character so he could quickly walk over to stage right and grab it. I wasn't paying attention. He came over to stage right and put his hand out. I just stared at it. When I didn't hand him the gun, he shook his hand impatiently as if to say "C'mon, hand it over…NOW!" I couldn't think fast enough and just stood there with a dumb look on my face. Finally, he muttered "Gun!" through his teeth, and I still just stood there. So he went back out on stage and pointed his finger and loudly said "Bang!" The audience never knew that this wasn't in the script as odd as it may have seemed. The play was a comedy, I believe. Or was it? Maybe I just made it one. That was my first and last experience working props for a play. No one will ever give me props for my props abilities, I'm afraid.

Julia Kidd

I think one of my funniest stage performances was the Julia Child skit that I performed for a church talent show. I wrote it myself. My inspiration was the Julia Child skit on Saturday Night Live where Dan Aykroyd played Julia and accidentally got her hand caught in a blender.

I practiced Julia Child's voice and mannerisms until I had them down. I wore a 1950's style housedress and a chef's apron and hat. I called myself Julia Kidd. I demonstrated how to cook a fresh chicken, potatoes in jackets and a cranberry soufflé. I told the audience that it was important to start with a fresh chicken. As I held up a rubber chicken I remarked to the audience that my chicken was so fresh that I had to slap it in the face! When I demonstrated how to cook potatoes in jackets I put on five jackets, one at a time, and then declared how hot I was. When I said that my soufflé called for the *entire* can of cranberries, I placed the entire tin can into the soufflé dish. When I told my audience that it had to be baked in a low oven, I bent really low to the ground and shoved everything into my make-believe oven, just a few inches off of the floor. I got many laughs. One lady's voice stands out above all others in the videotape of my performance. She laughed at almost every line and kept saying "Oh, my God!" I think that was the most gratifying audience acknowledgement that I have ever gotten.

The Mamas, the Papas and the Ham Sandwich!

The church that Lois and I both attended held annual talent shows. Lois and I were in all of them of them, performing together in comedy skits, dance routines and singing acts including "The

Joanie Carson Show" (a spoof on the Johnny Carson Show--I wrote the skit and played Joanie), "The Sweeney Sisters" (a cheesy lounge act a la Saturday Night Live) and "Ain't No Mountain High Enough" (based on the "Designing Women" performance of that song), just to name a few.

One year we paired up with two guys, Mark and Chuck from our guitar group, and sang "California Dreamin'". We dressed like The Mamas and the Papas and I think we sounded pretty much like them. I sang Mama Cass' part. I wore a big muumuu with a pillow underneath and a long brown wig, parted down the middle. During the part of the song where a solo flute or recorder plays, I swayed back and forth just like Cass used to do. We were so into our performance that Lois and I actually became Michelle and Cass, if only for a few minutes! After the song ended and the stage went black, all you could hear is me asking "Has anyone seen my ham sandwich?" and then the sounds of someone choking. Irreverent, perhaps, but it sure got a lot of laughs, which is what I always go for!

Rita Simmons

Perhaps my best theatrical accomplishment was the parody of Richard Simmons' "Sweating to the Oldies", a video that I created, produced, directed and starred in when I worked for Cash Bank (not the bank's real name). The video was shown at the regional sales meeting. I called it "Selling to the Oldies" as a way to gain recognition for the Telephone Banking Sales Department that I managed. I wrote parodies to three oldies. "Dancing in the Streets" became "Selling in Their Seats" and "Aint No Mountain High Enough" became "Ain't No Sales Goal High Enough". "It's My Party (and I'll Cry If I Want To) " was transformed into "It's My Product (and I'll Sell If I Want To)".

When I came to them for support of my project, our Marketing Department gladly agreed to pay for the recording studio time, because they were responsible for putting on a show at the big annual bank sales meeting. Two bank employees (both professional singers) and I recorded the songs. That part was so much fun. I felt like a bona fide recording star with my headset on, singing into the microphone in a real recording booth! The day of the video shoot, I wore short shorts, a tank top and a big Afro wig and called myself Rita Simmons. I led my Telephone Banking staff in three dancercise routines while the pre-recorded oldies played. After the routines, each of my sales staff members danced through a line and looked into the camera. We later added the text showing how many bank products they had each sold a la the "Sweatin' to the Oldies" videos that showed how much weight each "dancerciser" had lost.

The Rita Simmons video was shown at the regional bank sales meeting attended by the bank executives and all of the branch managers. I was never so proud of my staff. The branch managers were astounded by how many bank products my staff had sold. The Telephone Banking Sales Representatives didn't usually get credit for their sales; the branches did. I think after seeing these results they all had a little more respect for my department. My manager had been afraid of the reaction to my video when I had first approached him with the idea, but when the CEO of the bank came up to him at the meeting and congratulated him on having such talented people working for him, he was very proud

Are You Looking Up My Skirt?

I was attending another regional sales meeting, this time for the brokerage firm where I worked for eleven years, when I was randomly selected to take part in the murder mystery dinner play. Naturally I jumped at the chance to be on stage! My character actually turned out to be the murderer. I didn't have any lines. I was just supposed to stand over the dead body. While other characters were talking on stage, I happened to look down at the co-worker (a male) who was playing the part of the corpse. I had on a short skirt and saw him sneak a peek. Without thinking I ad-libbed the line "Are you looking up my skirt?" I brought the house down, as they say. After the play was over, they awarded us participants ball caps with the logo of the theatre group. When I went up to claim mine, one of the professional actors asked the audience for a round of applause for me. He said my line was the funniest one in the entire play. He said that I had gotten more laughs than he and the real actors had. If he had asked me to join the theatre group, I would have. But he didn't. Wouldn't that have been a fun side job?

Madonna of Edisto Court

In the early 1990's I had a karaoke machine. I spent hours singing and imagining myself to be a famous singing star. I must admit I was a little full of myself, giving myself credit for being far more talented than I really was. One day I stayed home from work, sick, and spent all day in bed belting out Madonna songs. The echo effect of the machine made me sound pretty good. The windows were open, but I didn't care if my new neighbors heard me. By the end of the day they were probably hoping, *just like a prayer*, that my singing would end! I am surprised I didn't hear somebody yell out "Take a *holiday*, Madonna!" But, even if I had heard them, I was a *borderline* psycho and would have just kept on singing.

One evening, I was in the front bedroom of our two-story house catching up on some ironing. I had about two hours' worth of ironing for me and Madonna to do. I had the karaoke machine on and I sang Madonna songs over and over for the entire two hours. Again, the windows were open. When I was finished with the ironing, I walked over to the window to close it. I glanced across the street and saw six people standing in front of their house. They were looking up at my window. It was the man and woman who owned the house, their two small boys and the man's parents. I waved and shouted "Hello". Then I asked "Could you hear me singing?" "We sure could!" was the answer. "We've been standing out here for about thirty minutes enjoying the show!" I had been dancing as well as signing. I was so embarrassed, but not so embarrassed that I stopped "treating" my neighbors on Edisto Court to Madonna songs. For the neighborhood Fourth of July get-together the next summer, I brought my karaoke machine out. Several of the wives joined me in serenading our husbands with Madonna songs while they readied the fireworks. Sometimes I wish I still had that machine.

Proud Sister Mary

I guess my last public performance was in October 2006 when I performed in a Red Hat Society Halloween party karaoke contest. I almost had a heart attack (really) during the rigorous performance, but at least I did win an engraved trophy. I was dressed as a nun and I sang "Proud Mary". I called my act "Proud Sister Mary".

As Tina Turner told us, this song starts out slow, and I started out reverently singing in a solemn, almost operatic voice. Then when the music sped up, I became a crazed dancing nun. I wore a red and purple scarf around the waist of my habit, and when the music got wild, so did Sister Mary. I whipped off the scarf and used it rather irreverently, I must confess.

I did a good job singing until I ran out of breath. As you know, that is one long-ass song. It is especially long if you are in your late 50's, singing as well as trying to dance like Tina Turner and you have a blocked artery that you don't even know about. I got through most of it, but when I started dancing like Tina, bobbing my head up and down like a maniac, I suddenly ran out of breath, started to feel dizzy and had to quit. This is just one of several times that I almost stopped breathing from too much exertion and blamed it on asthma. Looking back on this incident and knowing that I had to have a stent put into my heart eight years later, I wonder if I didn't almost "bite the dust" that day. At least I would have been dressed like a nun, so maybe St. Peter would have let me in past the Pearly Gates without question.

My Crazy Queen Stories

Whose idea was it anyway to write stories for every letter in the alphabet? This will be a short section. Maybe you should save it for those times when you need just a little something to read while you're waiting for an elevator or sitting in the john!

Amy and the Queen

My youngest daughter Amy's father is British. We had planned to name her Amy, but with a different middle name. But the moment she was born, being so proud of her half-British heritage, I declared that her name was Amy Elizabeth. As I looked at my husband I added, "For the Queen!" He looked very pleased.

One Christmas our family went to Wales to visit my in-laws and decided to spend a couple of days in London before leaving for home. My daughters were about four, eight and ten at the time. I remember that we all had sneakers on because we were going to walk all day. There was a foreign man on the double-decker bus who was laughing as he pointed to our shoes and saying something in his language. It appeared that he was making fun of our shoes. I guess they looked too American or something.

Our first stop was Hyde Park, famous for its Speakers' Corner. There was a Mc Donald's across the street from Hyde Park, which back then seemed like an odd juxtaposition of Modern America and Olde England. We walked all over London that day. We went to Madame Tussaud's Wax Museum where I posed next to the figure of the Pope and pretended to be picking his nose. We walked through the Tower of London. We walked around Piccadilly Circus and many more tourist sites. By late afternoon four-year-old Amy was really tired from all of the walking. And anyway, the sites that we were visiting weren't of particular interest to her. To keep her motivated, we kept telling her that we were soon going to see the Queen, meaning that we were going to walk to Buckingham Palace to hopefully see the changing of the guard, and maybe if we were lucky, catch a glimpse of the Queen walking her corgis. By the time we were actually headed to the palace in the afternoon, her little legs were very tired and she started to get cranky. "We're almost there, Amers. We're going to see the Queen!"

When we arrived, we were not in time to see the changing of the guards and of course, you can't really see a lot from outside the royal gates. We did not spot the Queen or any other member of the Royal Family out on the palace grounds either. Finally, little Amy had had it! She threw herself on the sidewalk in front of the gates and refused to get up. She screamed over and over, "I want to see the Queen!" The poor guards with their motionless, expressionless faces were probably thinking "Get that Yankee brat out of here!" We were all tired, and none of us had the strength to pick her up and carry her.

We finally pulled her off the ground and practically drug her away. She was still crying and demanding to see the Queen. I guess she thought we were going to be invited in to have tea and little finger sandwiches with the Queen or something!

Queen Latifah

I like to pray the rosary. Usually as I finger each bead, I pray for a different person in my life and their prayer intention. One morning on the way to work I decided to pray for each of my loved ones without actually using a rosary, because I was driving. I invented the Alphabet Prayer, which consisted of me thinking of the letters of the alphabet, one at a time. With each letter I prayed for the first few people in my life I could think of whose name begins with that letter.

When I thought of the letter A, for example, I immediately thought of my daughter Amy, my two Aunt Anns and a dear old friend named Agnes. Then I said the Hail Mary for those people's prayer intentions, whatever they might be. And so I repeated this process for each letter. I had no trouble thinking of multiple people for most of the letters of the alphabet, but when I came to the letter Q, I was stymied. I tried and tried to think of someone, anyone in my life, whose name began with Q. Then I thought, "Aha! I'll pray for the Queen of England. I kind of know her. Well, at least, I was at her house one time. But praying for a title, rather than just a first name, kind of bothered me. It was breaking the rule of my new prayer. And then it hit me. I did know someone whose first name begins with a Q. Queen Latifah! OK, so it's her stage name and not her given name. And I don't really know her, but I did enjoy watching her in that one television show, "Living Single". And even though I can't name one of her rap songs, I do like her singing. I was sure Queen Latifah could use a prayer just like anyone else. So, I pray for her every time I say the Alphabet Prayer. Who knows? My prayers may have helped her career a little. I wonder if I called her, explained how I often pray for her and asked to appear in her next movie, if she'd give a "sista" a chance?

My Crazy Reptile Stories

I hate reptiles so much I can hardly write these stories. I'm not kidding. Reptiles repulse me, folks! I actually have chills right now. Maybe the sisters in my Catholic grade school are to blame, because they told the story of Adam and Eve and blamed the snake for everything. I have hated them ever since (reptiles, not the good sisters!)

The Designer Chameleon

My experience with a chameleon is about as gross as it gets. My Aunt Ann (the donut Aunt Ann) took my sister Lois and me to the circus when I was five years old. You're not going to believe this, but they were selling live chameleons with safety pins in their bellies to be used as decorative pins on women's coats! I am NOT kidding! As you know, a chameleon changes his color to blend in with the background. I suppose it was considered fun to watch a chameleon change to the color of your coat, but I thought it was repulsive. I hated reptiles and I hated the idea of a woman wearing a live reptile on her coat!

My Aunt bought one for my sister to have as a pet and maybe to rescue the chameleon from having a pin in its belly. I politely declined the offer to have one of my own. Lois brought it home and put it in the basement. I think it just ran around loose. I don't know what she fed it and don't care. I don't know how long the dang thing lasted, but it was too long for me. I didn't go down to our basement the entire time Lois' chameleon lived with us. And I loved playing in our basement! I am shuddering as I write about it. Aunt Ann and Lois saved the chameleon from a fate of being live jewelry, but in doing so, they scarred me for life!

Revenge is SSSSSweet!

My little sister Linda knew how much I hated snakes. Linda was usually very sweet and well-behaved. I am nine years older and I was jealous when she was born because she had usurped my position as youngest in the family. When she was a baby I used to sneak into the bedroom and pinch her cheeks to make her cry. When my Mom came into the room to see why her baby girl was crying, I stood there with an innocent look on my face and declared that she had just started crying for no good reason; that I hadn't done anything. My Mom may have fallen for this once, but not twice. She noticed the red pinch marks on my little sister's face, and boy, did I get into trouble! I was pretty nice to Linda after that, but revenge is sweet. Linda waited for the right time to get her revenge for the pinched cheeks; in fact, she waited nine years!

I was in college, eighteen years old, when a nine- year- old Linda took her shot. I remember we were in the basement family room when it happened. I was listening to classical music, an assignment for my music appreciation class. Linda liked to hang around me in the evening, especially when I went downstairs to play music and try to focus on doing homework. (I inevitably ended up standing in front of the mirror and singing Motown songs into a fake microphone rather than doing homework).

That evening I noticed Linda had on a knit turtleneck top with a brown and tan snakeskin design down the front and on the sleeves. I had previously told her that I hated that top, because I hated snakes. The music I was listening to was soft and seductive like a snake charmer's music. It may have brought out the reptile in Linda. She stood right next to me, stared into mine with hooded Cobra eyes and started hissing softly. I screamed. She moved closer, still hissing. I screamed and screamed and finally had to turn off the music and flee the family room, because I was so "creeped" out! Linda had waited nine years to strike! She had waited like a snake in the grass. And she got me good! Moral of the story: Never pinch your baby sister, and never underestimate the power of a nine year old, especially if she's wearing a snakeskin print top!

Soapy the Serpent

When I was in my thirties, while giving my daughter Amy a bath, I had another horrifying reptile experience. Amy had a "Soapy the Serpent" bath mitt that someone had given her when she was a baby. (I should take a look in her baby book to see if I can find out who gave that horrible thing to her!) We had used the bath mitt numerous times and I had never really given any thought to the fact that it was a serpent. I had finished washing her and was watching Amy play in the bath water. We used to play a game where we would throw the wet wash cloth at each other's face. Amy put the soaking wet "Soapy the Serpent" bath mitt in her hand and threw it out of the tub towards me. We both laughed. It was part of our game. I bent over to pick up the washcloth from the floor and it was then that I took a good look at it. Suddenly I realized that it was a snake! I dropped the wet washcloth and screamed. Amy looked at me questioningly. I had to leave the room and got somebody else to take over getting Amy out of the tub. I'm not sure, but I think "Soapy the Serpent" slithered out of our house after my realization of what kind of mitt it really was!

Burial at Sea!

I'm not even sure what type of reptile in this next story was, but I gave it a burial at sea. Last year I saw something light colored on my dining room floor. At first I thought it was something my cat Edi coughed up. As I got closer, I saw that it was a lizard of some kind! I figured it had come into the garage and Edi, who had been playing in the garage, had killed it and brought it to me as a present. I screamed a little and went into the kitchen to get a wad of paper towel to pick it up with and throw it in the trash. As I grabbed it, I felt it move. I can't tell you how horrifying that was for me. I walked in circles and said out loud "What should I do? What should I do?" I was shaking all over with disgust. I then walked into the bathroom and gave it a swirly send off! One flush and it was gone. Some people think I should have just released it into my yard, and I guess that would have been the "humane" thing to do. But I panicked. Besides, it was not human. It was a horrible reptile!

My Crazy School Stories

Kindergarten Kapers

I was pretty well-behaved in Kindergarten. I didn't even mind the so-called naps, because all you had to do is lay your head down on your arms for a short time. I remember lifting my head a lot and peeking around to make sure I wasn't missing out on anything. The only "crazy" things that I remember doing in Kindergarten involved getting our vaccinations, sneaking a few licks of a lollipop when I wasn't supposed to be eating it and eating the white paste.

Getting the vaccination was a scary thing for most of the kids, but not for me. I was used to getting shots and they have never really bothered me. As I got closer to the front of the line on vaccination day I heard the nurse say to each kid, "Now this won't hurt much. It will feel like a mosquito bite." I stood there silently without flinching when she thrust the needle into my upper arm, but I thought to myself that it did hurt. It hurt pretty badly. Not ever being one to remain silent when I have something important on my mind, I said loudly enough for the kids standing behind me in line to hear, "Mosquito bite? Hah! That felt more like a snake bite!" I remember being told to hush as I was gently pushed out of the way before I could say any more. I was just trying to be truthful. When my parents asked me how getting the vaccination went, I told them what I had said. I was told that sometimes it's better to keep my opinions to myself.

The other two bad things I did in Kindergarten (at least that I can remember) involved eating.

I loved eating a little paste from the jar every time we had a project that involved pasting. I can still remember the taste of that school paste. It came in a big white plastic jar. My Mom told me never to eat that again when I told her about eating it. She said it had lots of germs in it and would make me sick. I didn't care. It tasted so good! I think "Kindergarten Paste" should be a featured frozen yogurt flavor of the week. Not many young people would choose it, perhaps, but I'll bet us old people would at least give it a try for old time's sake!

One day I had a lime flavored sucker. I don't know why I had it during class. Perhaps suckers were given out in class because it was someone's birthday? All I know is that the time for eating suckers was over and we were told to put our suckers away. I didn't want to stop licking mine, even though lime has never been my first choice of sucker flavors. I don't know if I didn't want to stop licking my sucker because I liked it or if I just wanted to outsmart Miss Erna (probably the latter), so I devised a way to sneak in a few licks. It was story book time, when we could silently page through story books. I don't think anyone in Kindergarten could read yet, because back then, believe it or not, kids didn't start learning to read until they were in the first grade. We knew the alphabet, but that was about all. I held up my story book in front of my face and started licking my sucker. I remember telling the kid sitting behind me that I had found a way to eat my sucker without the teacher seeing me. I felt kind of proud of myself for outsmarting her. Just then, Miss Erna started walking towards me. So, to avoid getting "in trouble" for eating my sucker, I quickly closed the book shut...sucker and all! Too late! Miss Erna had seen what I was doing. She grabbed the book out of my hands, opened it and saw the sucker. She pulled it off, kind of tearing the page a little. As she held it up for all to see, she gently scolded me, not for eating the sucker, but for making the book all sticky and causing it to tear. I learned my lesson that day and have never, ever eaten a green sucker while reading a book that didn't belong to me! I have accidentally dribbled a little food on library books, because one of my favorite pastimes is eating something really good while reading a good book, but I never again stuck a green sucker in another book!

Kicked Out of First Grade!

I remember doing two bad things in first grade. The first one was really bad.

Our class was divided into three different reading groups according to ability: red birds, blue birds and yellow birds. While the teacher was working with one of the reading groups who sat in wooden chairs in the very front of the room, the rest of the class remained in their desks and did "busy work" on their own. One day I decided to play a trick on Susan K., a fellow red bird. She sat in the front row of the wooden chairs, while I sat in the second row. Susan was kind of a mean girl. I remember one day she stepped all over my newly white-polished, fake saddle oxfords (we couldn't afford suede), saying "New shoes, new shoes!" in an annoying sing-song voice. My shoes weren't new, but they had been newly polished, because my

Mom never allowed us to wear scuffed up shoes. I hated polishing my saddle oxfords, because the polish always dripped all over, running down to the orange soles and smudging on the black "saddle" part. Besides hurting my toes, Susan was causing me to have to polish my shoes again that night!

I really don't remember if my action was in retaliation for something Susan had done to me or if I was just being as obnoxious as "Desperately Attention-Seeking Susan" was, but I decided to pull the wooden chair out from under her just as she was about to sit. I timed it perfectly. Susan's bottom hit the floor. Her face turned fifty shades of pink as everyone laughed at her, especially me! Sister Mary P. was not laughing though. Sister helped Susan up off the floor, made sure she was not hurt and then asked who had done this. After a few seconds, I raised my hand. There was no getting out of this one! There were witnesses. Besides, I was one of Sister's favorites. I probably wouldn't really get into trouble.

Sister was furious with me. She told me how I could have crippled Susan for life and then she banished me from the room! I was so embarrassed to be standing out in the hallway, and I was so afraid of getting in more trouble when I got home. My face was fifty shades of red from shame and fear. I could look into the room because there were glass panes in the door. Every once in a while someone would look out at me and give me the "shame finger". I could almost hear them "tsk-tsk-tsk-ing" me through the glass window. But mostly everyone, including Sister Mary P., ignored me, making me feel like an outcast. I was left out and that was something that I could never tolerate well. After a few minutes I had to do something. I desperately needed attention, so I pushed my sad face and hands up against the window pane and gently "mewed" like a puppy. That got me the attention I was seeking. The kids started laughing, and Sister Mary P. probably didn't want any more distractions, so she let me back into class. I went back to my red bird perch (actually, my wooden chair) feeling properly chastised. I never pulled that stunt again. Oh wait! I did do it again, when I was in my twenties. At work I pulled the chair out from under a woman, who rightfully got very angry. She told me I could have crippled her for life!

The other bad thing I did in first grade was to draw little teats on my people in the "Ten Commandments" booklet that I made. I drew the people in Moses' day as Native Americans without tops, because I had seen them in cowboy and Indian movies. I guess I thought that's what all "unsaved" people looked like in the olden days. I have always been a pretty good artist and I try to put a lot of detail in my drawings. So I drew little teats on the men standing around Moses. I did draw a robe on Moses, because he was the holy guy, but I drew the Israelites as Native Americans. Hey! I was only in first grade and hadn't had any history classes yet.

Twisted Bones

I had Sister Mary P. for second grade, too. (I bet she was thrilled!) I know you won't believe this, but one day I was "side-talking" too much. This is what I call talking to other students while the teacher is talking. Sister Mary P. caught me side talking one too many times and decided to make an example of me. She put tape all over my mouth. It wasn't duct tape or anything that stuck very well. It was just the ordinary one-inch wide plastic tape that we use to wrap presents or hang pictures on a wall. Sister resumed her teaching and I muttered through the tape, "Look, Sister, I can talk with tape on my mouth!" I felt very proud of myself for being able to do this. Of course, everyone laughed, even Sister Mary P.

The worst thing I did in second grade was when I almost hit Sister Mary P.! We were lined up for lunch dismissal. I went home for lunch every day. I thought a boy named Bobby, who used to tease me a lot, was standing behind me in line. I felt him tug at the back of my hair and I turned around with my hand up as though I was going to smack him. I wouldn't have really hit him, but I just wanted to show him that I wasn't in the mood for his shenanigans that day. To my horror, it wasn't Bobby. It was Sister Mary P. who had tugged on my hair! I don't even remember if Sister said anything to me or if she even noticed that had almost hit her, but I was genuinely horrified. I muttered something like "I thought you were Bobby!" The dismissal bell rang just then and I walked out of the classroom as quickly as I could.

All the way home I worried that I was really going to get "in trouble" when I got back to school. I didn't tell my older sister Lois about the incident. I kept it to myself. I could hardly eat my lunch, which was unusual for me, because lunch was the only meal I liked. My Mom must have noticed that something was wrong and asked me what was the matter. I wanted to tell her so badly, but I was too scared. I thought I was probably going to be expelled, maybe even excommunicated, for almost hitting a nun! In a few hours I might not even be welcome in my own home. How could I tell my Mom?

I started crying and I told my Mom that my chest hurt and that I couldn't go back to school. My Mom asked what I meant when I said my chest hurt and I said that I had twisted bones. "Twisted bones?" my Mom asked. "Twisted bones!" my sister exclaimed with delight. She knew this was going to get interesting. I went on to explain that I often experienced pains in my chest and that it was from the bones in my chest being twisted. It happened especially when we had tomato soup for lunch. My Mom explained that there was no such thing as twisted bones and asked me what was really going on. Lois kept reciting "Twisted bones!" over and over and laughing. I was crying. My Mom finally sent Lois on her way back to school and tried to get to the bottom of the situation. I kept repeating that I had twisted bones and therefore could not go back to school. My Mom kept asking what was really wrong, but I couldn't tell her. She was adamant that if I couldn't tell her what was really wrong that I was going back to school. She gently but firmly shoved me out the front door.

I stood out on the front porch, crying and beating on the door, but my Mom kept telling me to go back to school. I begged and pleaded to no avail. My Mom wasn't budging. I could tell she was right on the other side of the door, but she wasn't opening it. Finally I had to give her a dose of her own medicine. She had once told me a story about how her own mother had forced her to go to school when she didn't want to, and how she had been locked out of the house just as I was that day. She had yelled out to the entire neighborhood, "People, my mother is crazy!" over and over. Finally, because my grandmother was so mortified, she let my Mom back into the house. So I yelled over and over, "People, my mother is making me go to school with twisted bones!" My mother kept yelling at me from the other side of the door to be quiet and to get to school. I cried, I yelled, I screamed until I finally ran out of gas. I said one more time,

"People, she's making me go to school with twisted bones!" Then I started walking. I have to hand it to my Mom. She hung tough. I don't know if I could have withstood my child yelling at the top of her lungs about how bad a mother I was.

My chest really did hurt. I thought I probably had polio or something and that my mother was being so cruel, for making me go to school anyway. I dreaded facing Sister Mary P. I planned to tell her how sorry I was the minute I saw her. I wanted her to know that I would never hit her. But I was prepared to face the music. If Sister didn't believe me, I would be kicked out of school and maybe even out of the Church. I would not be welcome in my own home. And I had twisted bones! I would probably have to spend the rest of my short, miserable life roaming the streets, holding a sign that said "Please help me. I have twisted bones!" When the twisted bones got worse, I would probably become a cripple, just like I almost caused Susan K. to be. I guess it served me right.

I entered the classroom just as the bell rang, signaling us to take our seats. I had barely made it back in time. Sister was already standing at her desk in the front of the room and started to lead us in prayer. I smiled at her as she scanned the classroom and she smiled back. Nothing was ever said about my almost hitting her, and years later it was confirmed that I had indeed been one of Sister Mary P.'s favorite students. (I ran into Sr. Mary P. several years later and she told me she had kept my Ten Commandments booklet to show to her other students. She told me she loved my creativity with the Seventh Commandment, when I drew a cowboy robbing a general store in front of a barrel that was labeled "shuger". She gave the booklet back to me. I was so touched that she had kept it all those years. I sure wish I could find it, but I think it got thrown out years ago.)

Suddenly it was like a weight had been lifted off of my chest. It didn't hurt any more. The twisted bones were gone. After school, my Mom acted like nothing had happened, at least that's the way I remember it.

So That's Where All Those Beanies Went!

I was a mess in third grade. My little sister Linda was born on February 24th and I turned nine on March 1st. I loved having a new sister, but in gaining her I lost my position as the baby of the family. It was actually a miracle that she was born. My Mom had suffered multiple miscarriages before Linda was born, which had greatly affected our whole family. I guess it was an uncertain time for me, and it all really took its toll on my scholastic life.

In third grade I suddenly became very messy at school. I stuffed everything into the bottom of my desk. When the teacher asked us to take out a certain book, all of trash in my desk spilled out from my desk and into the aisle. I started writing really sloppily too. My penmanship had been really neat in first and second grades, but was almost indecipherable in third grade. I started stammering a little when I had to read out loud in class and avoided raising my hand. This was abnormal for me. I had previously been a hand raiser and always wanted the chance to speak and even sing in front of the class. It was also the year that I developed a little habit of sniffing and scrunching my eyes closed at the same time. (A nervous tick maybe?) My family noticed this new habit and even made fun of me. They took me to our family eye doctor and he gave me glasses. (Everyone who ever went to him walked out with a pair of glasses.) The glasses did not help. They only served to make me feel more insecure. And they didn't fit comfortably, so instead of wearing them, I stuffed them under my seat along with the trash and other stuff I had accumulated at school.

To make matters worse, our third grade teacher was sick a lot and we often had substitute teachers. A substitute teacher eventually took over as our permanent third grade teacher. I didn't even care for the original one that much and the second one didn't seem to really know me. When my parents came to school to get my report card, the substitute teacher asked which child was theirs. My Mom said that her daughter was "the little girl with the blue glasses". Then she added that I sat in the third row in the third seat. The teacher said that the girl who sat there did not wear glasses. When my parents came home with my report card, I had some 'splaining to do. Not only were my grades lower than usual, the jig was up when it came to my glasses! My parents said that I had to wear my glasses, so I devised a plan to ruin them. (The glasses, not my parents!) I took a black magic marker and painted them. When my parents saw them, I innocently explained that I was just trying to make sunglasses out of them. I naively thought that my parents would just say that I didn't have to wear them because they couldn't afford to buy me new ones. I don't know if they bought me new glasses or if the magic marker came off with some special cleaner, but soon I was wearing glasses in school, hating every minute of it.

At the end of the school year we had to clean out our desks and take everything home, except for the text books. I had so much stuff that the teacher had to assign another student who lived near me to help me carry it home. My sister Lois even had an armful of my stuff. I remember the three of us walking the three blocks to my house trailing trash and stuff all over the sidewalks. When I got home, my Mom went through all of the junk that included papers that I had forgotten to bring home, half-eaten PBJ sandwiches that I had brought for breakfast, dirty handkerchiefs, pencils and crayons that had been replaced numerous times because I couldn't find them, and three beanies. Part of our school uniform was a red beanie. My Mom had to replace mine three times that year because I had lost mine. She was pretty upset with me each time I had told her that I had lost it. Lois and I laughed days later we saw some of my desk trash still trailed all over the neighborhood. It gave Lois another thing to laugh about when it came to her goofy little sister. And, me? I just felt like a total failure. Third grade was one of the worst years of my life.

My Hero, Sister Emerita

In fourth grade, Sister Emerita, a petite, red-faced Irish woman, saved me. She remains one of the heroes of my life. She took an interest in me for some reason. Somehow she looked past my awkward exterior and saw my potential. Perhaps she knew that I had been a good student in first and second grade and guessed that my inability to read aloud and my sloppy penmanship were only temporary. One day she asked me to stay inside during recess. She stayed with me and had me read aloud to her. Then she had me practice my penmanship. She stood behind me watching and telling me how to slant my letters and making me practice various strokes until the rest of my classmates returned. We did this for many days. Every day she told me I was improving. I felt my old confidence coming back as I read out loud to Sister without stumbling, and I wrote with the finesse of an artist. Then one day she asked me to stand up next to my desk and read a paragraph out loud. I still remember where I stood. My desk was in the row by the windows and was the second or third one. I remember Sister looking at me with confidence that I could do it. I read without one mistake. Everyone clapped when I finished. I felt so triumphant. That memory is burned into my brain. And even to this day, I am told that I have beautiful handwriting, so thank you from the bottom of my heart, Sister Emerita!

PS: Through God's workings, many years later my BFF Barbara and I were privileged to be with Sister Emerita just hours before she left this world. I played her favorite song, "Barcarole", on my harmonica. I had sort of learned to play in Sister Emerita's fourth grade harmonica band, but only knew this one song. Barbara said the Irish Blessing prayer out loud to Sister. I think we gave her a good send-off. There were tears coming down her cheeks as she lay there in a comatose state. I don't know if that was from my poor harmonica playing or if she felt our love. I hope the latter.

I Plead the Fifth!

I have stories about my crazy fifth grade experiences in other sections of this book, so that's all I'm going to say here on the grounds that saying anything further may incriminate me.

The Red Sea and Vincent

In sixth grade I had a lay teacher named Marilyn W. (ironic, huh?) She was young, in her late twenties, I believe. We all really liked her, but my class was mischievous, so we did something one day to see if we could drive her crazy by having the whole class wear red one day. The girls had to wear uniforms (white blouses with Peter Pan collars and navy blue skirts, but we were allowed to wear any color of cardigan sweater). We planned that all of us girls would wear red sweaters and all of the boys would wear red shirts on one designated day. The plan was as soon as Miss W. entered the classroom we would all start swaying and softly chanting. We thought maybe she would be hypnotized and collapse to the floor, thereby making it impossible for her to teach that day, or that we would drive her totally mad and she would flee the classroom in a crazed state! Either way, we were pretty sure she wouldn't be able to teach that day. After several seconds, she looked at us and told us to stop. That was it. All of our planning and all of the effort we all made to wear red that day was for naught.

Sixth grade was the year that Father R., our religion teacher, gave us an assignment, which was due on March 17th, just two days before the Feast Day of St. Joseph. Father asked us to compose a prayer to St. Joseph, his favorite and namesake saint. Well, typical of me, I forgot all about the assignment until right before Father was to come to our class for our weekly religion lesson. In about ten minutes I quickly wrote a prayer to St. Joseph in the form of a poem. I don't remember it word-for-word, but I think it started something like this.

Dear Saint Joseph
Meek and humble
Teach us how to pray
We pray to you

For a happy death
Teach us what to say

There were a few more lines, but the original paper is long gone. I was just finishing up when Father walked into the classroom. He collected our prayers and read them. After a few minutes he declared the winner. It was me! I won a beautiful rosary. March 17 is now my lucky day because of this experience and the fact that I won a speech meet in my junior year of high school on that date. St. Joseph is my favorite male saint. I brought a little St. Joseph statue to several people as they lay on their death beds and I'm sure St. Joseph helped them during that difficult part of their journeys.

In sixth grade my mind was starting to move towards creative things and it became increasingly hard for me to pay attention in class. I stopped paying attention in math class and worked on my drawing skills instead. I even played a part in driving one teacher mad that year. She actually fled our classroom, never to return. We had a sister come in to teach us music that year. She was very old. One day she appeared to be at her wit's end. She kept scolding us for the slightest things and told us she had just about had it. Suddenly, Vincent B., who sat behind me and had a crush on me, rolled up his paper, held it to my ear and blew into it really hard. It startled me so much that I loudly yelled out "Aaah!" Sister Mary Nervosa (not her real name) threw her book down, said "That does it!" With that, she ran out of the classroom, slamming the door on her way out. All of us kids were stunned into silence. Some were looking at me with a look as if to say it was my fault. I knew it wasn't. It was Vincent B.'s fault. We waited for the Principal to come in and chew us out, because surely Sister Mary Nervosa was going to tell on us. Finally, the Principal (another sister) did come to our room to chew us out. She explained that Sister Mary Nervosa was very nervous and that when someone had yelled out, it was the straw that broke the camel's back. She demanded to know who it was. All eyes were on me. The entire class was waiting to see if I would own up to it. I sheepishly raised my hand. The Principal asked me why I had done it and I replied "Vincent B. blew in my ear!" I didn't get "in trouble", but Vincent B. did. I had been the innocent conduit that time.

Seventh Grade Was No Seventh Heaven

Seventh grade is kind of a blur to me. I hated it. It was the worst year of my grade school experience. I was extra ugly that year. I developed a cowlick in the back of my hair, my face started to break out with pimples, my humped back got more humped and I completely lost whatever cuteness I had ever had that year. To make matters worse, I did not like my teacher, because she was super strict. She was constantly poking me in the back and telling me to stand up straight, which humiliated me even more than I already was for being so ugly. And of course, she taught my least favorite subject--math. I still remember having to stifle vomiting every day when Sister Mary E. said "Boys and girls take out your math books." Besides being so awkward and inept in school, I tried to play basketball and failed miserably, just as I had tried and failed at softball. I couldn't do anything right in Girl Scouts either. We often made projects that I didn't understand how to make in the first place. I didn't follow instructions and I could never complete them on my own. The only thing I was good at was dreaming up stories and poetry, acting, singing and dancing. There weren't many opportunities that year for me to shine, so I didn't.

The summer after seventh grade I was invited to a pajama party. I didn't wear a bra yet, even though I needed one. I guess my parents were in denial about how quickly I was growing up. I knew that all of the other girls who were invited to the party wore bras. In fact, I may have been the only girl about to enter eighth grade to not wear one. I had heard that sometimes girls at pajama parties put each other's bras in the freezer as a prank. I wanted my bra frozen! I also knew that when I changed into my PJ's that some girl would notice that I didn't have a bra and would make fun of me.

I didn't have any money of my own and I was afraid to ask my mom if I could please get a bra, so I took matters into my own hands. My family always kept a big bag of clothes in the basement for donating to charity when the bag was full. I had seen one of Lois' used (very used) bras in the bag. The afternoon of the party I snuck down to the basement and put on the worn out bra. It was really pointy and I needed handfuls of Kleenex to fill out the cups. I proudly wore my bra to the party, hoping someone would notice that I now wore one. All evening I kept dropping hints by saying stuff like "Gee, my bra is really digging in", and letting a strap fall down my shoulder and making a big production about righting it. When it came time to change into our pajamas, I made sure my bra was on top of my pile of clothes for all to see. Nobody froze anybody's bras that evening. In fact, all of the other girls fell asleep before I did. I was too excited to sleep. After all, I was now one of the cool girls, getting invited to a pajama party and most of all, for wearing a big pointy bra.

I continued to wear the bra for days after the party. One day at the lunch table, my Mom looked directly at my chest and with a little laugh asked me if I was wearing a bra. I said "yes". She asked me where I had gotten it and I told her that I had snatched it out of the Father Dempsey (a Catholic charitable organization) bag. She told me it was way too pointy and that if I thought I needed a bra I should have just asked her about getting one. My Mom was sick and didn't feel like going shopping that evening, so she sent my Dad on mission. He took me to Sears. We walked right past the hot cashews and into the Lady's Lingerie Department where he loudly announced that his daughter needed a brassiere. I was humiliated beyond *measure*, especially when the lady actually did have to *measure* me. I walked out of the fitting room after being gaped at and groped, carrying my very first bra. It was actually bigger in cup size than the pointy one had been. My Dad loudly announced that we needed two. I wanted to crawl under a rack of slips, I was so embarrassed, but inside I was rejoicing so much that I didn't even whine for hot cashews on the way out of the store like I usually did.

Itching Powder Ruined my Romance

In eighth grade I felt a little less ugly and a little more confident than I had in seventh grade. Even though no one declared that I was his girlfriend, I felt that a few of the boys in my class were attracted to me. At least they thought I was funny. My way of getting a boy's attention was to act silly. If you can't be the prettiest girl in class, at least be the funniest!

I liked a boy named Jerry. One day he walked me home from school and I was sure we were going to be boyfriend and girlfriend.

He had seemed interested in me and he lived within view of the front of my house, on the other side of the vault company where I used to dance. (See My Crazy Childhood Stories). Jerry was known as one of the bad boys in eighth grade. He was in the other eighth grade classroom, so I didn't get to see him much during the day, but on this particular day he asked me if he could walk me home. That's where most grade school romances started - with "the walk home".

He didn't carry my book bag, but I was very excited. I had a crush on him because he was kind of cute and also because he was kind of a bad boy. Things were going as well as expected. I was shy back then, but I think I was holding my own in a conversation. I was probably using my humor to try to charm him. But then, he looked at my feet and asked me one of the worst questions I have ever been asked while in a courting situation. "Why do you have webbed feet?" I was horrified by his question. My feet are the ugliest feet in the world according to some man in my past, but Jerry hadn't even seen my feet. I had shoes and socks on! The front part of my foot is much wider than the heel, giving it a duck foot appearance perhaps, but for him to say that to me was totally devastating. Any self-confidence I had was all swept away by his question. I clammed up after that, and by the time we reached my house, I knew this was probably the first and last time Jerry would walk me home. Our romance was short lived, that's for sure. But I continued to have a crush on this bad boy with the bad manners.

Shortly thereafter I heard that Jerry had been kicked out of school. Apparently he had put some itching powder down the history teacher's back as she sat in her desk. Graduation was just a few days away when Jerry had been kicked out of school. Despite the webbed foot conversation, he was still looking at me like he was interested and I was giving him the same look back. I had planned to dance with him at our graduation party and tell him I liked him!

The night of the party, Jerry crouched outside of a parish hall window and watched the party. I had on a beautiful aqua lace semi-formal gown and my "permed" hair looked good that evening, too. I caught a glimpse of him looking in on me while I danced with someone else. He kind of smiled at me and I shyly smiled back, thinking how much I wished he was the one I was dancing with. If he had been allowed to attend the party, I'm sure we would have danced. And I would have forgiven him if he had accidentally stepped on one of my webbed feet!

Laughing Hyena

I always say that I laughed my way through freshman year in high school. There was one day in particular that really exemplifies this. I used to get really bad cramps. One time my Mom fixed me a hot toddy to relieve the pain. She mixed a little whiskey and sugar in some warm water and had me sip it like tea. It worked. One morning in freshman year I started to get cramps early in the morning, before I left for school. I remembered how my Mom had made me a hot toddy before, so I made one for myself that morning. I am notorious for not following directions, so it should come to no one's surprise that I mixed the hot toddy a little light on the warm water and a little heavy on the whiskey. Even though I had to walk three miles to school in the cold that morning, I was warm! When class started my cramps were completely gone and I was feeling no pain whatsoever. In fact, I was feeling really good! Something struck me funny during class and I started laughing. It was one of those laughing jags that you can't stop no matter what. I was gasping for air, stomping my feet and making noises trying to stifle the laughter. Sister Mary R. asked me what was so funny and I couldn't even answer her. She looked at me as if to say "That girl is crazy!", and then resumed class. I am so glad she didn't get too close to me; otherwise, she would have smelled the whiskey on my breath. That could have been the end of my Catholic high school experience!

Another time that year, also in Sister Mary R.'s math class, I got the giggles again and couldn't stop. This time it wasn't whiskey-induced, it was just my usual silliness that started a laughing jag that wouldn't stop. Sister walked right up to me and said in front of the entire class that she was challenging me to one entire minute of no laughter. She stared me down. The whole class was staring at me. You could hear a pin drop. It felt like a showdown in the Old West. I lasted a few seconds and then, out of nervousness I'm sure, started laughing uncontrollably again. Sister declared that she had known I wouldn't be able to go one minute without laughing, called me a laughing hyena and resumed math class.

Sophomoric Smart Alec

My sophomore year was my least favorite year of high school. I hated all of my subjects except for English. We had a really cool teacher, Sister Lenore, who sometimes asked us to compose stories as a class. We started by picking a subject. One time we picked "beaver" as our subject. We told poor Sister Lenore that we chose that subject because we were a class of eager beavers, especially the girls! One by one, each student would come to the board and write one sentence that made sense in view of the subject and the sentence before it. The day that we wrote "The Beaver" was one of the highlights of my sophomore year!

I have always been stubborn, wanting to do things my way, even when my way is actually harder than the "right" way. Case in point: in sophomore year we had a big Latin vocabulary test. Instead of spending an hour the night before to memorize words, I spent at least three hours rigging up a system to outsmart the teacher!

I wore a knife-pleated navy blue uniform skirt that year. I decided to write each Latin word and its English translation on a narrow strip of paper and then pin each strip inside of the pleats of my skirt. That would enable me to kind of flip a pleat to see a vocabulary word. How I was going to remember which pleat held which vocabulary word, I do not know, but at the time I thought my idea was genius. It was time consuming and tedious to prepare though. First I had to write out each word and meaning; then use straight pins in such a way that the strips of paper would be hidden from view and that would not stick me when I sat down on them. Once that was done, I had to steam press each pleat until it would stay down and kept the strips of paper hidden. After hours of work, my skirt was a masterpiece to behold. I even thought that I should patent the idea and make a fortune on it. I could almost hear the commercials advertising my Smart Skirt. "Tired of not making good grades on those pesky vocabulary tests? Tired of studying your heart out only to freeze on the test? Try our Smart Skirt. All it takes is a little time to write out the answers, pin them to the Smart Skirt and then iron them into perfect pleats. No one but you will see the answers. Your parents and teachers will be amazed at your grades! Get your Smart Skirt, a box of straight pins and a package of paper strips right now for only $19.99. Call the phone number at the bottom of your screen now. Operators are standing by!"

The next morning, while walking the three miles to school with my BFF Barbara, I bragged about my system. I didn't mention that the straight pins were kind of scraping against my bare legs and that I was a little worried about getting caught. I just proudly explained how I was going to ace the vocabulary test and had "skirted" the whole studying issue.

During the test I recalled most of the vocabulary words on my own. Writing them on the strips of paper had actually been a kinesthetic method of studying, but I didn't know about learning styles then. I did consult my skirt during the test just to verify a few of the answers. As I deftly opened the pleats and stole glances, I noticed that some of the kids who sat behind me were watching me. I just kind of gave them a superior smile as if to say "Bet you wish you would have thought of this, you poor studying saps!" and confidently wrote my answers on the test paper. All was going well until I sensed someone standing behind my desk. I looked up and saw Sister A. M. watching me intently. She asked me what I was doing. I explained that I had devised a way to use my school uniform skirt as a study guide and that I was just situating the pleats in a way that the straight pins wouldn't stick me. She seemed to be buying it. Then she asked how long it had taken me to rig up the "study guide", and I told her about three hours. When she asked how long it would have taken me to just study in the normal way, I got it. My way had taken me three times as long. I think Sister A. M. was a little "off", because I did not get into trouble for cheating as I should have. I think she really thought that I had only used my skirt as a study tool and not as a reference during the test. I was always waiting for her to give us an "open skirt" vocabulary test, but she never did.

I have always been mischievous and still am. In sophomore year we had a priest by the name of Father William P. come into our class for a religion class once a week. He was serious and his lessons were kind of dry, so I got a little restless one day. They were renovating the school building that year, and for Father's class I sat in a desk right next to a wall. There were some exposed bricks within an inch of my desk. One of them was loose, which gave me an idea. I tore off a piece of notebook paper and scribbled a little note. I then wedged the scrap of paper into the space made by the loose brick. Right in the middle of class I raised my hand and Father P. asked me what I wanted to say. I pulled the little paper out of the wall and said, "Father, I found a note in the wall. Can I read it?" I don't think I even waited for permission. I just read the note out loud, "I was here. Signed Little Willy P.". The whole class laughed. Father was not laughing, but his eyes kind of were, I thought. I don't remember what he said in response, but I know that I did not get "in trouble" for interrupting class. I think he thought it was kind of cute.

Decades later, I finally realized that I had been working with Father P.'s sister Jennie for years. She had always talked about her brother Bill, the priest, but I had never made the connection before, even though their last names were the same. I told her the story about the note from Little Willy P. and she told me that she thought her brother, now deceased, would have certainly thought what I did was funny, but that he would not have let on, because he was a serious priest.

Another memory that I have of my sophomore year is that it was my least favorite year of high school, that I generally felt like a failure and that I begged my parents to send me to public school. They refused to allow me to go to a public school and I am glad, because I think I needed to be in a small school. Saint John's High School had a total of about 500 students when I went there, as compared to the nearby public schools that had probably 2,000 students.

DMWTJ!

"Don't Mess with the Juniors!" was our class motto that year. We were a high-spirited class. It was my favorite year in high school!

In junior year, I had Speech Class, which was my favorite high school class ever! I have already talked about how I won the Junior-Senior Speech Meet that year with a humorous speech. Mr. Kuppinger, whom we fondly called Mr. K., taught Speech class. Mr. K. recognized my comedic acting ability through this class and later cast me in one of the lead roles in our Senior Play and also in a couple of plays that he directed for my parish CYC group. I remember performing a serious speech one time in his class that turned out to be a humorous speech because of the accent that I used. He said, "Marilyn, that was supposed to be a serious speech, but you changed it to be so funny!" I got an "A". Mr. K. told me that he would make sure I won a scholarship to Webster University because of my acting abilities, but sadly, this did not pan out. I would have had to take Drama Class in my senior year in order to qualify, and due to a schedule conflict I was not allowed to take the class. Instead I was forced to take Spanish, which to this day has not helped me succeed in life like being an actress would have.

There was one speech that I had to deliver that year that I did not feel good about. It was a serious speech that I had to write myself, and it had to be based on a political subject. I chose to speak about the war in Viet Nam. I did not really understand the war or anything about the politics behind it. There was nothing funny about the subject matter whatsoever, and I really did not feel prepared to give my speech on the day it was due.

I felt so unprepared and anxious that I couldn't even eat my lunch on the day of. The speech didn't make sense, I couldn't remember half of it and I knew it would be a disaster. I didn't want to disappoint Mr. K. nor jeopardize my grade in his class. I decided that I needed more time to prepare for it so I feigned being really sick. During lunch time I went to the restroom and applied green and purple eye shadow under my eyes. Then I went up to the sister who was monitoring the cafeteria and told her I was very sick. She took one look at me and agreed that I did not look good. She sent me to the Nurse's Office. She assured me that she would send word to Mr. K. as to why I would not be in Speech class, which was right after lunch.

When I entered the Nurse's Office, the sister in charge asked me what was wrong with me, and recorded it in her big log of sicknesses. I told her that I was experiencing really bad cramps and that I felt like I was going to die. She took a look at my horribly colored face and instructed me to lie down on a cot. I laid there for a long time, feeling so relieved that I had avoided Speech class, thanking God for the reprieve and promising him and myself that I would improve my speech and rehearse it before the next Speech class. The period (class period, not my fake one) was almost over when another student came into the Nurse's Office. I heard her say that she had really bad cramps, and then she started crying from her pain. Sister mentioned that this must be the day for bad cramps and instructed the other girl to lie on the other cot. This girl was crying and moaning and carrying on so much that she was making me look bad, like I was faking it. So I stepped up my game. For every moan I heard from that girl, I saw her moan and raised her two. After not making a sound for over a half hour, now I was moaning and groaning like a woman giving birth to triplets! Soon the end-of-period bell rang signaling the end of my period, too. I jumped up from the cot, miraculously healed of my affliction. I wiped off the under-eye shadow and ran to my next class.

As it turned out, Mr. K. did not allow me to make up the missed speech after all, but my grade did not suffer. I still got an A in his class. And I deserved an A, if for nothing else, than for my stellar performance in the sick bay.

Senior Year

My senior year would have been so much more fun if not for my mother's tragic death in August, right before the school year started. I still enjoyed many things about my senior year, but naturally, it's kind of hard to have a lot of fun when you have a broken heart. Luckily, I was young and full of hope for what life had in store for me, so I was able to sometimes forget my problems and enjoy a few events, such as dating, the prom, the senior play, graduation and of course, being an upper-classman.

One of the classes I had in senior year was called Current Events. I did not (and still do not) enjoy the news (except for celebrity news) any more than I enjoyed math. There was no textbook for this class, but we were expected to read the daily newspaper and Newsweek Magazine. I read the daily newspaper, but only the comics, advice columns and the movie listings and reviews. And I read any celebrity news that was covered in the weekly magazine, but barely glanced over the other (boring) stuff like the Viet Nam War and political news.

Our teacher, Mr. S., was barely out of college. He was handsome enough I suppose, but a little too dorky for my taste. Being so young, he seemed to get embarrassed easily, especially when one girl used to hike up her skirt and sit with her legs sprawled out during class. (Yes, I did attend a Catholic school, but in spite of what the nuns and priests tried to teach us, we were still randy and raucous teenagers after all).

Mr. S. used to pass around a copy of Newsweek Magazine during class with notations he had made on some of the articles that he wanted us to read. I sat in the second desk from the front in the row on the left side of the classroom, where he always started the magazine circulation. In other words, I was the second one in the large classroom to get the magazine. One day as I paged through the magazine, I saw a picture of a pole-vaulter in action and got an idea! Underneath the picture, I printed a caption. It said, "Oh, my jock strap just ripped!" Spurred on by an appreciation of my own humor, I started writing captions under many other pictures, all of which (my captions, not the pictures) were either lewd or otherwise inappropriate. As the magazine reached the back of the classroom, ripples of laughter could be heard. This gave me great satisfaction. When the magazine had gone about halfway through the classroom, Mr. S. began suspecting that something wasn't right. He demanded to know what was so funny. Then he demanded to see the magazine.

It was handed over and Mr. S. sat at his desk in silence as he leafed through it.

You could hear a pin drop as he paged through the magazine. If anyone suspected me as the one who had written the innapropriate remarks, all they would have had to do is look at me and be assured of my guilt. There were beads of sweat on my brow and my face was probably beet-red. Finally, Mr. S. stood up, magazine in hand, and faced the class. He asked "Who is responsible for this?" I waited a few seconds, remembering those awful times in grade school when I had gotten kicked out of class for misbehaving and wondering if this punishment would be even worse, before finally raising my hand. Mr. S. looked at me and slowly started to smile. Then, holding up the Newsweek Magazine, he said, "This is some of the funniest stuff I've ever seen!" Then he added "But don't do it again, okay?" Class resumed and I breathed a sigh of relief.

I didn't do it again; at least not while I was in high school. But I can't say I haven't written funny, even lewd and otherwise inappropriate captions in other books and/or magazines. If ever you are in a public library or look through a used book at a flea market, and you see this type of notation, maybe, just maybe, it was me.

Oh, and feel free to make lewd or otherwise inappropriate notations in this book. Ha ha!

UMSL - University of Marilyn Still Laughing!

Going to the University of Missouri-St. Louis right after graduating from high school was a waste of time and money for me. I didn't know what I wanted to be when I grew up. I still hated studying. I still liked having fun above anything else. I was there to find a boyfriend or two, to party, dance and play cards; and I was there because I wasn't ready for life in the real world yet!

Freshman Fun

In between classes, I hung out in the student lounge in Benton Hall, the only building on campus with classrooms at the time. It was a big open room with sliding glass doors and big windows overlooking Bugg Lake (named for Chancellor Bugg). We had a lot of good times in that lounge. One day my friend Bill fell asleep like he did nearly every day. He worked a full time job at the bank (where I eventually worked with him) at night and didn't get much sleep. I decided to give him "the hot foot" to see if that would wake him. With all eyes on me, I ceremoniously stuck several matches in the space between the leather uppers and the soles of his shoes. When they were all in place I quickly lit each one. Everyone in the lounge was watching and laughing. Soon Bill started to feel the heat and stomped one of his feet a couple of times. There was more laughter, but then the laughter subsided. We were sort of scared that he would get burned or that we would start a big fire. Somebody ran and got some water and we doused out the flames. Bill was just starting to wake up when the water hit him. He took it good-naturedly, but that is one of my pranks that could have been disastrous. Some of the guys used to like to light farts with hairspray in the student lounge also. It's a good thing they weren't doing that the day that I lit Bill's shoes up!

We liked to play cards in between classes. That's where I learned to play "Hearts". We played every day. Sometimes if I was involved in a game of Hearts, and it was time for class, I would skip the class in order to continue playing. Soon I was skipping classes in order to play, not just because I was in the middle of a good game. And eventually, I even dropped one class because it interfered with my card playing. At the end of my first semester, my report card was sent to my Dad. He wasn't even paying for my schooling. A small scholarship and my own money were paying for it entirely. I never understood why the report card was addressed to my Dad and not to me. I came home from school one day and my Dad was in the kitchen reading the mail. He held up my report card and asked what in the heck was going on. It said I had missed one of my classes 99 times. It was the class that I had dropped. My Dad just kept shaking his head and repeating "Ninety-nine absences". I tried to explain that 99 indicated that I had missed all of the classes, because I had dropped it, and I pointed out that there hadn't even been 99 classes anyway, but my Dad was not buying it. He was so hung up on the 99 absences that he barely said anything about my grades, which were mostly C's. He didn't know that I had spent more time in the student lounge than I had in any of the classrooms that semester. Unfortunately I do not even remember how to play Hearts now, but if I had attended each and every Ancient History class, I'll bet I wouldn't remember anything about that subject either.

My Grades Weren't the Only Things Sliding!

One day we had a freezing rain and the steep hills between the parking lot and Benton Hall were very treacherous. Hordes of students were walking down both hills. I was at the top of the steeper of the two hills (not to be confused with the Touhills) with my grade-school friend Debbie who had driven me to school that day. I had slippery bottomed shoes on and I started sliding. My body twisted and I slid the whole way down the hill on my stomach. My knees were scraped and bleeding, but what was really hurt was my pride. There were at least two hundred students walking towards Benton Hall when it happened. My friend Debbie came down to where I had landed and tried to help me up, but she was laughing so hard that she kept dropping me. Everyone was staring. Some people were laughing. Debbie couldn't stop. I kept trying to get up but kept slipping back down. Finally, one of my grade school classmates who had been walking down the other hill, which was about a half of a football field away, came over and helped me up. I was grateful of course, but embarrassed that so many people, even those on the other hill, had seen me make a spectacle of myself. Earl said he had noticed the commotion and when he saw that it was me, thought to himself that he had better help me out for old time's sake.

I went to my Psych class after a trip to the restroom to try to wipe off some of the blood and mud from my light blue skirt. I took my usual seat next to a girl that I always sat with. She was from a wealthy part of town and always had expensive-looking clothes on. I on the other hand, didn't have many clothes, and the ones I did have were certainly not expensive. Even though she was very friendly with me, I often caught her giving my clothes the once-over. That day I had on one of my best outfits that I normally didn't wear to school. It was a light heather blue cardigan and a matching A-line wool skirt. It was ruined after my fall. I was upset about the fact that I had ruined my best skirt and had just made a spectacle of myself in front of the whole school. I hoped no one would notice the blood and mud on my skirt. My friend looked at my skirt and said with a look of horror on her face, "Oh, my, what an unusual pattern on your skirt!" I was in no mood for her judgment that day, so I said "Oh, haven't you heard? It's a new fashion craze called mud and blood!" I opened my book and looked straight ahead. I think that was the last time we talked. I wonder if she went shopping after class that day, looking for something in "mud and blood".

My Crazy Travel Stories

There's Something Wrong with the Plane!

It was August 15, 1969, six days after Charlie Manson's followers had murdered Sharon Tate and friends, and I was going to California on my first airplane ride ever! I was very excited, but a little scared because of the murders.

Terry, my fiancé, was in boot camp at Fort Ord in Monterey. It was a middle of the night flight, and I had just worked from 4:00 to midnight at the bank, but I was too excited to be tired. I boarded the plane, taking in my surroundings with awe. I easily found the row listed on my boarding pass. I was disappointed to see that my seat was on the aisle. Since this was my first flight, I wanted to be next to the window. There was a man in that seat. His eyes were closed, but that didn't stop me. I brazenly tapped him on the arm and said, "Sir, this is my first flight. Could I please have the window seat?" He muttered something and moved to another row.

I'll never forget the thrill of my first ever take-off! It was how I imagined being shot out of a cannon might feel! Once we got to the right altitude, the other passengers closed their eyes, but not me. I didn't want to miss a thing. I looked out the window for the entire flight, imagining where we might be. When the pilot announced that we were finally flying over California, I noticed lights on the horizon. Were they the lights of Hollywood, I wondered. Would I soon see the big "Hollywood" sign? Now I know that we were still flying too high to be able to see anything, but at the time, I really thought the lights were from some big Hollywood complex. And it crossed my mind that they might even be the lights at the Tate residence! Surely they would have lights on if they were investigating the crime scene. Why they were probably recreating the crime right at this very moment! I strained my eyes to see if there were detectives swarming the place. I wished we could get a little closer, so I could see what was going on. Then maybe I'd even be able to see blood stains on the lawn! A lot of time went by and we were still hovering over the crime scene. It wasn't normal to hover in one spot like this, was it? I wondered what was going on, so I hailed a stewardess.

I said to her in a low voice, "I don't mean to alarm anyone, but do you know that we have not moved for the last half hour?" She looked at me like I was crazy and asked me why I thought this. I stated emphatically, "See those lights on the landscape? I haven't taken my eyes off of them for a half hour. We haven't moved!" I wondered how a trained stewardess could be so stupid as to not realize what was going on. Or was she purposely playing dumb so as not to alarm me or the other passengers that something was really wrong? She looked at me like I was deranged and said in a sarcastic voice, "Those are the lights at the end of the wing, you moron!" Her mouth didn't say "you moron", but the expression on her face did.

I still remember the thrill of the landing of my first flight. The way I remember it, first we swooped down towards the ocean and then kind of circled back towards the airport. At first I thought we were going to land right next to the ocean. I believe the ocean is about twenty-five miles from downtown LA, so it is quite possible that I did see it. But as whacky as I am, who knows if I really did see the ocean that night.

I had plenty of time, hours in fact, to kill between landing and having to get on the next plane to San Francisco. From San Francisco I was going to take a bus to San Jose and then a cab to Monterey. I decided to hunt for movie stars. Surely the airport would be swarming with them. I searched faces for celebrities, but saw none. Then I saw a coffee shop and decided to sit in there and have breakfast. Maybe I'd sit next to a movie producer or director who would strike up a conversation with me and ask me to be in a movie. I remembered that Lana Turner or some Hollywood star had been discovered at the counter of Chasens, or was it the Brown Derby? So, why couldn't a would-be actress from St. Louis be discovered in the airport coffee shop?

I ordered a donut and coffee and just sat at the counter taking it all in. No one spoke to me or really even looked at me. I still remember what I had on. It was a blue and green watch-plaid sleeveless empire waist dress that was really short. My long legs were bare and kind of tan and I had on two and a half inch heels, which were flattering. I was proud of my legs back then and often got compliments on them. So I crossed my legs, kind of hiked up my skirt just a little, and subtly swung my exposed leg back and forth, hoping to attract a casting agent or someone who would realize that I had star potential. I got nothing. I was about to get up and start walking around the airport to troll for movie stars again, when I heard an announcement. "Will Paul Peterson please come to Gate X. Paul Peterson, Gate X, please." That was music to my ears. Paul Peterson, the actor who had played Donna Reed's son Jeff Stone on the Donna Reed Show until 1966 was in the house! All I had to do was find Gate X. I would introduce myself to Paul, tell him I was his biggest fan, and before you know it, I'd be reading for the part of his girlfriend in a spin-off of the Donna Reed Show. I asked someone where Gate X was and determined that it was too far away, so I decided to concentrate on being at the right place at the right time to board the next plane.

Somewhere along the line I found out that the flight to San Francisco had been cancelled due to fog and that the airline was taking us to San Jose by bus. I thought this was perfect! I'd be able to really see California. Maybe we'd pass right by a hippy commune or something. I think it was about 8:00 or so in the morning when we finally boarded the bus. I sat next to a young lady named Cathy. She lived in Washington State and was on her way to Fort Ord to visit her new husband. I didn't understand why she had to go south and then back north to get to Fort Ord, but then again, I didn't know much about air traffic, routes or really anything about flying. She and I talked all the way from LA to San Jose. I really liked her. She told me that she was going to be staying on base along with some other wives. Since I was not an Army spouse, I was not eligible to stay on base. I was staying in the Flamingo Hotel in Monterey. Cathy and I agreed to share a cab once we got to San Jose. I remember being dropped off from the cab first. I felt grown up and a little nervous to be checking into a motel by myself. I also felt a little embarrassed because of the name of the motel. It sounded kind of tacky.

I remember walking from the motel to a Denny's Restaurant. As I walked down the road, I felt such freedom! I was in California! And I loved being on my own with no one from the establishment judging my every action! Maybe I'd stay in California and become a hippy since the Hollywood thing hadn't worked out. I knew I really wouldn't, but it was fun to pretend that afternoon. I had never heard of Denny's before. I sat at the counter and ordered a big chef salad. I had never had a big salad before. It felt so Californian!

On the way back to the motel I shopped in a little dress boutique and bought myself a really, really short mini-dress. It was so short that when I later showed it to my Dad he said "That is NOT a dress. You better tell me that's a top!" I told him that it was a top and actually wore it over my bell-bottoms when I left the house. Then I removed the bell-bottoms as a co-worker and I rode to work, and wore it as a dress. I remember that it was too short for me to be able to do my job that night. Just the slight motion of reaching for the tray of checks hiked up my skirt so that my underwear showed. I worked with mostly boys and got quite a few comments on my new California mini-dress that night. I finally told my supervisor that the only part of my job that I could do that night was the part where I sat at a desk. That was the only time I wore that dress as a dress. From then on I wore it over my bell-bottoms and kept them on. My California "top" was purple, green and orange horizontal stripes with a zipper in front that had a big ring as the zipper pull. I wore it with my bright Kelly green corduroy elephant leg bell bottoms. It was one of my favorite outfits ever!

The Not So First Class Flight Home

After getting married in October, 1969, I joined Terry in Germany that December. Terry and I only lived in Germany together for about seven months when Terry was ordered to go to Viet Nam. The trip home to the States was probably the worst trip of my life, thanks largely to our Siamese cat Charlie. I left Germany on a Wednesday afternoon and didn't get home to St. Louis until Saturday afternoon! There was a lot of scratching, bloating and general mayhem in between.

Terry drove me and Charlie to the airport on a Wednesday morning, even though my flight didn't leave until early evening. It was a two hour drive to the airport in Frankfurt. Foolishly, we did not have a travel cage for Charlie. I guess we naively thought he would sit docilely on my lap for the entire trip to the airport. Charlie freaked out on the autobahn! He flew back and forth from the front seat to the back seat like he was possessed. He kept jumping onto Terry's head while Terry was trying to drive. I did my best to restrain Charlie, but to no avail. I don't know how many times he jumped onto my head and dug his claws into my scalp. When we got out of the car after a couple hours of hard battle, I had bloody scratches all over my face and arms, my hair looked like I had combed it with an eggbeater and my nylons (precursors to pantyhose) were ripped to shreds. We dropped Charlie off at the Pan Am Airlines terminal for his flight, and then Terry took me to the hangar where the Army plane was waiting for me. Terry's military direct flight to St. Louis was scheduled for Friday evening, so he went back to the base in Bamberg and our apartment in Litzendorf to wrap things up.

It was an overnight flight of at least six hours. When I finally arrived at JFK Airport in New York the next day I looked like a casualty of war. Not only was I all scratched up and disheveled from the car ride from hell, but being almost eight months pregnant, I was swollen like I had been stung by a thousand bees. In fact I looked like a big, bloated bumble bee, because I was dressed in a bright yellow maternity jumper that may have fit when I was six months along, but was now really stretched across my swollen belly.

I had two pieces of heavy luggage that I had to carry myself. I didn't know about luggage carts or airport motorized vehicles. I had been limited to a total of forty pounds of luggage for the trip to Germany, and I was bringing all of that back plus some stuff I had acquired in the eight months that I lived there. I had to go to the Pan Am terminal to pick up Charlie and then get the two of us to the TWA terminal for the flight to St. Louis. I had no idea how far away Charlie was. I schlepped the fifty or so pounds of luggage through the terminal and had to keep stopping to rest. I didn't think I could take one more step. I was exhausted! People were passing me by without a glance. I had heard that New Yorkers were cold and uninvolved, but I thought it was disgraceful that out of the hundreds of people passing me by, no one offered to help me. As I struggled to continue moving forward with great difficulty, I suddenly lost my cool. I slammed my two suitcases to the ground and shouted at an innocent man who happened to be passing by. I said, "You! Pick up my bags!" I must have looked so bizarre that he was afraid of me. He picked up my bags and carried them all the way to the information desk of the TWA terminal. That's where I learned that the Pan Am terminal was clear across the airport. I would have to take a cab to get there.

I walked outside of the terminal to hail a cab. Several cabs stopped and asked where I was going. When I said I was going to the Pan Am terminal, they sped off. Finally a policeman came up to me and asked what was going on. When I told him that no cabbie would take me to the terminal, he explained that the cabbies wouldn't take me because they wanted a longer trip so they could make more money. He told me this was against the law. He then hailed a cab for me and told the driver to take me to the Pan Am terminal. The cabbie gave me a dirty look and begrudgingly drove me to the terminal. I don't remember if I gave him a tip or not. I was pretty naïve and unsophisticated, so I may not have known to do so. I probably ruined that guy's day.

Once I arrived at the terminal I learned that Charlie would be transported to the TWA flight by airport personnel and that I didn't have to carry him there myself, so my cab ride had been unnecessary. I could have had TWA call Pan Am to make that arrangement. I also learned that there was not enough time by then for Charlie and me to get back to TWA in time for our scheduled flight. I didn't know what to do. They suggested that I keep Charlie in their care while I arranged for another flight. I went to the Pan Am Information desk with tears in my eyes and asked if they could help me. I remember that the lady at the desk had a thick foreign accent. She called TWA to ask about the next flight to St. Louis. She found out that there were no more flights to St. Louis that day and the flights on Friday were all booked. The next flight I could get on was on Saturday at noon and only first class tickets were available. She said she would help me and Charlie get booked on that flight.

While she was helping me, she was interrupted by a Hispanic woman who seemed to be in dire straits. Wanting to help the woman, but apparently not understanding Spanish, the Pan Am agent asked those of us standing around the information desk if any of us knew Spanish. Wanting to be helpful because the Pan Am agent was being so helpful to me, I raised my hand and proudly said "I do!" (After all, I had taken a total of four years of Spanish in high school and college.) The Hispanic woman seemed to be in a panic as she spouted off in Spanish. I did not understand a word she was saying. I continued to listen to the words that were coming out of her mouth, but they were words that I didn't understand. To show I was listening I wanted to say "yes", but instead of saying "si" I kept saying "ya." Being in Germany and speaking a little German for the past eight months had apparently really mixed me up so that I could no longer speak Spanish! (Truth be told, I could never converse in Spanish very well.) I searched my brain for questions in Spanish that I could ask in order to understand what the woman needed, but all I could think of was "Donde es la biblioteca?" (Where is the library?) This question didn't seem to be particularly helpful in this situation, so I threw up my hands in surrender and told the Pan Am agent that I couldn't help after all. I explained that my eight months in Germany must have messed with my multi-linguistic skills.

The female agent must have been done with me, so she had a male agent take over. I told him that I didn't have any money other than a few dollars to pay for a cab back to the TWA terminal. I couldn't afford a hotel or any meals. I pictured myself spending the next two nights on the airport floor with my head propped up against my suitcases, hungry and exhausted, but unable to sleep for fear that some mean New York gang members would rob me of my last few dollars. He asked if I knew anyone in New York that I could stay with since my flight wasn't for two days. I started to cry. I didn't know anyone in New York City. At this point, the male agent looked as desperate to figure out what to do with me as I was. All of a sudden a light bulb came on in my head and I realized that my brother-in-law lived in upstate New York. Maybe he could pick me up and let me stay at his house! The agent offered to call my brother-in-law for me. The trouble was, I didn't have my brother-in-law's phone number or exact address. The agent looked in the phone book and found the phone number. He talked to my sister-in-law, Ann, and explained the situation. He arranged for her to come and get me. It would be a couple of hours, but she would be there as soon as she could, the agent explained to me.

I didn't really know my brother-in-law or sister-in-law. I had talked to them on the phone a few times, had seen pictures of them and their kids and heard all about them for years, but had never met them in person. What a way to finally meet! Poor Ann had to drive about fifty miles to the airport with her three little girls, since Bud was still at work. I can only imagine what Ann was thinking when she first saw me. By then I was even more swollen and disheveled, and I had tear streaks on my face and was shaking from hunger and fatigue. After the long drive to their house, we sat down to dinner. Ann had made a roast beef with mashed potatoes. As she fixed my plate, she admonished me not to eat too much because of the salt content of the meal and the fact that I was already alarmingly swollen. Ann got a phone call from my brother-in-law while we were eating. When she left the room to take the call, I warned my three little nieces not to tell on me as I loaded up my plate with "seconds".

The next morning Ann had to go grocery shopping and insisted I go with her. My feet were so swollen from two days of travel and all of the salt I had eaten that I couldn't get my shoes on. I wanted to go barefoot, but Ann insisted that I wear a pair of her shoes. She wore a larger size shoe than I did, but I barely got into them. Her shoes were long and pointy and I remember thinking that I looked like I was on skis. I still wore the outfit that I had worn since leaving Germany, since my suitcases were locked and I had somehow locked the keys inside. (We had to bust open the suitcases and ruin them when I finally arrived in St. Louis). So I went to the store looking like a freak: a great big fat bumblebee with scratches all over and wearing skis!

On Saturday morning I finally boarded the TWA flight to St. Louis. Charlie was safely tucked into the underbelly of the plane, having been delivered from the Pan Am terminal. It was day four of traveling and I was still wearing the damned bumblebee outfit. Luckily the swelling in my feet had gone down enough so I could get into my own shoes. As I walked through the first class section trying to find my seat, I noticed that all of the other first class travelers were men. They glanced up from their Wall Street Journals to see a very nervous young lady who looked like she had been run over by a truck. I felt so self-conscious and intimidated that I decided not to sit in first class. I kept walking until I found an empty seat in the economy section. When the stewardess checked my ticket and informed me that I was in the wrong section, I asked her if I could stay where I was. I explained that I did not feel comfortable in the first-class section with "all those business men". She looked at me like I was nuts, but she let me stay there. While they were probably eating filet mignon on china and sipping champagne in first class, I was eating dried-out chicken on a little plastic dish, sipping a Coke and thinking how glad I was to finally be going home. Later, when I told Terry how I had sat in economy, he threw a fit. "Who pays for a first class ticket and then sits in economy?" he asked. A self-conscious, inexperienced, scared and exhausted, giant, pregnant bumble bee, that's who!

Hey, Donkey _____!

In the early 90's when I worked for a local bank as a Telephone Banking Department Manager I was allowed to attend a few telecommunications conventions. I signed up for one in Chicago and asked my friend who worked as one of my department supervisors to accompany me. Since I had attended several sessions before this trip, I decided to blow off the part of the seminar that was redundant to me. Karen and I had a nice afternoon in Chicago, eating, shopping and sight-seeing. We rode the El and made our way through the urine smells of the underground. We saw plenty of derelicts and even some vigilante group members patrolling the underground. As we made our way back to the hotel at the end of our day, we stopped by a neighborhood store for some "party" items, since once we got back to the hotel, we would be in for the night. We bought several scandal magazines, Diet Dr. Peppers, chips and even a pack of Virginia Slims. Neither one of us smoked, but we felt so free and a little mischievous.

It was late afternoon when we got back with our "wild party" goods and decided to sit out on the balcony for a bit. We puffed away on Virginia Slims as we read the magazines and just relaxed. Even though I was a former smoker and had asthma, I smoked that day as a way to assert myself as an emancipated woman, echoing the slogan of Virginia Slims, "You've come a long way, baby!" Karen and I puffed and laughed over something that I don't even remember. I started coughing and wheezing a bit. The sun was going down and it was getting chilly with the wind whipping around our eighth floor balcony. We decided to go inside. I tried to open the sliding door, but could not. I tried several times, thinking it was just a heavy door, when all of a sudden I realized with a sickening feeling that the door was locked! I gave the news to Karen. She stood on a chair that she had pushed right up to the railing in an attempt to look into the room next door and try to get someone's attention. When I looked up and saw her teetering on the chair I screamed. My scream startled her so that she almost fell off the chair. Luckily she did not. Then we both started laughing so hard that I was really wheezing.

We continued to shout to our neighbors, but the room was dark and it eventually seemed unlikely that we were going to rouse anyone. So I started yelling down to the ground where there were a few people walking on a pathway from the convention center to the hotel. I yelled at several groups, but no one gave any sign of hearing me. The wind may have been carrying my voice in another direction, we were eight floors above them and there was a noisy generator competing with my voice. I have never been accused of talking too softly. In fact one of my neighbors, referring to when I called my children in for supper, once remarked that I was the loudest woman he had ever heard. Still, no one seemed to be hearing me.

It was getting dusky and increasingly colder. Karen and I were no longer laughing. We were actually close to tears. I started to feel like I was going to have an asthma attack, and my inhaler was in the room. The passersby were fewer and farther in between, too. Karen continued looking into the neighbor's room and searching for some signs of life, while I kept watch for another passerby. Finally I saw a fat man dressed in what looked like a custodian uniform walking on the path. I mustered up every last bit of oomph in my voice and called out to him. "Hey, you! We're on the eighth floor and we're locked out!" I yelled this several times. Nothing. Finally, in total frustration I yelled out, "Hey, Donkey _____! We're on the eighth floor and we're locked out!"

And wouldn't you know it. He looked up. I repeated my message, only this time leaving out the way that I had initially addressed him. He motioned that he had heard. I then yelled out our room number and he nodded. Karen and I expected him to appear at our balcony door in a few minutes. Karen was still peering into the neighbor's room in case someone was in there, when all of a sudden she let out a blood curdling scream. There in the window of the neighbor's room was a huge grey blob! It took us a second, but we finally figured out that it was the custodian's belly pressed up against the glass. He opened the door and assured us that he would have our door opened in a minute. I guess he had misunderstood the room number that I had yelled down to him, or knowing me, perhaps I had given him the wrong room number. Either way, help was on the way. Ole Donkey _____ was at the rescue!

In a minute, Old Donkey _____ had opened our balcony door from inside and we gathered up our party goods and ran into the safety of our room. Once inside and after thanking Ole Donkey _____ profusely, I thought about the situation and got mad. I told Ole Donkey _____ that there should not be the kind of lock that automatically locks when you close the balcony door. He explained that it was for safety reasons that it automatically locked, because some people might accidentally leave it unlocked at night. "But what if children were out on the balcony?" I asked. He humbly agreed that this could be a problem without saying that there should never be unattended children in a hotel room in the first place. When he left, the more I thought about it, I got myself quite worked up. What if I had suffered a full blown asthma attack while locked out there? (Never mind the fact that I was smoking). What if Karen had fallen off of the balcony? What if we had had to spend the night out there in the cold? I decided to call the front desk and complain. I told Karen that I thought we deserved a complimentary weekend from the hotel for all of our trouble. You would think that we would question ourselves about staying in that hotel again, but the prospect of a free weekend in Chicago took precedence.

When I reached the front desk clerk I told our story, emphasizing that Karen could have fallen off of the balcony and fallen to her death and that I could have died from an asthma attack from all of the stress. After I finished my tirade, the clerk (female) said in an uninterested tone of voice, "Ma'am, what do you want me to do?" I told her that I was seeking fair compensation and I suggested the free weekend stay. She said that she could not do that and then offered to send some hot tea to our room for our trouble. "Tea? You're offering us tea, when we could have both been killed?" "Yes, Ma'am, I'd be happy to send up some hot tea." I told her she could keep her hot tea and slammed down the phone. I did not want "Tea and Sympathy" I wanted a free weekend in "my kind of town"!

Alarming Stays in Boston!

When I worked for a different financial institution in the '90's I traveled to Boston a couple of times, staying at a fancy hotel. Both stays included middle-of- the-night false fire evacuations. The first one that I experienced occurred around 1:00 AM. I was not asleep when the alarm sounded, otherwise I might not have heard it. I am a deep sleeper, but that night I was wide awake from too much chocolate! I have never been able to resist hotel honor bars even when they charge $5.00 for a pack of M and M's. That night I had M & M's, a mini bottle of Bailey's, a Snickers Bar (which I don't really even like) and God knows what else. I was full of alcohol and chocolate, not conducive to sleeping. When the alarm sounded I knew I had to quickly evacuate, and I knew I wasn't supposed to even stop to change out of my nightgown. I hesitated just long enough to grab my purse and room card key before running out of the room in my nightgown. My co-worker, Janet, had also fled her room wearing only her nightgown. The hotel was on a very busy street and I felt like everyone in downtown Boston was gaping at us in our nightgowns. The next morning our boss told us that this hotel was known for its middle-of-the-night fire alarms, so that's why he hadn't even bothered to evacuate.

The second time that I stayed at that same hotel we had a middle-of-the-night fire alarm go off. I had left a pair of jeans and a tee shirt on the floor next to my bed just in case my boss had been right about this hotel. This time I was a little calmer. I took the time to get dressed and grab my purse. I thought this was just another false alarm until I opened my door. I didn't see any smoke or flames, but what I did see was bedlam. There were ten to twelve Chinese men all dressed in look-alike pajamas running down the hall in single file and muttering what sounded to me like "Chin, chan, chow, chee, chan!" in urgent but calm voices.

I felt that I had better take the lead, because some of these men looked scared and after all, they were in a foreign country and may not have known what to do. It was my responsibility to lead them to safety. I took my place at the front of their line and motioned for them to follow me. I "ran-walked" ahead of them and headed for what I thought was the stairwell. When we got to the end of the hallway I saw that the door that I had assumed led to the stairwell was just a closet door. I motioned for them to stop, turn around and follow me again. The "Chin, chan, chow, chee, chan" got a little louder and more urgent as I finally led them to the real stairway. Even though I was a little scared, I had to laugh to myself at what it must look like to see me leading these PJ-clad men. Once again we were told to return to our rooms and that the alarm had been a false one. Some of the little men thanked me before returning to their rooms. Or at least, I think they were thanking me. They may have been cursing me for leading them astray for all I know. Does anyone know what "Thank you" is in Chinese? Does it begin with an "F"?

Out the Window!

In the late '90's I was working for a big bank as a Private Banking Trainer and was new to the team. It was during the winter and my team had to go to a two day training session in Charlotte,

N.C., the national headquarters of the bank. We stayed in an old historic hotel where the training sessions were also held. I arrived in the late afternoon of the day before the training began. When I checked into my room I could tell that someone had smoked in the room. The residual smoke was so strong I knew I could not stay. The hotel promised to move me into another room as soon as possible. It was time to go to dinner with my teammates. When we got back to the hotel a few hours later, I was told that I could move my things into a new room. It was kind of a pain to have to move to a new room at night, since we had to be up early the next day, but I figured it was worth the effort to avoid the smoke and get a good night's sleep. I still had trouble getting to sleep, though, because the new room was too hot.

The next morning as I got dressed, the heat in my room was so unbearable that I had to pause in the process and call the front desk to complain. They assured me that someone would come to my room after the breakfast rush (while I would be in class) and adjust the heat for me. During a break I came down to my room to check the heat situation and it seemed to be okay. After the training ended for the day I came into my room to get changed for dinner. When I opened the door I was hit with a blast of heat. It was even hotter than it had been when I had first complained. I called the front desk to ask if they had tried to adjust the temperature in my room, and if they had, I was going to ask to be moved to another room. It was that unbearable. I was informed that they had done all that they could to make the temperature more comfortable in my room and also informed me that they would send someone to my room to carry my things to yet another new room. They explained that it might be awhile before they could send someone, and that if I was that hot, I should just open a window. I had taken off most of my clothes by this time, and was wearing just my bra and pantyhose. I decided to take their suggestion to open a window before I put the rest of my clothes back on.

There was a beautiful antique desk sitting right in front of the only window in the room. It was too heavy for me to move out of the way, so I cleared off the top of the desk and knelt on it to reach the window latch. The curtains were open, but my room faced a convention center across the street and there were no windows on that part of that building. I didn't see anyone on the street, so as I knelt on the desk and struggled with the window latch I felt fairly confident that no one could see into the room. And I thought "Too bad if they could see me!" We Yankees can't take this much heat! I finally got the latch open, but was still having a very difficult time opening the window itself. It had been painted shut. Now, keep in mind that I had on slippery panty hose, my skin was wet with sweat and the desk was highly polished. My back was being strained and my shins were getting sore from kneeling. With every ounce of effort I could muster, I pulled the window handle really hard. The window suddenly flew fully open. I slid across the shiny desk and nearly flew out of the third floor window in my underwear!

Can you imagine reading the headlines of the Charlotte Observer (or whatever they call their newspaper) the next morning? "Middle-Aged Midwestern Matron Hurls to Death Wearing Only Bra and Pantyhose!" There would be an accompanying photo showing me splayed out in the street, face down, with all of my upper back fat and flat butt exposed to the world! The caption would say

"Charlotte Convention Center event goers gaze at the ghastly sight as they exit, while street workers try to scrape up the unsightly debris in time for the evening's event at the Center." I am so grateful to have been spared that embarrassing demise.

As I recovered from my near death experience there was a rap on my door. It was someone from the hotel housekeeping staff offering to help me open the window. From the other side of the door the person explained how the windows tend to stick and I might require help with it. I politely declined the offer, stating that I had managed it myself, and that I no longer wished to change rooms. I was too exhausted!

My team members were all southern belles and were used to being pampered, because as they often said, trainers work so hard. On the previous evening while we were at dinner, they dominated the dinner conversation with their travel "war stories" in order to let me know (in case I didn't realize) that I was new and not nearly as experienced as they were. But that night I had a "war story" of my own to tell. How many of them had nearly flown out of a third floor hotel window? They laughed as I described my near-death experience, but they still had plenty more of their own "war stories" to tell. None of their stories were funny. They were mostly accounts of how a certain hotel did not have a bath tub (how barbaric!) or how a particular restaurant did not offer any fine imported wines (how unacceptable!) or how a hotel's towels were too nubby for their delicate lily-white arses!

I never did "fit in" on this team, and soon I was asked to move to another department. Instead I left the bank.

Grub Burgers, FEMA Trailers and the Big Flash

My daughter Amy and I went to Gulf Shores, Alabama for the first time in September, 2009. We rented a two-bedroom condo in Gulf Shores from Saturday to Saturday. Amy drove and I attempted to keep us on route by referring to a notebook where Amy had written the driving directions. We took off from O'Fallon, MO on a Friday morning, around 8:30, I believe.

We drove and drove and started to get really hungry around noon, but we were on a long stretch of road that had nothing but trees for quite a long way. Our stomachs were so empty by about two o'clock that they were starting to digest themselves. (That's my way of saying we were very hungry and not all that picky about what we were going to eat.) We finally saw a restaurant. It was the Scenic Café at the side of the road somewhere in Tennessee, shortly before you cross over into Mississippi. It was a small, old structure with lots of old stuff lying around outside. We weren't picky, though, just very hungry.

When we walked in I felt like I was walking into a "Deliverance" type movie set. There was an old man sitting at the counter talking to the cook behind the counter. They both eyed us. I couldn't tell if they were eyeing us suspiciously or sizing up their victims. We were told to seat ourselves at one of the few tables. Soon a weird-looking young man came over to take our orders. We noticed that it was just about two o'clock and the place was about to close. We were grateful at the time that the young man had offered to serve us and had not turned us away. (Looking back, he would have done us a big favor if he had quickly hung up the "Closed" sign as soon as we pulled in.) The sign outside of the café and the menu both referred to their famous grub burger. I asked the young man what a grub burger was.

He proudly explained that during WWII when meat was scarce, people in those parts had added a lot of cornmeal to their hamburgers and then fried them in lard. He said they were delicious. People loved grub burgers so much that even well after the restrictions of WWII were over, they continued to serve them.

Feeling adventurous and ravenous, I decided to give grub burgers a try. Amy ordered fries with hers, but soon lost her appetite for them when she saw the cook using the same grease to fry the grub burgers and the potatoes. When the young man delivered Amy's fries to the table, they were swimming in dark brown grease. The whole time I was eating my grub burger, which tasted like they probably sounded to you when I described how they were made, I noticed the young man and the cook were huddled in the kitchen staring at Amy and me. The old man at the counter had left. I felt very uncomfortable. I mentioned to Amy how their staring at us was making me feel weird, but did not mention that I was afraid they were going to kill us. We asked for our bill and got out of there as quickly as we could, lying through our greasy teeth when they asked us how we had liked the grub burgers. Once we got outside, Amy and I shared that we had both felt like they might have been about to kill us. Maybe they really did try to kill us with that grub. Amy got sick after eating all that grease, because her system is not used to it. I, on the other hand, didn't really feel sick, but I will certainly never order another grub burger, even if I am starving.

After lunch as we drove into Mississippi, we passed a group of little metal structures that I later realized were yard sheds for sale. I remembered that Hurricane Katrina had damaged parts of Mississippi a few years prior, so I blurted out, "Look Amy! FEMA trailers!" Amy laughed so hard she could hardly keep her grub-fries down. Just because we were in Mississippi (and nowhere near where Katrina had hit), I thought I was seeing something historical. (This reminds me of how sure I was that I was seeing Sharon Tate's property from the airplane, when I had flown to California in August, 1969). We decided that the notebook with the driving directions should also serve as a log of Crazy Marilyn-isms. I wrote the first one about the FEMA trailers in the notebook. Later, I thought I saw a pack of wild dogs crossing the highway, when in reality it was no more than three stray dogs. So I added "Look, Amy! There's a pack of wild dogs!" to the log of Marilyn-isms. I know there were many other crazy statements made on our trip, but I can't find the notebook right now.

The only other crazy thing that I did on this trip that Amy and I can remember is the flashing incident. Amy and I drove to nearby Florida for dinner one evening. The place where we ate had outdoor seating, which we chose. It wasn't that comfortable because we had to sit on a picnic bench, but at least it was outdoors. I had on a fairly short skirt that evening. When we were finished eating I very awkwardly got out of the picnic bench in front of several other diners who just happened to be looking my way. Suffice it to say that if these people ever returned to that restaurant they definitely would have chosen indoor seating; in other words, a table *without* a view!

The Claw Hand

Twice when I went to Gulf Shores it was with my daughter Amy and my daughter Nancy and her family. One evening we went to dinner at Ribs and Reds. On previous trips to this restaurant I had ordered ribs, but this time I decided to try the reds. I am allergic to lobster, crab and scallops, but at the time had never had any signs of allergies to shrimp. (Just recently I found out that I am allergic to shrimp!) I was very disappointed when I got my reds. They were way too difficult to open and I didn't even like the taste of the tiny bits I was able to get out of them. I only ate about two and gave the rest to my son-in-law Grant, who loves them. After serving us our food the young waiter brought us bowls of lemon water to cleanse our hands. I get pretty wound up when I'm on vacation, and I love to make my grandchildren laugh, so I decided to have a little fun with the waiter. As he passed by our table I got his attention. I told him how much I had enjoyed the lemon soup. He just looked at me like I was crazy. (I am used to that look). My grandchildren laughed, so mission accomplished. We were still eating when all of a sudden I noticed that my right hand was seized up with spasms. I made a comment about it and tried to ignore it. But then it got really bad. It seized up like a claw and was quite painful. It wouldn't stop "spazzing" out. At first it was kind of funny, but after about five minutes, I started to wonder if I was either having some type of stroke or maybe a weird allergic reaction to the reds.

The waiter passed by our table again and I stopped him to ask what I should do about my claw hand. He looked at me like I was crazy and suggested that maybe I could soak it in the bowl of lemon water! I don't think he was trying to be funny or smart-mouthed. I think he just didn't know what else to suggest. My hand eventually stopped seizing up so I could get a good grip on my credit card to pay for the meal. Looking back, perhaps I should have caused a bigger scene and had my family lead me out of the restaurant with me shouting, "My hand! My claw hand!" Maybe in all of the commotion the young waiter would have forgotten to give us the bill.

Last year Nancy and family went back to Gulf Shores and ate at Ribs and Reds. Rachel told me they had a good laugh remembering how I had commented on the delicious lemon soup and the spectacle of my crazy claw hand.

My Crazy Underwear Stories

The first story that comes to mind when I think of underwear is the one about me flinging my panties in my doctor's face, but I'll save that story for last.

Fake Bra

I was very self-conscious when I was in the fifth grade. That was the year that I turned eleven. My body was changing and I was slowly turning from a little girl into a pre-teen. Some of the girls in my class started wearing nylons by that age, but my parents considered me to be too young for nylons so I continued to wear bobby socks, even to my Aunt Marcella's wedding that year. I felt so envious of the girls that were allowed to wear nylons. Nylons looked so fancy. Wearing bobby sox with a dress looked really dumb I thought. My parents obviously considered me too young to wear a bra, too, although many of the other girls my age were wearing them. I felt so left out when I saw other girls wearing bras. They had passed into their pre-teens while I was being held back in childhood. It was pretty obvious which girls wore bras and which ones didn't. It wasn't so much the size of their busts as it was how a bra showed up underneath their clothes. We wore white uniform blouses to school. A bra looked a lot different underneath one of those blouses, with its straps and band, than a white undershirt or the top of a full slip did. I no longer wore undershirts, thank God, but I wore a full slip underneath my school uniform.

The boys sure seemed to be able to spot a bra when they saw one. They had a habit of coming up behind a girl in school and "snapping" her bra by grabbing the elastic band through her blouse of course, pulling it out a little and letting it snap back. It was considered kind of a big deal if you got your bra snapped by a boy. It meant he recognized that you were becoming a woman. Maybe it meant that he liked you, too. Yes, I felt very left out. I was never snapped. So, knowing my parents would never let me wear a bra, I devised a way that I could still get snapped and feel like a part of the cool girls club. I had an elastic belt that I wore over my leotard in dance class. It was pale pink and would show nicely through my white uniform blouse. Never mind that it was about three times as wide as the band of a bra, unless we're talking about an eight- hook bra, if there is such a thing. It had a big clasp that wouldn't really look like the hook closure of a real bra, but I was hoping no one would notice that. It was elastic and would snap. That's what was important.

So one day, I got dressed for school leaving off my full slip and wearing my faux bra instead. I wore a cardigan over my uniform blouse so my Mom or sisters wouldn't see what I was wearing, and went to school ready to be snapped at last! But it never happened. During class I made a big production about it being too hot for my sweater and took it off. I bent over as much as I could hoping everyone could see the outline of my faux bra across my back, just begging to be snapped. But either no one saw it or they didn't know what the heck it was. They could have thought it was a mini back brace or something for all I know. I soon tired of wearing the belt. It was getting kind of tight and a couple of times it almost unclasped. That would have been hard to explain.

Even though I soon really needed a bra it would be a few years before I finally got to wear one. (See the story titled "Seventh Grade Was No Seventh Heaven" in My Crazy School Stories). Until I wrote these stories I never realized how a little thing like not being allowed to wear a bra could affect a girl's self-esteem and sense of identity.

Flinging My Panties

I was in my twenties, pregnant with my second child (Nancy) and should have been comfortable going to the OB-GYN by that time, but I wasn't. I still got very anxious when I was asked to assume the position in the stirrups. Truth be told, it still makes me anxious. It was in the last trimester of my pregnancy, when they do an internal exam at every other visit. The physician's assistant instructed me to remove all of my clothing and to put the paper gown on. I wasn't paying that close of attention to what she was saying. I was lying there on the table waiting for the doctor to come when I heard the assistant's words in my head. I thought to myself, "Oh, no, she said that I should take off ALL of my clothes, and I still have my underwear on!" I don't know why this seemed like such a big deal to me, but I guess because I was young and shy, I definitely did not want the doctor to walk in right as I was removing my underwear. I quickly wiggled out of my underwear under the cover of the paper gown and drape, and hoped that I could fling them all of the way to the corner where my other clothes were piled on a chair. Just as I aimed and threw them with all my might, the door opened and the doctor walked in. My underwear grazed his face as they flew by.

I was so embarrassed. I apologized, explained how I had forgotten to take off my underwear and kept saying how embarrassed I was. He just laughed and then told me a story to reduce my embarrassment. He told me that one of his patients had been lying on the examination table waiting for him to come in when she decided to freshen up a bit. She, too, had been worried that she may get caught in the act. She quickly reached into her purse for a Kleenex, not realizing that some trading stamps were also in her purse and that they had gotten stuck on the Kleenex. She did her thing and then wadded up the used Kleenex and threw it in the waste can just seconds before the doctor had entered the examination room. When he proceeded with the examination, he started laughing. The patient asked what was so funny. The doctor showed her the trading stamps that had been left behind. The doctor and I both laughed and I forgot all about my own embarrassing incident.

My Crazy Vomit Stories

I hate to throw up. I mean, I really hate it. When I was a kid I vomited at least once a year. It always sent me into a panic. My family used to make fun of me, because it always went the same way. I would kneel in front of the porcelain throne, kind of whimpering while I waited for it to happen. Just as I started to feel it coming up I would call out in an urgent voice, "Mom, come here. Please come here!" My Mom would run into the bathroom, usually with my nosy older sister on her heels, and then I would violently scream "Get out! Get out!" just as it really started coming up.

My Poor Little Red Shoes

In first grade, just a few days before my class was making our First Holy Communion, we were walking down the alley behind our school to the church to practice for the big day. Maybe she was nervous or maybe she had a stomach bug, I don't know. All I know is that Susan H. hurled as we were walking down the alley and it got all over my red leather school shoes! Seeing and hearing her vomiting instantly made me gag. Then it made me up-chuck in the alley, too.

At least I didn't puke on anyone's shoes! Not to be outdone by me, Susan hurled again. By this time we were in church. I looked down at my beloved red leather oxford style Buster Brown shoes and saw chunks of Susan's puke stuck in the stitching on the top of the shoes. The sight and smell made me so sick that I vomited again. Susan heard me barf and that must have set her off again. Errrrp! I saw her errrrp and raised her one! Errrrp! Errrp! Sister Mary P. grabbed Susan and me and led us out of church, up the alley and back into the school building. I remember that she had us both kneel in front of the same toilet while she held our hair back and gently told us to get it all out. By that time both Susan and I had puked probably four times each and were done. Susan and I were both crying. I don't know why Susan was crying, but I know why I was. My favorite shoes were going to have to be thrown out. Sister helped us clean up a bit. I took a handkerchief out of my uniform blouse pocket to wipe off my beloved shoes. It was either the Thursday or Friday handkerchief from my day-of-the-week handkerchief set that I had received for my birthday that year. The hanky would have to be thrown out, too, I guessed.

When I got home I cried again as I told my Mom all about the vomit-fest that Susan H. had started, and how I was so sad that we would have to throw my shoes and hanky away. My Mom assured me that she would clean both, and that they would definitely not be thrown away. We couldn't afford another pair of school shoes, especially right before First Communion Day. We had already spent a small fortune on my dress, veil, shoes, purse, rosary and prayer book, not to mention the bakery cake and other food for my First Communion party on Sunday. So, when my Dad came home he had the dubious honor of cleaning my shoes. I noticed that he gagged several times while doing so and I hoped he wouldn't puke on my shoes, too. My Mom returned the 95% clean shoes to me and told me that my Dad had done the best he could. I noticed the stitching on my shoes was stained a little and not 100% clean. I tearfully explained that I could never wear those shoes again. But that fell on deaf ears. When I returned to school on the next Tuesday (we had Monday off), I was wearing the red shoes. And when Thursday - or maybe it was Friday – rolled around again, I had the freshly-laundered appropriate day-of-the-week hanky in my pocket.

Whenever I saw Susan after that, I couldn't help but remember our shared experience. We also shared a birthday. I was invited to her birthday party one year, but I don't think she was invited to mine. I couldn't take the chance of her puking all over my party!

Tomato Soup and Cottage Cheese

I have always loved playing pranks, and my Mom was such a good sport that she often found herself as my victim. One Friday when we were eating lunch I got an idea for a prank. I know it was a Friday, because when I was a kid we Catholics were not allowed to eat meat on Fridays. We had tomato soup and cottage soup for lunch that day. I was not enjoying it at all, because tomato soup gave me twisted bones (see "Twisted Bones" in the My Crazy School Stories section) and I didn't care for cottage cheese. My Mom got up to answer the front door and I was suddenly inspired to put the tomato soup and cottage cheese to better use. I ran into the bathroom and poured about half of each into the toilet bowl. I ran back to the table just in time and told my Mom that I felt really sick all of a sudden. I ran into the bathroom and made retching sounds. I even called out

"Mom, come here!" and she came running as she always did. This time I did not yell at her to get out of the bathroom, because my fake puking was already done. I pointed to the lumpy, pinkish stuff in the toilet and said, "See, I told you I can't eat tomato soup and cottage cheese!" For a minute my Mom believed it and started asking me when I had started feeling sick since I had seemed just fine before she had gotten up from the table. Right about the time she started to doubt me, I started laughing. She laughed and softly slapped me good-naturedly. I had made my point. No more tomato soup and cottage cheese for lunch!

No Green Beans, Please!

My first baby (my daughter Karen) was overdue by almost two weeks, so my OB-GYN told me to come in the next day to be induced. He told me to not have anything to eat or drink after midnight and to be at the hospital at 8:00 in the morning on October 7th. I was living with my in-laws at the time, because my husband Terry was in Viet Nam. In fact, he had just arrived there about a week before. My mother-in-law cooked a big dinner. I'm not sure what the meat was, but I remember eating a lot of mashed potatoes and gravy and loads of green beans, my favorite vegetable. In the evening I had a huge ice cream sundae with plenty of toppings and whipped cream. I wanted to eat as much as I could before midnight!

Shortly after eating the sundae, I kept going into the bathroom and staying in there for a long time. My mother-in-law noticed and asked me what was going on. I told her that I was trying to "go to the bathroom", but nothing was happening no matter how hard I pushed. "You're in labor!" she declared, and then she yelled out to my father-in-law, "Al, get the car. It's time to go to the hospital!" My father-in-law took the bumpiest route to the hospital that he could find, and we got there in half of the normal driving time. When they examined me they said there was no time to even register, and that I was ready to go. I think that bumpy ride had really speeded things up!

I had pretty hard labor, but it didn't last very long. Within two hours of first going into labor I was in the delivery room. There was no time for me to get a shot or anything, so they just gave me gas. I woke up just in time to see my OB-GYN bending over me and telling me it was a girl. I responded by projectile-vomiting right onto his face! I was so gassed up and excited about having just given birth that I wasn't even embarrassed. They handed me my beautiful baby girl and I forgot all about everything else. Later my mother-in-law, who had been right outside the delivery room, told me that the doctor had said, "I see someone had green beans for dinner!" She told me that he hadn't seemed mad or anything. I guess stuff like that happens to doctors all the time. But I wonder if the next time he instructed a patient to not eat after midnight, he added, "And no green beans, please!"

Final thoughts:

The doctor who got the green beans in his face was the brother of the doctor who got my underwear flung across his face. (See My Crazy Underwear Stories). The brothers were in their OB-GYN practice together. I wonder if they ever compared notes about their crazy patients?

My Crazy Writing Stories

I don't really have any *crazy* writing stories per se, but I do have a crazy song lyric. I write song lyrics all of the time. They help me express what's on my mind. Here is a sample of a song that I recently wrote in about ten minutes one Saturday morning as I was fixing my breakfast, which consisted of only two pieces of bacon and one lonely egg. Picture a country boy and his hefty girlfriend in a little country diner as you read the lyrics.

She Eats Like a Man

Two pieces of bacon
And one lonely egg
Ain't no breakfast for my girl
She's got a hollow leg!
Better double that bacon
And fry another egg
And maybe add some flapjacks
Hey, does she have to beg?

Better get her some biscuits
And red eye gravy and ham
That's a breakfast for my girl
Cuz she eats like a man!
Don't give her no oatmeal
She'll take a bowl of grits
Don't give her no prune juice
It always gives her the "bleep"!
Just think of a cowboy
Or a great big lumberjack
And give her their breakfast
Or she ain't coming back!
Better git her those biscuits
And her red eye gravy and ham
That's a breakfast for my girl
Cuz she eats like a man!

My Crazy X-rated Stories

I fooled you, didn't I? There are no X-rated stories from my life; at least not that I will ever tell! If this is the first chapter you went to and/or if you got out your reading glasses faster than Wyatt Earp could pull the revolver out of its holster in order to read this, you ought to be ashamed of yourself! LOL!

My Crazy Yacht Stories

I'm sorry to mislead you if you thought I was really going to tell you some stories about my experiences on a yacht, but if this would have been my real intention with this section this page would be blank. Actually this is my miscellaneous section; the place for some random stories that didn't fit into any other category.

Knocking, Chirping and Vibrating!

Living alone and not being skilled or experienced with home maintenance can sometimes be a real challenge for me. Simple chores such as opening a pump bottle of liquid soap or loosening a light fixture so I can get the burned out light bulb out can bring my attempt to fend for myself to a halt. Recently my saint of a brother-in-law (my dear departed sister Lois' husband) helped me with those very things that had me stymied. Whenever Don comes over I have a list of a few things that need his attention. I call it my "Donny Do" list. He always graciously helps me. He is a God-send for this widow who can at times be quite helpless, but who hates to ask for help. But Don lives over twenty miles away and is a busy man, so sometimes things happen around here that need the immediate attention of a man, like the following.

Knocking

I was watching television one evening. It was about 10:00 PM when I heard the knocking. It was loud, intermittent and sounded like it was coming from the basement. In fact, it sounded like someone was standing beneath the floor right under the recliner I was sitting in. I tried to think of what could reasonably be causing the knocking sound and could not. I had been out earlier that evening and I figured that someone may have broken into my house while I was gone and was in the basement trying to scare me by knocking on the living room floor. After several minutes of this taunting, he was probably planning to come upstairs to kill me. I tried to calm my over-active imagination and think rationally about this noise, but there was no other explanation. Someone was knocking on my basement ceiling!

I called my next-door-neighbor John who is my "go-to guy" when I need something. Like I said, I hate to ask for help, but this was too important to put off or put on a list for Don to do the next time he came over. I dialed John's number, but there was no answer. Next, I dialed my other next door neighbor's house. Eddie works as a police dispatcher, so he'd know what to do for sure. Unfortunately, his wife Elizabeth said he was at work. She told me that she would call him at work and then call me back. I was a tad unsure of what was really going on, because I know I have an overly-active imagination. I can't tell you how many times in my life I have misperceived something and ended up looking like a fool. (Read the stories in the My Crazy Childhood Stories about the times Judy H. and I summoned the police to check out a dead body that we found, and to intervene in the strangling of the old lady in the tower). So I thought I'd try one more neighbor before I would resort to calling the police. The knocking was still happening, almost in a pattern. This guy was really giving me a lot of warning. Maybe it was the sick ritual of a serial killer on the loose. They probably call him "The Knocker". I did not want to be "knocked up" by him, but I also did not want to make a fool of myself over something silly, if that's what this turned out to be.

I summoned up my courage and called a neighbor across the street. I explained to Laura that I was hearing knocking coming from my basement and was a little frightened, even though I was pretty sure it was something explainable. Laura said she'd send her husband Jeff over right away. It was about 10:30 PM by that time. When I opened the door I saw that Jeff had brought his teenaged daughter Shannon with him. Was Shannon there to provide extra protection from the man in the basement or was she there to protect her dad from me, I wondered. The two of them cautiously entered the basement while I steeled myself for one of two things: Jeff and Shannon running up the steps yelling "Call the police!" or Jeff and Shannon coming up the stairs laughing. Actually neither happened. Jeff explained that they hadn't seen anything out of the ordinary in my basement and hadn't heard any knocking while they were down there. But they were so nice to me and assured me that they hadn't minded coming over at all. My police dispatcher neighbor called me back and I told him all was well. I have such great neighbors!

PS: Some time later I heard the knocking again and instantly recognized it as my water pipes banging. My perception of sounds may depend on other things besides hearing. Perhaps when I am tired or in a certain state, I perceive things differently.

Chirping

Rich across the street may take the prize for the neighbor with the most patience and persistence when it comes to helping me with a problem. Last summer my old electric smoke detector in the hallway suddenly started chirping, even though it had been disabled a year or more before. At first it was few and far between chirps, but then it ramped up to every few seconds. I put up with it for many hours before I almost lost my mind. There is an active battery operated alarm right next to it. I disabled that, but the chirping persisted. I have several smoke battery-operated smoke detectors in my home. In fact, my brother-in-law Don had just installed one in each of the bedrooms. I have one in the hallway and another in the basement, both next to disabled electric ones. I checked all of them over and over, disconnecting them one by one and still hearing the chirps that seemed to be coming from the hallway right outside of the bedrooms and my home office.

I went out to get my mail and saw my neighbor Rich outside. He works from home, and in the summertime, often works out on his front porch because he gets better cell phone reception outside. After he was finished with his call I asked him if he wouldn't mind coming over to see if he could pinpoint which of my smoke detectors was chirping, because I had tried to isolate the sound and could not. By this time I was already half deaf and 100% frustrated. It takes a lot for me to break down and ask for help. That day the hours of chirping had broken me down.

Rich agreed that it sounded like the chirping was coming from the hallway, but did not think it was possible that it was coming from the old disabled electric detector. He disconnected the batteries from the battery operated detector next to it. The chirping continued. One at a time, he disconnected the batteries in the other "active" detectors, one in each bedroom and one in the basement. The chirping continued. I kept following Rich around, talking about what I thought was happening, while he patiently kept testing each active detector several times. He kept saying he was sure it was not the disconnected electric detector in the hallway, but I kept suggesting that perhaps it was. I could see that Rich was getting a little frustrated. Maybe he was wishing I'd stop chirping about my theory! Rich suggested that he could move the battery operated detector in the hallway to cover the wires that were hanging down from the old disabled electric one. It took him several tries. The screws in the alarm cover and the hanging capped wires just wouldn't co-operate. I felt so sorry for Rich. He was up close and personal with the deafening chirping, and standing and reaching up for any length of time is really hard on the neck, shoulders and back. He finally got it.

I thanked him for at least taking care of the hanging wire situation and suggested he let the chirping problem go, because I could see that he was really getting frustrated. Rich told me that he loves to solve problems and that it was really getting to him that he couldn't solve this chirping problem. His frustration must have refueled his determination, because he told me he would methodically eliminate each detector, one at a time until he found the culprit. Rich then took each detector out of the house, came inside and waited to see if we would hear a chirp. One by one, the detectors were placed out on the front porch and each time we could still hear chirping that seemed to be coming from the hallway. Finally they were all outside and we could still hear chirping inside. Rich reconnected all of them and went into each room to listen, and came up with different originating locations almost every time. I remained steadfast with my opinion that the chirping was coming from the old disabled smoke detector in the hallway, even though it had been totally disabled. Rich was really frustrated by this time and said he had to get back to work, but he hated leaving me with this problem. We both wondered out loud if it was poltergeists!

As he was leaving he suddenly got an idea. He asked if I had any carbon monoxide detectors and where were they. I mentioned that I had one in the basement, which we checked out, and one in the living room which also checked out as not being the culprit. I was in the home office and Rich was leaving when all of a sudden I remembered that I had one in that room, too. It was sort of hidden on the extra desk just two feet behind me. I picked it up and sure enough, it was not working. The battery had died. Just as I discovered this, we heard another chirp to confirm our suspicions. It came right from my hand this time.

Poor Rich was exhausted from his ordeal and I felt like a fool. I told him I owed him one. I thanked him over and over, but he very humbly said it was nothing and that he was glad to have been of help. I believe him. He is a nice neighbor! I told him that the next time I had a problem I would try another neighbor, but that I was running out of them. I'll have to be on the lookout for new neighbors. I need a fresh, yet untouched crop of Good Samaritans!

Vibrating

John next door has helped me so many times I have lost count. He started cutting our grass when Jerry got sick, and that was twelve years ago. He has cut my grass once a week from April through October for all those years! And that's just one way he has helped me.

I will never forget one time that I enlisted John's help, and neither will my plumber! It was several years ago. I was taking a shower and had just turned off the water when I heard it. It sounded like the water pipes were vibrating and about ready to blow! I dried off, dressed and then went down to the basement to inspect the pipes. I didn't hear much going on down there, but when I came back upstairs it got louder. I went into the bathroom and it got louder still. Not that it was a loud sound at all, but it was clearly a kind of vibration that I was hearing. And to me, a vibrating water pipe didn't seem to be a good thing.

So I called my "go to" neighbor John. As always when I call him, John was over here in a minute. He walked into the bathroom and heard the noise that I had described. Then he went down to the basement to turn off the water. We still heard the noise. We were both puzzled. It was then that I decided to call Mac, my plumber. Mac is a very nice man who lives in the subdivision.

John and I were sitting in the dining room when Mac arrived. We explained where the noise was coming from (the shower) and mentioned that John had turned off the water. Mac said he'd take a look at the shower. A minute later Mac came out with something in his hand and a funny look on his face. "Is this what you're hearing?" he asked. And there, in his hand, was my still vibrating (wait for it!) razor. Yes, it was one of those vibrating razors that I had neglected to turn off after I finished using it in the shower. The vibration of the razor against the metal shower caddy is what I had been hearing. We all had a good laugh and Mac didn't even charge me for the visit.

I have called John and Mac numerous times since that day for one problem or another. Neither one hesitates to come over, at least not that they let on, but sometimes I wonder if they think it's another wild goose chase when I call them. I never wanted to be the crazy old lady in the neighborhood, but it's starting to look like I might be.

There's an Earthquake in my Basement and I'm Folded in Half!

(I'll bet you have never seen a title like this one before!)

It was the summer of 2008. I had just had the new driveway, sidewalk and patio put in. I had confronted the guy who owned the company that did the work about several issues. They had driven their big tractor through my side yard when the grass was soaked after several days of hard rain and had left a long deep rut. And they had knocked into my neighbor John's wooden shed and damaged it. They had damaged several areas of siding on the back of my house and repaired it very poorly. They had not followed the drawing of the patio that I had designed. The tamping design did not meet the house and looks really dumb. When they stained the concrete it looked like they had just thrown it and didn't bother to blend it in. The driveway cracked immediately and they did a poor job of grouting it or whatever you call that process. And they did not seal the driveway. And then there was the daylight showing in my basement where the new patio didn't quite meet the bottom of my house! I may have even left some of the problems out, there were so many of them.

All of this was on my mind one Saturday. My daughter Amy and I were going to spend the day at the subdivision pool and we decided to include my two oldest grandkids, Alex and Justin. I went to pick them up and when Justin folded the front seat down in order to get into the backseat of my two-door, it got stuck. Once the kids were settled in their seats, I tried to unfold the driver's seat and get it into its upright position, but I could not get it to unfold. I tried and tried and finally decided to just try to squeeze into my seat the way it was. I could barely fit into the seat, but I did. I proceeded to drive the several miles to my house all folded over in the front seat. The three of us were laughing so hard at first and I kept saying "I'm folded in half, kids!" Then after a couple of miles it got kind of uncomfortable. I persevered though, because I couldn't wait to get into that pool!

I somehow managed to get us home. When I got out of the car, I just had to tell Amy all about it. Amy was already at the pool and in the water. I went up to the fence and loudly called out to her that I had driven home all folded in half. As I explained that my seat was broken, the other swimmers, my neighbors, looked at me like I was crazy. Amy looked at me like she wished I would just stop talking. I had the kids get into the pool with Amy while I went inside to call my car dealer about the broken seat. When I asked if it could be fixed the guy at the dealership told me that the whole seat might have to be replaced. Then he asked me if my seats were leather and if they were heated seats, to which I responded yes. He then explained that unfortunately that would make replacing the seat very expensive. He asked me to bring it in on Monday and they would see if they could repair it rather than replace it. I was pretty upset. I had just paid way too much for the driveway, sidewalk and patio and they had made a mess of the project, and now I was probably going to be gypped again by the car dealer. I was almost certain they would tell me that the seat would have to be replaced.

I went to my basement to get some beach towels, and the minute I stepped in I noticed daylight streaming into the basement from the back of my house where the patio was. There were several gaps. That probably meant I would have to fork out more money for some foundation work! Then I looked at the basement floor. There were several cracks that I had never seen before, and they were wet! With horror I thought, "There's been an earthquake, and my basement floor is about to erupt like a volcano!" I know this doesn't make any sense to you normal people, but in my world my first perceptions of many events or things are a ten on the Richter scale of my emotions. My whole world was falling apart. First, the disastrous patio project that had damaged my lawn, part of the siding and now the foundation of my house, then the expensive car seat replacement, and now this earthquake damage in my basement! Or had the patio people broken a water pipe? Either way, I had three disasters to deal with!

Just then I heard Amy's voice. She was laughing. She had come over to get the towels. I called her to the basement. She was laughing so hard she could hardly talk. She told me that the seat in my car was not broken. She had gotten it to sit upright on her first try! Then through her laughter she heard me say that there was an eruption of some kind going on right then in my basement and that it was ready to blow! I pointed to the basement floor, which in my twisted and hysterical mind looked like it was raised near where the new cracks were! This all made her laugh even harder. I pointed to the wet cracks on the floor. She told me that those cracks had always been there. Just then we saw several large drops of water coming from above. Right away, perhaps because she is normal, she knew that condensation on the overhead pipes were causing water to drip on the basement floor, which had in turn made the cracks that had always been in my basement floor appear darker. And the floor was not raised. That had been a figment of my vivid imagination!

Well, I felt better then, at least about the car seat and the non-existent earthquake in my basement, but I still had to deal with the crumbling foundation of my house. I told Amy to go back to the pool without me so I could call the patio guy and chew him out! He already knew about the other problems and had already heard me threaten him with a lawsuit if he didn't remedy everything right away. The list of my complaints was already in the mail to him along with a scathing letter. I screamed into the phone that he could add one more problem to that list; that his crew had damaged my foundation. He said he'd be right over to inspect the damage.

When he arrived within ten minutes and I took him to the basement and showed him where the sunlight was coming in. He told me that he couldn't see any such thing and I assured him that I could see it and that he must be blind. He said that all houses have sunlight coming in at the foundation and that it was no big deal. I strongly disagreed. Then he challenged me and said we could probably see gaps in the foundation on the other sides of my house that had nothing to do with the patio. We walked all around the other parts of the basement and saw none. "Well, Mrs. Winka," he said in his usual condescending tone when he was talking with me, "I couldn't see the ones you claim you saw, but I assure you they are all over, and they have nothing to do with anything we (meaning his crew) did. I told him in no uncertain terms that these gaps in the foundation were non-existent until the patio had been put in, and that it was looking more and more like I was going to have to retain an attorney. With that his eyes cleared up and he admitted that he could now see a little sunlight coming in from where the patio was. He said he was still not convinced that this had anything to do with them, but told me he would go get some foam sealant and take care of the situation for me. He said this all in a very condescending tone of voice and acted like he was doing me a big favor for giving up his Saturday afternoon to help me out.

He went to the hardware store and came back with a can of the foam and complained that I was keeping him from a family barbecue. I told him that I was sorry for him, and that I was missing time with my grandchildren at the pool. I didn't really feel sorry for him because I knew he had caused the problem himself by his shoddy workmanship. And I detested the way he always made excuses and told lies rather than own up to his mistakes. He filled the gaps. I had my doubts that this was a permanent fix, but I have not experienced any problems with leakage or any other foundation problems since, so perhaps he did fix that problem. Even after he paid to have my lawn graded and re-seeded, after he sort of (half-assed) fixed the siding he had damaged and gave me two sections of sidewalk and sealed the driveway for free, I am still very angry about him and his home "improvement" company. Every time I look at my patio I think of that jerk! One of my neighbors asked me two summer s ago if I would recommend the company to him for his driveway, and I said "Absolutely not!" Unfortunately, the neighbor didn't listen to me and hired him anyway. I'll have to follow-up this summer and see if his driveway looks as bad as mine did after only a couple of years.

I finally got to join Amy, Alex and Justin at the pool that day. We had a lot of laughs over my imagined problems, which took my mind off of the things that really did happen. I have never again had to drive "all folded in half". In fact, I had to trade that car in last year and now I have a four door. Every once in a while when I am in the basement, I look at those cracks in the floor and laugh to myself about the earthquake. Hey, I was right about one of the three mishaps at least!

My Crazy Zoo Stories

Orangutan Means Danger!

When I was a freshman in high school, one day we had the afternoon off so we could attend Field Day, which was held at a park a few miles from our high school. The girls that I hung around with decided that we would go to the zoo instead. I'm pretty sure my Mom believed that we just had the afternoon off and didn't know that we were really supposed to be attending Field Day. Surprisingly she did not verify why we had the afternoon off and she let me go to the zoo with girls she did not know that well. I was afraid she wouldn't approve of my new high school friends.

Cathy, Bettye and Linda (the gang members I referred to earlier in the book) all had big, teased hair, wore white lipstick and dark eyeliner, which was all the rage then, and more sophisticated than my look. I did tease my hair and used hairspray, but my hair wasn't as big as theirs, at least not yet. The girls passed the mom test and after walking to Barbara's house to pick her up, the five of us took two buses and finally arrived at the zoo.

With that makeup, hair and raucous laughter we must have looked and sounded like a pack of escaped hyenas as we scampered around. We went to the monkey show and probably attracted as much attention as they did with our monkey-like appearance and actions. I'm not sure what else we did, but I assure you that we attracted attention. We wanted people to think we were from the boonies and that we were in the big city for the first time ever. We talked in these stupid "country bumpkin" accents, which probably fooled no one. One of the girls loudly read the sign in front of the orangutan in a loud phony country accent. "O-rang-u-tan--that must mean danger in a foreign language!" I don't know why we thought that was so funny, but we did. I still laugh to myself whenever I see that word, which by the way, I have always pronounced as "orangutang" as though there is a G at the end.

Now, whenever I see teens being loud and acting obnoxious in public, I get very annoyed until I remember how I acted when I was their age. Fourteen-year-olds are just trying to find their identities and want to shake up "the establishment" a little, just like we did. We thought we looked so good, just like the kids who dress "Goth" or dye their hair bright pink these days do. I wouldn't really want to go back to those days, with all of the insecurities and mistakes, but when I do go back in my memory I have to laugh. We thought we looked and acted so cool that day at the zoo, when in reality people, and maybe even the animals, were probably looking at us and shaking their heads at how goofy we looked and acted.

Too Dumb for the Zoo

When I turned sixteen I decided that I needed a summer job. I heard that the zoo was looking to hire a lot of kids and that they were holding a testing session. What fun it would be to work at the zoo. Just as long as I wouldn't have to be a pooper scooper, I thought it would be a great summer job. I would earn money and get to see the animals every day. And better yet, I'd get to see plenty of boys every day!

I talked my friends Barbara and Janet into signing up to take the test too, although I don't think either of them really wanted a job that summer. On the day of the test I was pretty nervous. There were an awful lot of kids taking the test. I felt the pressure. I was surprised at how hard the test was, at least for me. Some of the questions were word problems, which I hated, and some of them involved knowing how to count out change, which I didn't know how to do then. (Later, when I worked at Famous-Barr I was trained to give out change. They don't do it like that anymore, which is a shame, I think). Counting out change was math, and as I have mentioned in "My Crazy School Stories", math and I did not get along. There were animal science questions, too. And as I have admitted, I don't know that much about animals. One question stated that a marsupial had escaped its cage, and it gave multiple choices as to what you should do. I remember I chose the answer "Grab it by its tail". I was so proud that I knew that a kangaroo was a marsupial, and since I knew kangaroos had tails, I was certain I had picked the correct answer.

Well, I'll never know for sure if I chose the correct answer to that question or not, but I think I probably answered it incorrectly. The correct answer was probably "call an attendant" or "report it to a trained specialist". Why would a sixteen year old be expected to help with catching an escaped zoo animal? It was a trick question and it had tricked me right out of a summer job. I must have had many answers wrong, because I flunked the test. Yes, I flunked the zoo test. Barbara and Janet both passed the test, but like I said, I don't think either of them really wanted to work at the zoo. I was devastated that I flunked the zoo test. It was a very humbling experience for me. It made me feel like I hadn't yet evolved from a primate.

Do Birds Mate Through Their Mouths?

About ten years ago I went to the zoo with Amy and my grandson Jake. We stopped at the bird cage where they had specialists answering questions about birds. We were standing around one of the specialists, along with a few other zoo guests, when it suddenly occurred to me that I didn't know how birds mate. So, thinking that I was asking an intelligent question, I loudly blurted out "Do birds mate through their mouths?" There was complete silence and all eyes were on me. The specialist just stared at me with a dumbfounded look on her face. I was so embarrassed that I wished the bird she was holding would suddenly fly over and peck my eyes out so I wouldn't have to see everyone looking at me like I was a moron. The lady never did answer me. The Q and A session was apparently over. The other zoo visitors, the specialist and her bird all walked away, leaving me with Amy, my grandson and my unanswered question. The next day at work I asked my co-workers if anyone knew how birds mate? No one answered. They pretended that they had not heard me. I had to Google my question, and what I found out, in case you are also wondering how birds mate, is that birds (male and female) have a vent called a cloaca which becomes swollen during mating season. I lost interest at that point. Suffice it to say that birds do not mate through their mouths.

PS: I still do not see what was so odd about my question.

THE CRAZY END!

My Crazy Epilogue

While editing this book, two of its characters passed away. One was a main character in my life, my ex-husband Terry. The other was the Father of Rock and Roll, Mr. Chuck Berry. Ironically, they passed away on the same day, March 18, 2017. St. Louis, and all of us, lost two great men that day. RIP, Terry and Chuck!